MEANING
A
LIFE

An Autobiography

MEANING
A
LIFE

An Autobiography

Mary
Oppen

—

Expanded edition
Edited, with an introduction, by Jeffrey Yang

—

A New Directions Paperbook

To George, whose life and mine are intertwined

—

Grateful acknowledgment is made to the editors of *Ironwood*, *Montemora*, and *Occurrence*, in which sections of this book originally appeared. Further acknowledgments can be found in "A note on the text."

An excerpt from the introduction with color plates of Mary Oppen's art was first published in *Poetry* magazine (February 2020).

Manufactured in the United States of America
New Directions Books are printed on acid-free paper
First published as a New Directions Paperbook (NDP1477) in 2020
Book design by Eileen Bellamy

Library of Congress Cataloging-in-Publication Data
Names: Oppen, Mary, 1908-1990, author. | Yang, Jeffrey, writer of introduction.
Title: Meaning a life : an autobiography / Mary Oppen ; introduction by Jeffrey Yang.
Description: New York : New Directions Books, 2020. | Series: A New Directions book
Identifiers: LCCN 2019055163 | ISBN 9780811229470 (paperback) | ISBN 9780811229487 (ebook)
Subjects: LCSH: Oppen, Mary, 1908-1990. | Oppen, George. | Authors' spouses—United States—Biography. | Poets, American—20th century—Biography.
Classification: LCC PS3529.P55 Z46 2020 | DDC 811/.52 [B]—dc23
LC record available at https://lccn.loc.gov/2019055163

10 9 8 7 6 5 4 3 2 1

New Directions Books are published for James Laughlin
by New Directions Publishing Corporation
80 Eighth Avenue, New York 10011

ndbooks.com

CONTENTS

INTRODUCTION

—

The words do not illuminate the poem;
the poem illuminates the words.

—ST. JOHN OF THE CROSS
(translated by Mary Oppen)

—

Some books we can read over and over again through the years with renewed delight. Our initial encounter with such a book feels like our first experience with a place we love, or like the first sight of shore or sea—that particular, that vast. Our emotions swirl with promise, hope, jubilation in a miraculous moment of recognition that enlarges our world. How lucky we are to have found this book! How impossible it is now to imagine our life without it! I think of this special-collection library that grows as we grow as our autobiographical canon—resistant to trends, conditioned by intuition and whim, and open to any language or genre.

Mary Oppen's *Meaning a Life: An Autobiography* merged into my autobiographical canon through her husband, George Oppen. I was working for New Directions on a posthumous selection of his poems, edited by Robert Creeley, who asked if I could write a chronology of the poet's life to run in the book. I was a fledgling editorial assistant, the "first stop on the whipping post" of our office, and the request came as a bit of a surprise. High on the challenge, I dove into the chronology with zeal and, after wrestling with it for a few weeks, sent a draft off to Creeley for his approval. Without comment, the Black Mountain master gallantly nixed it. It would be better, he decided, to have someone else do it. Still, all was not lost, as my research had led me to Mary's book, a copy of which was nearly impossible to track down at the time.

Meaning a Life was originally published in June 1978 by Black Sparrow Press—a California-based literary house built from the ground floor of Charles Bukowski and up through the contemporary American avant-garde—together with George Oppen's last book of poems, *Primitive*, which came out earlier that spring. George was already suffering the symptoms of what would later be diagnosed as Alzheimer's disease and, as Mary told an interviewer a few years after his death in 1984, "He couldn't get [*Primitive*] ready for the publishers. And he finally said, 'If you can do this, please do it.' He said, 'I can't do it.' So I had to put them together and get the typescripts presentable, and probably lots of things he'd have done differently." Her autobiography opens with the dedication "To George, whose life and mine are intertwined"—an echo of George's dedication in his *Collected Poems* of 1975 "For Mary / whose words in this book are entangled / inextricably among my own"—with the entirety of his "Anniversary Poem" as epigraph, one line of the poem questioning, "How shall we say how this happened, these stories, our stories." What objectively appears to be a rare, celebratory occurrence—the simultaneous publication of a couple's new books from the same press, both praised later that year in the same review by Michael Heller in *The New York Times*—with the Oppens feels both ordinary (the common light) and fated (the shining rays of a binary star).

Mary Oppen was born in the kitchen of her parents' frontier home in Kalispell, Montana, on November 28, 1908, and died on May 14, 1990, in Alta Bates Hospital in Berkeley, California. *Meaning a Life* was her first book; she turned seventy the year it was published. As she tells the story, she found poetry at the same time she and George found each other. She was eighteen when she met him in a poetry class at Corvallis State Agricultural College (now Oregon State University). On their first date George picked her up in his roommate's Model T Ford and they stayed out all night, "in the bright / Incredible light" of the moon, as George describes it in his poem "The Forms of Love." They "sat and talked, made love, and talked until morning . . . talked as I had never talked before, an outpouring," as Mary describes it in *Meaning a Life*. She returned to her dorm the next morning and was expelled (George was suspended) for breaking the curfew. She left school, George followed her, and they decided to flee family to make a life of their own, "complete, a mated pair, with the strength of our intelligences, our passions and our sensibilities multiplied by living our lives together," and with a shared vision of "conversation, ideas, poetry, peers." They were eighteen! Armed with Conrad Aiken's anthology *Modern American Poets* and writing, both soon getting poems published in the same Texas newspaper, for which they each received a check for $25. Then, almost as soon as she had begun, Mary stopped writing. While hitchhiking to New York, they made it as far as Dallas before she got sick, had an abortion, didn't recover, and returned to George's father's home in San Francisco. She talks about writing and not writing in her autobiography:

> The time and the urge to write did not come again to me until I was working on translations of St. John of the Cross in 1971 or 1972. I have quite often translated poems I wanted to read from the original French or Spanish. The St. John translation was so poor in every version I could find that I began to make what I called "transpositions." From that I began to write again; my readings in the prophets brought me back to a search for my father, who had read Sirach, Ezekiel, the Psalms, the Song of Songs and other parts of the Bible to me. It was as though pent-up emotions were waiting to be released—I wasn't aware of all I remembered until I tapped at the door and memories came flooding in. Apparently nothing is forgotten, but all is waiting to be called forth; I think I have reached a safe age from which to release these memories which have troubled me over the years. Perhaps they would not have been released for the asking when I was younger.

In an unpublished piece dated December 4, 1975, she shares a little more: "I started to write with the rise of the women's movement . . . without the women's movement my writing would not have been respected, in the first instance, enough to break through the male writing world. . . . I have chosen to write at the time culturally prepared for me. . . . I am happy to be writing, very pleased with the loss of shyness that took almost sixty-seven years to accomplish."

More publicly known is that George Oppen, too, stopped writing from 1935 to 1958, a choice initially connected to what he witnessed as the "catastrophe of human lives" in 1930s America. After spending a summer in Mexico, where the Oppens had witnessed a poor country undergoing a dramatic transformation through socialization, "from colonialism and 'peonage' into equality and nationhood," Mary says about their return to New York: "The city had an air of disaster; the unemployed were the refugees who had exhausted their resources and did not know where to turn." They also "did not find honesty or sincerity in the so-called arts of the left"—with Mary's exception of Bertolt Brecht and certain Soviet films—and instead joined the Communist Party and Workers Alliance in Brooklyn, organizing and demonstrating and participating in sit-ins in the Philippine, Puerto Rican, Syrian-Lebanese immigrant neighborhood of Borough Hall, mediating between the relief bureau and poor Southerners in Bedford-Stuyvesant, going to party training school in Utica, and there organizing union meetings and talking with industrial workers and farmers. The stories and observations Mary shares about those difficult times give a poignant account of the daily challenges grassroots activists faced in Depression-era America. Though shocked by the announcement of the Stalin-Hitler pact in 1939, they remained active party members through the war. Writing to a friend in 1959, George pointed to another reason for not writing: the birth of their daughter, Linda, in 1940—"Julian: there were only some fifteen years that political loyalties prevented me from writing poetry. After that I had to wait for Linda to grow up."

Words arrived before the life. Meaning a life lived close to the roots, meaning into words, words a measure of the life, in pursuit of meaning, meaning through seeing, listening, thinking, "to find a way of life in which the poetry we felt within us could come out of our lives." The first two chapters of Mary Oppen's book—a beautifully discursive and concise prelude—lead up to the moment of their romance. She recalls her childhood in isolated Kalispell, a place "where children and Indians were the only natives," a homesteading railroad and lumber town in the Rocky Mountains settled by families from the east, Germans and Scandinavians, three Chinese laborers, Protestants, Lutherans, and Catholics. Vivid memories of growing up in the woods with three older brothers; Papa, a postmaster and later a Ford dealer, then an investor in Chinese imports; and Mama, of Norman Catholic ancestry who worked multiple jobs and ran the house: "Rhythms from ancient times still held everywhere in the weekly order of household work." The seasons pass with the day's milk delivered by horse and wagon, smudge-pot summers at Flathead Lake, getting a pair of soft deerskin moccasins made at the coulée Indian encampment, preserved eggs checked against a light box in the basement, a lit candle gently placed in a snow-dome, watching the Aurora Borealis with Papa before bedtime, the Chinook wind of spring and the sound of snowmelt.

After a short stretch in Seattle, her family moved to Grants Pass, Oregon, when she was twelve, a one-street town settled by prospectors, farmers, and lumberjacks, though if you were black, she notes, you weren't permitted to stay overnight. It was the start of Prohibition, which as Oppen reflects, "incited lawlessness and added an air of secrecy and license, an air of drunkenness, to sex." She talks about teenage courtship being "the flushed and struggling girl finding no safe, satisfying or honorable outcome." It was the dawn of the Nineteenth Amendment. An impoverished, filthy old couple with a derelict farm lived on their block, along with two families of Osage Indians who were oil-rich, dignified, "their beauty almost burned the town." Oppen read everything "from Maeterlinck to Sax Rohmer" in the town's "pitiful" library and planned her escape from a place that "held for me the greatest danger I could conceive: to be trapped in a meaningless life with birth and death in a biological repetition, without serious thought or a search for life with more meaning." At fifteen her father died from cancer and she was suddenly plunged into a loneliness neither wilderness nor sex could alleviate. She worked and saved money for college.

What is essential, what is formative in a life recollected? Is it the nonessential that gives memory its unconscious form and awaits whatever remembrance warrants? Mary Oppen's book is subtitled "An

Autobiography," the sign signifying the life at the heart of its literary enterprise, as the etymology goes: *autos* (self), *bios* (life), *graphein* (to write, to record). In both the East and West the practice traces back to the fourth century, with Tao Qian and Saint Augustine, both impulses coming out of disparate traditions of written biographies. The poet Robert Southey is mistakenly credited with coining the English term in 1809, long after and during the erasure of America's oral autobiographers, the written stories of the indigenous not materializing until the 1830s in a complicated collaborative process that usually involved at least one native informant-translator and a white anthropologist-writer (Paul Radin's *Crashing Thunder: The Autobiography of an American Indian* comes to mind as a particularly fascinating example). Anna Robeson Burr's landmark *The Autobiography: A Critical and Comparative Study* appeared in 1909, the same year William Dean Howells, the "Dean of American Letters," called autobiography in his *Harper's Monthly* column "a new form of literature" and "the most democratic province in the republic of letters." Not an original opinion though still a mark of its rising popularity. Indeed, autobiography seemed made for America. A handful of sources are often pointed to for ballpark numbers: Richard G. Lillard's *American Life in Autobiography* (1956) lists 440 titles published in the first half of the twentieth century; Louis Kaplan's *A Bibliography of American Autobiographies* (1961) lists 6,377 titles published before 1945; Mary Louise Briscoe's *American Autobiography, 1945–1980: A Bibliography* (1982) adds 5,008 titles to Kaplan's list; Patricia K. Addis's *Through a Woman's I: An Annotated Bibliography of American Women's Autobiographical Writings, 1946–1976* (1983) lists 2,217 titles; Russell C. Brignano's *Black Americans in Autobiography* (1984) lists 710 titles.[*] From early colonial chronicles, settlers' narratives, captivity narratives, spiritual-conversion narratives, slave narratives, suffragist narratives, and on with the rise of literacy and work-play diversification, through "descent with modification," as Darwin described evolution, the autobiography in America has become game for any hook, vocation, or identity,

---

[*] See *American Autobiography: Retrospect and Prospect*, edited by Paul John Eakin (Madison, WI: University of Wisconsin Press, 1991), and *American Women's Autobiography: Fea(s)ts of Memory*, edited by Margo Culley (Madison, WI: University of Wisconsin Press, 1992).

from supertramp to robber baron, open to all and anyone who can write down their memories and tell their own story, publication self-guaranteed, a dream of the song of myself woven by everyone themselves.

And like any dream it comes with risks, which is perhaps why, even today, the genre is still treated like an unwanted guest in the glass house of belles lettres. For one, it is easily prone to the "calculated distortion and tactical offhandedness" that Theroux accuses Kipling of in *Something of Myself*. I think of Gulliver's reply to the Shropshire Captain who urged him to put his story "in Paper" upon his return to England: "My answer was that I thought we were already overstocked with books of travel; that nothing could now pass which was not extraordinary; wherein I doubted some authors less consulted truth than their own vanity, or interest, or the diversion of ignorant readers." For "books of travel" read "autobiographies," a genre that has always existed on the outskirts of literature, written, or read, more as an afterthought to the "real" creative work at hand. A sentiment Ezra Pound must have shared when he wrote in a letter to the New Directions publisher James Laughlin, "When a man writes his meeemoires that's a sign that he's finished." Still, at age thirty-five Pound did write a short one in the guise of a book of travel, or "Harzreise" as he called it (an allusion to Heinrich Heine's account of his journey to the Harz Mountains), titled *Indiscretions: Or, Une Revue de Deux Mondes*, a humorously coded, racially cringeworthy romp through his family annals; he also wrote/compiled a gem of one based on his friendship with the artist Henri Gaudier-Brzeska, subtitled "A Memoir." Pound's daughter, Mary de Rachewiltz, also wrote one, *Ezra Pound, Father and Teacher: Discretions*, that came out in 1971, the year before her father died, in which she interspersed lines of *The Cantos* throughout as luminous evidence of the lived life embedded in the lifelong poem.

As Basil Bunting says in his masterwork *Briggflatts*, "A strong song tows / us." Even devoted fans of his delicately structured poem might have forgotten its original subtitle, "An Autobiography." Bunting's poetic aspirations are expressed in the poem itself as reverence for the Italian composer Domenico Scarlatti, who "condensed so much music into so few bars / with never a crabbed turn or congested cadence, / never a boast or a see-here." Oppen is likewise studious of condensation in her prose, her understated, carefully attentive sentences always testing the truth of her experiences without overreaching. She relates their chosen life together—the life that fills the rest of her book beginning with "Love & Escape"—in this way:

> We were in search of an esthetic within which to live, and we were looking for it in our own American roots, in our own country. We had learned at college that poetry was being written in our own times, and that in order for us to write it was not necessary for us to ground ourselves in the academic; the ground we needed was the roads we were traveling. As we were new, so we had new roots, and we knew little of our own country. Hitchhiking became more than flight from a powerful family—our discoveries themselves became an esthetic and a disclosure.

It is a youthful, romantic vision, as well as a serious statement about the relationship between art and life, bound to their times—an aesthetic of discovery that seeks a life in art and art out of life.

Romance (against romanticism) is what encapsulates *Meaning a Life* most for me, a romance of the mind and heart, not a fairy-tale romance, though at times it almost reads like a fairy tale, but a romance with real ups and downs, immersed in the empirical world, lived through their travels in France by horse and cart, through the rise of fascism in Europe that they saw firsthand, through the Great Depression, the Second World War—when George worked a seventy-hour week as a machinist in an airplane factory in Detroit before being drafted into the army at age thirty-six, then sent to fight in the Rhineland for a year before getting seriously wounded in a foxhole, his fellow infantrymen killed—and on through nearly a decade of political exile in Mexico in the 1950s, due to the real threat of persecution under the Smith Act for their work with the Communist Party. A twentieth-century American romance of consciousness on the open road; a book of travel where the autobiographer is not the usual singular self at the center of the story but the union of two individuals. Unlike, for example, Nadezhda Mandelstam's devastating memoir *Hope Against Hope*, written as a testament to her husband, the poet Osip

Mandelstam, while the externals of her own life remain undisclosed or inconspicuous. As Mary writes, "It must be remembered that we were always *two*; we learned from reading and from what we saw, but conversation never ceases between us." She echoes this in a journal she kept on their visit to Israel in 1975 at the invitation of the mayor of Jerusalem: "Of course I am *I* and George is most certainly *George*, his accomplishments are his and mine are mine, *but* the composite life we live is *us*."

"The composite life" meaning to place with, or together. Of their beginning, setting out on their new life into the unknown, they would quote a line by Sherwood Anderson: "we wanted to know if we were any good out there." They recalled this line in letters and interviews, as George did in 1973, writing to Dan Gerber, "the cadence produces the statement of 'out there' as a thing that exists, the line has more than a novelistic quality." It also appears in a poem in *Primitive*, and it comes up in Mary's book when she's recalling their four-year stay in France with their dog Zee-wag during their early twenties. Before that, in the "strange limbo" of George's stepmother's drawing room in San Francisco, his stepmother who required Mary to wear a girdle and gloves when she visited, she mentions reading Lewis and Clark's accounts of their Northwest expeditions, Robert Louis Stevenson's *Travels with a Donkey*, and Charles Doughty's *Arabia Deserta*. Again, they fled George's domineering family for New York, sailing a catboat from Lake St. Clair in Michigan, navigating the rivers to the Erie Canal and through its system of locks, to Albany and down the Hudson River to Seventy-Ninth Street, the whole journey accomplished with only a road map as their guide.

While in New York she mentions reading Proust ("sinking deep into his memories and awakening to intuitive knowledge of my own"), Henry James, and Virginia Woolf ("her writing meant to me the flash of insight while a leaf falls, the knowledge of complex relations that comes in a moment of understanding"). At a party they met the poet Louis Zukofsky, who introduced them to the poet Charles Reznikoff, both poets becoming two of their closest contemporaries, particularly Reznikoff with whom they took long walks around the city and would visit often, and whose verse, Mary wrote after his death in 1976, "remained with me since I was twenty years old." Zukofsky would edit a special issue of *Poetry* magazine in 1931 that was focused on a group of poets, the "Objectivists," whose work he thought sought the "objectively perfect" in "the direction of historical and contemporary particulars." He pointed to Ezra Pound, William Carlos Williams, Marianne Moore, T. S. Eliot, Wallace Stevens, E. E. Cummings, Reznikoff, and Robert McAlmon as practitioners, and included exemplary poems by George Oppen, Basil Bunting, Reznikoff, Williams, and Martha Champion, among others, as well as Emanuel Carnevali's translations of Arthur Rimbaud. Furthering his statement about the meaning of objectivist, Zukofsky refers to "the lens bringing the rays from an object to focus," that the aim of the poem was to achieve "the totality of perfect rest" as formed by "sincerity, the accuracy of detail in writing," for "in sincerity shapes appear concomitants of word combinations, precursors of (if there is continuance) completed sound or structure, melody or form." In an interview Zukofsky described it simply as "thinking with the things as they exist." Reznikoff related the term to a quote by the eleventh-century Chinese writer Wei T'ai that the translator A. C. Graham had used as an epigraph to his *Poems of the Late T'ang*: "Poetry presents the thing in order to convey the feeling. It should be precise about the thing and reticent about the feeling, for as soon as the mind responds and connects with the thing the feeling shows in the words; this is how poetry enters deeply into us." Or as Mary quotes George who attributes Zukofsky:

> the necessity for forming a poem properly, for achieving form. That's what "objectivist" really means. There's been a tremendous misunderstanding about that. People assume it means the psychologically objective in attitude. It actually means the objectification of the poem, the making an object of the poem . . . the attempt to construct meaning, to construct a method of thought from the imagist intensity of vision. If no one were going to challenge me, I would say, "a test of truth." If I had to back it up I'd say anyway, "a test of sincerity"—that there is a moment, an actual time, when you believe something to be true, and you construct a meaning from these moments of conviction.

All of this bears significantly on Oppen's autobiography—her intellectual interests, her approach to prose, how she distills her memories and experiences, proceeding chronologically as a whole while moving back and forth in time within. In some respect her writing makes me think of the nineteenth-century Maine-lover Sarah Orne Jewett—her deep interest in local folks, her plainspoken narratives, her generous spirit, her lack of artifice. While the method, in her own graceful way, feels objectivist inclined, which is not to say that it lacks warmth and humor as that would be untrue.

In France they used Henry Adams's modernist treasure *Mont-Saint-Michel and Chartres* as a guide, his philosophical travelogue through medieval architecture, poetry, and glass, a Baedeker of the luminosity left of Mary in Majesty, her reign in a time when "theology turns always into art at the last, and ends in aspiration." They read Leon Trotsky's *History of the Russian Revolution* while Jewish refugees poured into Paris. Before they had left New York, they decided to start a press with Zukofsky called To Publishers, using some of the inheritance money George received from his mother's family when he turned twenty-one, and while in France printed three paperback titles: Zukofsky's *An "Objectivists" Anthology*, Williams' *A Novelette and Other Prose*, and, in one volume, Pound's *How to Read* and *The Spirit of Romance*. Zero copies sold and the press folded. They visited Pound in Rapallo, when Basil and Marian Bunting lived nearby with their two children. Pound introduced them to Constantin Brancusi, Auguste Rodin, and Ossip Zadkine in Paris; Mary, who had turned to drawing and painting when she stopped writing, studied with other artists at Hilaire Hiler's studio.

Hiler, an American expat who lived in Paris for fifteen years, also pops up in Anaïs Nin's *Diary* and the Canadian poet John Glassco's *Memoirs of Montparnasse*. Glassco probably wrote most of his book long after his three-year jaunt with a friend in 1920s Paris, though he claimed to have written it in his early twenties; it first came out in 1970. Hiler, described by Nin as "big, loud, overflowing," appears pseudonymously in the *Memoirs* as Sidney Schooner, "gigantic American painter . . . lover of whores"; McAlmon also plays a part in Glassco's moveable feast, as a sort of foil for the memoirist. (Memoir, I've gathered, can often be understood as autobiography's more confessional twin, both born from the union of diary and history.) Glassco says that he wrote his reminisces "to record, and in a sense relive, a period of great happiness," the happiness of exchanging prostitutes in a brothel with Schooner and friends, and dining on snails, or Welsh rarebit, with them. A circus of savory literati parades through his loosely fictionalized pages, giving readers, as the poet Stephen Scobie once noted, "the image of the self he never and always was." For Oppen, "Happiness comes in the conversations and the learning that I have to master, even in the barest knowledge of how to get from here to there." She steers clear of the sensational; measures the actual with the particulars of her memories; probes for insight and clarity without complaint or passing judgment. Here are two different approaches to autobiography, neither more "correct" than the other, both welcome in the autobiographical canon, Oppen occupying the actual in the historical and reflective, Glassco the fictive.

The short chapter "1938–1941: Transition" must have been one of the most difficult for Oppen to write. She says,

> Birth . . . I think I am afraid to try to write of it. In childbirth I was isolated; I never talked about it even to George. He was surprised to learn that giving birth was a peak emotional experience and so entirely my own that I never tried to express it. Exposure of the experience has been attempted, and although I concur with the attempt, I do not think it has yet been told in a form in which it is whole. I would wish it to remain whole, and I have preserved the wholeness of my own experience of birth by not telling it; it is too precious to me.

She proceeds to write around birth by confronting death. She speaks about her many stillbirths—holding one dead fetus in a hospital pan—about an infant who died in the cradle at six weeks, the guilt, isolation, and loss she felt because of those deaths, and how she became obsessed with desire for a child. The chapter was published in the journal *Feminist Studies* the same month her book came out, with different opening and closing paragraphs bracketing a similar middle section, and titled "Breath of Life." It is a more private, more personal piece, written on the day Bird died, the small, lifeless body of their pet blue budgie recalling the smallness of their baby boy's death years before. "Transition," like the rest of her autobiography, deftly threads together inner and outer moments, moving seamlessly between public and private matters so that, for instance, Chamberlain's signing of the Munich Pact, celebrated when they are in Utica with the ringing of church bells, occurs while she's struggling with the desperate desire to have a child. Novelists have been doing this for ages, often as a strategic way of using historical events to give the personal greater significance, but it doesn't come across like this in *Meaning a Life*. In an unpublished review of the book, Anita Barrows writes about the Oppens' "sense of life engaging both inner and outer worlds, where neither is overwhelmed by or absorbed by the other." Through Mary's words, the reality of their inner life converges with external events as one continually changing occurrence.

Choosing to write again during the period of second-wave feminism, Oppen benefited from a fertile field of twentieth-century women autobiographers like Jane Addams, Ida B. Wells, Emma Goldman, Edith Wharton, Gertrude Stein, Kate Douglas Wiggin, Mary Austin, Zora Neale Hurston, Dorothy Day, Mary McCarthy, Simone de Beauvoir, Maya Angelou, Margaret Mead, Maxine Hong Kingston, Angela Davis, and the naturalist Sally Carrighar, whose *Home to the Wilderness: A Personal Journey* Oppen quotes in a journal entry: "One's mind has to be emptied, then it fills in an unaccustomed and very rich way." Their work, among many others, opened up the autobiographical form to a multiplicity of subjectivities that inhabit and engage the world in formerly unwritten spheres of thought and experience. Their lives made way for their words; their lives and their words "culturally prepared" the times in which Oppen returned to writing. "In defying the traditional injunction to silence for women," Margo Culley notes in her edited collection *American Women's Autobiography*, "the autobiographical act itself contests WOMAN."

When Oppen turned from writing to the fine arts in her early twenties, it wasn't a passing phase but became a devoted practice of making pictures until the end of her life. She did have some gallery success early on, and, something she fails to bring up in her book, later in life was even included in the 19th National Exhibition of Prints at the Library of Congress in 1963. The public side of the enterprise, however, didn't sit well with her. This is the entirety of an unpublished piece she titled "Fame":

> I know ambitious women, so I know that not only men are ambitious for worldly fame, but women do with less, at least in these times. Other things than fame satisfy me: the fame of the world let into my life threatens me, I don't really want it. I am uncomfortable with it, I don't want to meet the world eye to eye nor do I want to maintain a public stance. I would have to learn, master, become that. I prefer the grace of my life, lived with an ambiance that is familiar— It is a romantic vision, and that is what my life is; it is not only the vision, but it is what I've made, I would defend it, do it again. The public fame for me would have been hell. One person's heaven may be another person's hell. I'd choose my own way again, and it is heaven.

Fame as a threat, as hell in opposition to its lack being heaven, inverts the usual order of our contemporary aspirations. It feels like a particularly radical inversion for our times, a choice proscribed for self-preservation as an act of self-forgetting, true to her sense of individuality and freedom.

Oppen's papers are archived in the Mandeville Special Collections Library at the University of California San Diego. Besides drafts of poems, stories, and essays with typed corrections on pasted paper strips, vignettes of people she knew, journals pasted with scraps of real estate listings, notebooks filled with diary entries, poems, dreams, pasted recipes, and quotations (Camus, Teilhard de Chardin, Rilke, Chekhov, Thomas Traherne, Nietzsche, Kierkegaard . . .), there are nearly two hundred pieces of finished artworks, along with numerous sketchbooks and photograph albums. The images are constructed from a variety of materials and mixed-media, and are of the things Oppen saw around her: cityscapes and seascapes, trees and poppies, canyons and cordilleras, portraits of women and dancing girls, abstract figures, a still life of vases, a conch shell, clothesline, torso, kitchen, bulrushes, ports, and flowers. Watercolor, oil, gouache, acrylic, charcoal, crayon, pencil, or ink are rendered on paper, cardboard, wood, particle board, or tissue on paper. A tree is stitched onto burlap, a swan stenciled on cut paper; there are etchings of horses, owls, a frog, and a Greek goat, an embroidery of a tree, as well as collages, mostly of flowers, and most strikingly an almost two-by-two-foot portrait of George. There is a collage-like portrait of a boy looking down at his yellow tie, raised gently with his fingertips as if sewing; he might have just used it to wipe his red upper lip, the subtly shifting colors of his face a landscape of moods and reflections.

Mary Oppen talks very little about painting in her autobiography, save for a humorous anecdote about an art class in Paris, a brief aside on Hiler, and then later, as political refugees in Mexico, she says that they both took classes at "an art school," without mentioning it was actually the renowned La Esmeralda National School of Painting, Sculpture, and Printmaking, where José Clemente Orozco, Diego Rivera, Frida Kahlo, and many other prominent artists taught at some point or another. Instead, Oppen's lifelong engagement with painting is more immanently evident in *Meaning a Life*, in the writing itself, through her vivid observations, her imagistic compression, her distillation of memories in a nonlinear linearity, and through the very structure of her book, which Barrows fittingly describes in her review as "a series of portraits." Barrows writes, "So the meaning of a life: not necessarily the obvious, not 'narrative' in a strict sense, but rather a series of portraits where outstanding details tend to capsulate the whole. More than a style of writing, I think, this is a way of seeing: a kind of integrity evident as much in the facts of Mary Oppen's life as in the work, refusing to dramatize, exaggerate, defend, but allowing experience to stand for itself." Meaning an honest record of experience, of not wanting to forget, that enriches our life. Meaning constructed from moments of conviction, extracted from memories, the meaning of life *meaning* a life.

I visited Mary Oppen's archive twice, first in December 2011 and then in August 2018, to see if there might be more autobiographical material she had written in the last decade of her life. Some of this work appears in the appended section of this book, "Other Writings." The following three fragments from her papers I've included here as they each speak to a different aspect of her autobiography. The first reproduces the text of a scrap of newspaper clipped inside a red folder that contained a draft of *Meaning a Life*; the second reproduces a typed page titled "To See"; the third reproduces the last section of a typed, three-page piece in a folder titled "At Home in the World":

> Physicians teach that dashed expectations set in motion four recognizable stages in the process of grief: denial, anger, a search for knowledge, and resolution. If the process is not honestly confronted, then the involved individual or group—or even nation—is often suspended too long at the stages of denial and anger.
>
> Denial characterized the nation's attitude toward the Vietnam veteran from the 1960s until the dedication last November of the Vietnam

—

> To see, not to travel everywhere, but to see and talk, and think, and understand. George and I have spent our lives at it. It will never be understood, we try, but we change, and life changes, it's a new eye we see with every time we look, and a new aspect of the universe presents itself to our changed eye. But this is our search: to understand as much as we are able of the universe we are part of.

—

> Michael Hamburger wrote to me, "It is a mistake to carry one's account too far in time, to the point where memory ceases to act as filter." I shall have to live to be eighty to write of all the years and their times that I have lived—I plan to live long, and I find that a perspective of time makes it possible to choose from the wealth of memory, that storehouse of what I have thought, what I have seen, and heard. Memory returns this to me, purified by time, made safe for me and those close to me, safe from my sometimes capricious thoughts and judgments. Time and still

more time. I was writing when I met George and only began again a few years ago. The long span of years was not silence—it was life.

When I began to write, a few years ago, I asked George, "Do you remember any of my early poems? I have forgotten them." George recited two poems to me. The only ones I have from those early times.

—Jeffrey Yang

A NOTE ON THE TEXT

This expanded edition of Mary Oppen's *Meaning a Life: An Autobiography* contains the original text published by Black Sparrow Press in 1978, with a few minor typesetting corrections. Related prose and poetry from Oppen's archive at the Mandeville Special Collections Library at the University of California San Diego has been added in the section "Other Writings." "Re: Maine" first appeared in *George Oppen: Man and Poet*, edited by Burton Hatlen (Orono, ME: National Poetry Foundation, 1981). The other prose pieces in this section were transposed from typed, corrected versions in the archive—an indication of Oppen's possible intention to publish them. Three of these pieces ("Nassau + My Trip to Visit Andy," "After a Conversation with G.," and "'Does she think she is a legend?'") first appeared in a slightly different form as part of a folio, "Sketches of Life," in *North Dakota Quarterly* 2.3 (Summer 1994–95), edited by Rachel Blau DuPlessis from handwritten pieces she found in one of Oppen's spiral notebooks. The poems first appeared in *Poems & Transpositions* (New York: The Montemora Foundation, 1981), a supplement to the literary journal *Montemora*, edited by Eliot Weinberger, and the letterpress chapbook *Mother and Daughter and the Sea* (Madison, WI: Black Mesa Press, 1981). Oppen's long journalistic meditation about their trip to Jerusalem and her mini-sketches of sites visited in Greece, among other vignettes and character sketches in her archive, were not included in this volume as they either overlapped with the autobiography, seemed incomplete and rough, or were too far afield from *Meaning a Life*. A future edition of her writings, as well as of her numerous artworks, awaits an auspicious scholar.

Thanks to Lynda Claassen, Nina Mamikunian, and Robert Melton at the Mandeville Special Collections Library and Archive for New Poetry for their gracious assistance. Thanks also to Rachel Blau DuPlessis for her generous feedback on the introduction and the selection of archival material, and to Eliot Weinberger for all of his conversations about Oppen's work over the years. Thanks to Lindsay Garbutt, Don Share, and the rest of the staff at *Poetry* magazine for publishing an excerpt of the introduction with color plates of some of Mary Oppen's paintings, etchings, and collages—to my knowledge, the first published folio of Oppen's visual art. And to Linda Oppen—without her help, patience, and enthusiasm this new edition of her mother's book would never have been published: Thank you!

MEANING
A
LIFE

An Autobiography

ANNIVERSARY POEM

        'the picturesque
common lot'   the unwarranted light

Where everyone has been

The very ground of the path
And the litter grow ancient

A shovel's scratched edge
So like any other man's

We are troubled by incredulity
We are troubled by scratched things

Becoming familiar
Becoming extreme

Let grief
Be
So it be ours

Nor hide one's eyes
As tides drop along the beaches in the thin wash of
          breakers

And so desert each other

—lest there be nothing

      The Indian girl walking across the desert, the
sunfish under the boat

How shall we say how this happened, these stories, our
        stories

Scope, mere size, a kind of redemption

Exposed still and jagged on the San Francisco hills

Time and depth before us, paradise of the real, we
        know what it is

To find now depth, not time, since we cannot, but depth

To come out safe,   to end well

We have begun to say good bye
To each other
And cannot say it

—George Oppen

A BEGINNING

1908–1917

In our photograph album I have pictures of my two grandmothers, Mary Merchant and Emma La Marr. I did not know my grandfather Colby, so for me it is Mary Merchant who heads my Colby family. Colbys made their way westward from Deer Isle, Maine, and in the Historical Society on Deer Isle I once read an account of Laura Colby, who received a handbill from a passing sailboat with the news that the Americans had won the war against the British. Her sons rowed her the ten miles to Castine to tell the British commander the news.

Gabriel Colby was a banker in Des Moines, Iowa, at the time of the Civil War, and at his death his wife Mary was left with her fifteen-year-old son, ten daughters, and my father Ora, the younger son. Mary managed the bank and in wartime became prosperous. She survived through wartime speculation but after the war was land-poor. She married off nine of the daughters, but she kept the youngest to care for her and outlive her, still unmarried. Each year my grandmother Colby came to visit us for three days and I felt the tension between her and my mother. When she was with us she became the head of the house.

My grandfather Thomas Conklin went from upper New York State to join the Union Army. At war's end he collected his back pay and started walking west. After meeting my grandmother Emma La Marr in Ohio, he walked farther west to Montana, where he took a homestead near Kalispell. Emma went out to Kalispell from Ohio and they lived a frontier life. Grandfather, who played the fiddle, started a singing school, and they sang with a few neighbors who gathered together from their homesteads in the vicinity. My mother's memory of farm life was that they all worked far too hard. Grandfather went to town only to buy what they could not grow on their own land. My mother wanted a silk dress and a gold ring when she was six years old; "A gold ring won't keep you warm," her father told her, "but I will buy you a piece of silk as long as the paring you can peel from an apple."

Family farms were large—one hundred forty acres of wheat-land was my grandfather's homestead. Anyone could take a homestead grant of land from the government; the only requirement was to improve the land, which meant building a dwelling, living in it and putting the land into production. A photograph pictures my oldest brother, a baby, sitting with my mother's youngest sisters in front of the family log cabin. My grandparents must have lived long hard years in that cabin in a struggle with the land to make it support them and their fourteen children.

Mama had the face of her mother and of her Norman ancestors. I have seen my mother's face in Normandy—the same blue blue eyes, strong hawklike nose and high cheekbones bright with color. Born Alice Carrie Conklin, she had the features of some far-off Viking ancestor. Mama felt free and capable, and the atmosphere in our home was an atmosphere of equal work, but all her life she wanted diamonds, and a fur coat was a symbol to her. It seemed to me that her stories of her childhood were eventful, but she felt deprived. When Mama left the homestead to go back east to a teachers' college, she worked to support herself in my grandmother Colby's house, baking bread for the large family. At sixteen she graduated and took her first job near Coeur d'Alene, Idaho, where she lived with a family who had children in the school. She rode her horse side-saddle back and forth each day to the school. When she was eighteen and my father Ora was twenty-one, they married and moved to Big Fork, Montana, where Ora had an appointment as post-master and Alice taught the first school in the new settlement.

I think that my father's older brother had not made room for my father in the family business in Des Moines, or perhaps Ora would not stay in Des Moines; Ora and his brother were not friends. That first year in Montana, Ora had a crippling rheumatism, and he spent long hours in the summer sun, baking out pain. In the newly settled wilderness in Montana my parents' neighbors were the Indians, and that summer Ora became friends with the Flathead Indian chief, Drag-Your-Tail-Feathers-Over-the-Hill. He would invite the chief to visit and the very next day the chief would be waiting beside the door and they would spend the day together. The chief took from the table any food that was not eaten, for food was traditionally taken home to women and children from any feast.

(In 1974 I read of Indians forming an organization to save themselves from further degradation, and one of the leaders is a man from Montana named Drag-Your-Tail-Feathers—maybe a grandson or a great-grandson of my father's friend.)

At the time my parents went to Big Fork in 1896 the northwest was being settled by waves of immigrants from Germany and Scandinavia. Land had to be wrested from wilderness; virgin forests could still be found when I was small, although in 1908, when I was born, lumbering was already a big industry. Farmhouses built by these northern people resembled the white-painted, gabled farmhouses left behind in the old country. A farmer was judged by his barn: if the barn was in good repair and was big, cared for and used, if he had hay in the loft and cows in his stalls, he was thought to be a good farmer, though his house might need paint and the porch might be sagging. Wheat, potatoes, and apples were the main crops, and every farmer fattened a few pigs as well and kept at least a few cows to supply butter, milk, cheese, and meat.

These north European farmers brought their customs with them. Most of them were Lutherans, and they built their small white-steepled church in the town near our house. In back of the church was a long shed for sheltering the horses and buggies that brought the families to church. The influence of New England was manifest in the town—Kalispell had the Chautauqua Circuit, a touring cultural organization that came in summer for a few weeks and again in the winter. My family subscribed, and we all attended lectures, opera, recitations, singing, a strange assortment of entertainment; Protestant and Catholic churches, singing societies, several fraternal societies, and a Carnegie Library also existed in the town. Somewhere near Kalispell a Chinese graveyard with its peaked monuments held offerings of food and flowers on certain days. The graveyard must have dated from the time when Chinese men came over in large numbers to build the Great Northern railway, completed from coast to coast in 1896; the Chinese had been ruthlessly exploited, so stories tell, and the graveyard marked their many deaths.

When I was due to be born our house was not yet finished, and Papa hurried to get the kitchen ready in time for my birth. Mama and Aunt Dill (who was going to care for me for a few days), Dr. Fisher and Papa were in the new house when I was born in the finished kitchen, and a chestnut tree was planted for me in a corner of our new front yard. The street was new, the town was new except for a small section of Main Street and the depot of the railroad. Kalispell is on a river in the Rocky Mountains, and I think it is still on the main line of the railroad. Highways for automobiles were not continuous in the same condition of roadway until fairly recently, and we traveled, when it was a long distance, by train. Kalispell was isolated; the adults felt a nostalgia for homes back east—New York State, Ohio, or Iowa for my parents and grandparents. For others it was New England, but for many it was Scandinavia or Germany, and for three Chinese it was faraway China—not east but west across the Pacific. From the Orient came nearly all our bowls, baskets, lacquer trays, boxes, and my dolls, especially the small ones I liked to sew for. The one restaurant had a Chinese cook, although the meals that were served were mashed potatoes and a boiled vegetable with meat and gravy. A Chinese man was also the only laundry man in town. Chinese were scattered throughout the northwest, lonely without their women and children.

The railroad station was the most important place in Kalispell. Men who hung about the livery stable ("hired men" who were hired on farms when they were needed) moved off, when a train was due, toward the station, where baggage cars rumbled on the wooden platform, and sometimes there was a job for one of the jobless men, a trunk to move or a wagon to load. The train arrived in a cloud of steam and screeching brakes, whistling and tooting; everything that came to Kalispell came by that train.

Once Mama and I traveled from Kalispell to faraway Spokane to visit Mama's sister. It was night when we arrived in Spokane, and I stepped down from the train to a street lit by electricity. Lights! and signs!—a pig jumped up and down and put a whistle to his snout. I watched entranced, and I'd have stayed watching, but my aunt came toward us and the grown-ups moved toward a streetcar. A streetcar! At each new thing I wanted to stay and ponder and stare. The streetcar lurched and lumped along until we came to a house with cousins I did not know, a household with different smells and, it seemed to me, with no rules for behavior. I was buffeted by the strange cousins; I was disturbed at not being left alone to see or to think or wonder at all that was new. At last I began to cry, and Mama had to cut short her visit. Again we went on the streetcar and saw the dancing pig and the lit streets. We slept at night in a Pullman car in a snug berth made up for us by a Negro porter. All was quiet and the other passengers had disappeared when I looked out from our curtains to see the train aisle transformed into a dark green corridor in which ladder-like steps for climbing into the upper berths had been placed. The curtains swayed with the train's motion, and the only light was at the end of the car where the porter sat. A little hammock hung from head to foot beside our window for our clothes, and in the corner of the berth was a reading light which I turned on and off. I raised the tightly-drawn window curtain and the mountains flashed by. I had never imagined, when the train come tooting and whistling into Kalispell each day, that inside the train was an enchanted life with a ritual of service, a ritual that makes me sleepy still to recall it.

Alice in Wonderland seemed to me not only a foreign child, but a child hampered by too many petticoats and interfering adults. I felt not very different from her but much more free. Dorothy of Oz was closer to my feeling for myself. She knew Kansas as I knew Montana, and she met adventures outside her barren home surrounded by her powerful friends and companions just as I felt protected by Papa and Mama and three older brothers.

At the railway station I used to talk to the engineer and the fireman in their long-billed caps as they leaned from the windows in the engine and coal-tender, waiting for the loading of coal, water, mail, and baggage. Papa was the postmaster in Kalispell, and sometimes I watched the sorting of the mail while townspeople stood around talking and waiting for their newspapers from back east. The arrival of the train was the moment in the day in Kalispell when people met, when they talked and thought about the rest of the world out beyond the mountains.

Many families in Kalispell kept a horse and many had a cow as well. My family had owned a horse named Maude, but by the time I was born we had an automobile. Papa and several other men in town wanted Fords, but Henry Ford would send cars only to a dealer, so Papa agreed to be the dealer. He ordered the cars, and after they were delivered he gave up the agency. My oldest brother Wendell is still bitter—he says, "Just think what a Ford agency would have meant to us boys." Wendell spoke of my father in an aggrieved tone, but I don't think my youngest brother and I ever found any lack in our father. I felt he was there for me, and for me to imagine him to be different would be to imagine the world into which I was born a different world.

The Ford had straps to the front of the hood to hold the top forward; in fine weather we folded the top behind the back seat. The car was high, very like a horse-drawn carriage, with running-boards serving as steps and with a tool-box fastened to the running-board. Papa made all the repairs himself on the spot usually, wherever we were. On summer evenings Papa would say, "Let's go for a drive," and I would run quickly to hunt for his cap which was always mislaid. He drove the Ford (later it was the Maxwell and then the Overland) trundling along at twenty miles an hour, chatting, looking, and stopping if there were new flowers, a pig with new piglets, or a sheep with new lambs. He drove as far as the steel bridge which had replaced the ferry. At home, when we climbed down from the car, I could still smell our horse Maude; she had lived in the stall where we now kept our car.

When I was five my friend took me to school with her to visit. The teacher placed a small chair for me near my friend, and as the children worked with crayon and paper she backed slowly down the aisle looking at each child's work. I gave her skirt a yank—I wanted her to look at my friend's paper. She turned, picked me up, and put me outside in the cloak-room. She didn't want me! I took my bonnet from a nail, put it on, and left the building. As I walked home I passed a house where my mother had taken me to call, and the man of the house had given me stereopticon slides to look at while the adults talked. I climbed the steps, I rang the bell, was invited in and given the viewer and a stack of cards. School dismissed, the children went home, and an alarm was raised to find me.

Next year I was in school. Miss Telgener, whose skirt I had yanked the year before, gave each of us a large white lump of library paste on a little piece of paper. We used a finger to spread it where needed for our paper work, on paper lanterns, chains or baskets. The paste had an aroma of cloves and a delicious taste, and I asked, "May I have more?" I had eaten mine—it was cool and smooth and the flavor burned a little. I wonder, do they still serve it in first grade?

My parents and my brothers built a summer house, Mereshack, at Flathead Lake. In our album is a photograph of my mother with me, an infant, on her lap, while my brothers fished nearby on a rocky point above the lake. In summers at Flathead Lake I used to stare into the grasses, and I could sing as Robert Louis Stevenson sang about his childhood in Scotland:

> *And all about was mine, I said*
> *For me the bees come by and sing.*

I loved Mereshack. Walking to our nearest neighbor's house, I took a path through the woods, our dog Zeewag accompanying me. Grandpa Wade told me stories of his Civil War days and how he had received the wound from which he still limped. I loved the paths, but my ancient friend preferred the smoother walking of the road, a new road in a new nation, and with his cane he chucked the rocks that fell from the hillside, as he walked to Mereshack with me.

Wendell was our fisherman, and he took his pole and creel with a can of worms or grasshoppers for bait to spend the day by himself, fishing the stream from high up on the mountain until it tumbled into the lake and he was near home, his creel full of brook trout. We ate trout fried crisp for dinner, with wild strawberries brought from an upper meadow for dessert, and next day we all went to gather more berries, cans, and pails tied to our belts. A cedar tree bent toward the water from a steep bank near our cabin; we would climb out its trunk, and as the tree bent lower we kept the motion going and the tree would rise and fall, rise and fall, dipping a little into the lake. I also had a swing from the first branch of a giant fir tree, and when I swung out over the lake high in air I could see a rowboat passing or a launch moving slowly down the center of the lake from a lumber town at one end to the other end, where a road entered the Flathead Indian reservation.

Mosquitoes and No-see-ums (black flies) were a nuisance in June. I wrapped my legs in tissue paper and pulled my long stockings over the paper to protect my legs. People who had to go out of doors at that season swathed themselves like beekeepers. We kept smudge-pots going on the corners of our big front porch even in July and August, and we seldom lit a lamp because the insects swarmed to the light.

Papa came on weekends, and in the dark he told a story or Mama sang, and we sang too—"In the Gloaming" or "It's a Long Way to Tipperary." After my brothers were grown we no longer went to Mereshack; Mama did not want to go there for the whole summer with only me for company.

At Papa's vacation time we went on camping trips in groups of four or five families. An accordion-like rack on the running-board at Papa's left hand was the riding place for Zeewag, who strained forward into the wind and was the first to jump down when we stopped. Zeewag was even more eager than we were to go camping; he made a quick sally to greet each of us before running off on his own investigations. For all of us it was a joyful passage through tall timber with snow and glacier-capped mountains high above us. The roads we traveled were dusty or muddy; saplings or logs laid across marshy places in the road made what we called "corduroy," over which our wheels rumbled as we passed. Sometimes the men in our party cut more saplings to lay over deep mud. Bridges which had been built for horsedrawn lumber-wagons were thrown across streams or ravines by lumber-workers. The roadway on these bridges was of planks laid over an under-structure of logs, with no side rails; we dismounted before crossing to lighten the load in the car, and someone always walked in front of each car to make sure the wheels stayed on the planks. I then crossed to the other side on foot, aware of the drop to a sometimes roaring river far below. Wide rivers had a ferry, usually manned by a father and son who lived nearby. The road which slanted steeply down into the river was visible on the other bank, rising steeply to continue into wilderness. We passed horses with caution, as they were still unused to seeing cars and might bolt. We seldom met another car, and we never passed one; Papa usually slowed down to wait until the huge clouds of dust had settled. If it had rained, sheets of water flew out as our wheels passed through puddles in the road. Before a trip, Papa inquired at the Post Office until he found someone who had recently been over a road we planned to go on, because roads washed out, bridges gave way, marshy places became bogs, and ferries were sometimes not running. A trip in any direction from Kalispell was an adventure.

One vacation, we camped the first night in a big shed at a lumber camp where the owner was Papa's friend. Hay was spread in the barn, and we slept in a long row, twenty or more of us. I awoke to a shot. Papa was sitting up and by the light of his flashlight he was shooting wood rats! In the wilderness beyond the camp, before Papa stopped the car at our next camping place, Mama saw a grouse and she jumped out, shot the grouse, and had it ready for the pot by the time the fire was burning.

Next day, another child and I started across some shallow rapids with a young woman from another tent holding us each by one hand. As she lost her footing in the swift current she let me go, and I was swept downstream. One of the men heard our screams, jumped in and rescued me. I don't remember fear—perhaps it happened too fast—what I do remember is the strange assortment of clothing that was found for me until my own dried out.

On our way home an electrical storm broke over our heads with a cloudburst. We were on a high road overlooking Flathead Lake; the road was slippery red clay, only one car wide with an occasional turn-out for passing. Our car had hard tires with big wheels, and we slipped and slid, coming perilously near the cliff edge, but we stayed on the road and slithered our way to the bottom. As always when a storm broke, we had a discussion: should we put on the isinglass side curtains? If we put them on we all had to get out as the curtains were kept under the back seat. We struggled with fastenings which fitted badly and kept out little rain. It was dark long before we reached Kalispell and Papa lit the carbide lamps, which made a bright light; yet, the road was dark and we were wet and cold. We climbed stiffly down from the car in our barn at home and I still remember the smell of carbide as Papa turned out the lamps.

I remember this trip particularly as the best thing our family did together. My brothers have yearned for the spirit of those times, and they have lived close to the forests all their lives, but I think it was my father's spirit that made our way of life—and now, writing this, I add my mother's spirit too.

One time Mama and I went to the Indian reservation so that Mama might take the medicinal waters and bathe in the hot sulfur baths. Papa drove us to the reservation and helped us set up our tent on a platform provided for tent-floors; we chose one near a stream. The baths were of sulfur-mud; soda-water and sulfur-water were drunk for the cure. People came to treat a variety of ailments—a girl my age, crippled from polio, became my friend, and after her daily bath we played together. Our friend Mr. Haines, an elderly man, helped us build a water-wheel and a little dam on the stream near our tent; our little wheel turned in the current and our dam of rocks made a pool into which we put our feet.

An Indian Pow-wow was held while we were at the hot spring. Flathead Indians came to the ceremony with their sick and ailing from long distances. As they arrived, all the women were walking, with the many dogs running alongside or under the wagons; eligible maidens and the young braves were on horseback. I watched them set up camp—the many teepees made a village around the hot springs—and they prepared for the dance. One boy my age had a red vest entirely covered with bear-claws worked into a design. Everyone wore beaded moccasins for dancing; men wore head-dresses with feathers trailing down the back. They danced, a stomping dance, to drums, and sometimes the dancer turned around and around, again dancing in the circle of men. Men left the dance and returned, campfires smoked, women were busy at the fires, children ran in and out of teepees. The dancing was a religious ceremony, danced with reverence by the Indians, but I did not understand its meaning when I saw it. Probably my attitude reflected that of the grown-ups around me—they held the Indians in contempt. We were even there on their reservation, without thinking to ask permission!

The trip home must have been long and tiring, but I remember my growing excitement as we came nearer to Kalispell. Traveling has always made the return tense for me; excitement builds until I cannot bear to be met, but want to savor the return all the way from the station, all the way home! For a day or two I prefer to be alone, to look newly on all that I know from a previous time, to see the changes, try to glimpse the meaning of what has happened and is happening, to hear with a stranger's more alert ear the voices I know well, to see with that more acute eye all that I jealously claim as my own. It is perhaps one of the chief joys of traveling: to come home.

In early years no limit was set on game to be taken, although a hunting season was declared and we always had a full allowance. A large part of our meat for the winter was game, especially venison, of which Mama made mincemeat. She canned some of the meat with a pressure cooker; haunches were taken to the butcher, who smoked them for us and sliced them thin, and he also kept fresh meat for us in his lockers until we needed it. We sent meat to friends in town who had no hunter in their household; fish or small game was shared too. In my household of four hunters, with my mother sometimes making the fifth, we always had plenty of game. Papa sometimes took visitors from back east on these hunting trips, and after the hunt we had a feast of the game they brought home. One time a heap of ducks lay in the middle of the kitchen floor, and Mama sat pulling the feathers while the ducks were still warm. She looked up, and a duck, bare of feathers, rose from the pile and staggered across the kitchen before it fell, dead.

Papa carved and served at all our meals. I sat at his right hand, and Mama sat at the other end of the table laden with food for the feast. All the hunters were seated, including the friends from back east who had joined the hunt, and neighbors and friends were invited. All of us were talking, waiting for our plates to be served. Papa finished carving a duck, served a plate, and passed it to the most important guest. He started to carve another duck, and it slipped—it flew across the room to land beyond Mama's shoulder on the side-board among the dishes!

The visitors from back east kept my parents in touch with families and friends. At times chance visitors to Kalispell whom Papa met at the Post Office were invited to the hunt and the feast; any traveler was welcome at our table.

I used to sit on my parents' bed watching Mama dress to go out in the evening. She wore a different corset from her everyday corset, and she looped the strings over the bedpost and backed away from it to pull the waist in tighter, making her bosom and hips seem large, her waist small. Under the corset was a chemise; over the corset she put on a camisole which tied under her bosom with a string and was elaborate with embroidery and lace at the top. She then pulled on under-drawers edged with lace at the knees. Petticoats came next, several if they were starched and lacy, or she sometimes wore a beautiful taffeta petticoat that changed color from purple to green and rustled, almost whistled. Sometimes she wore a white sequin-covered evening dress, which was her finest. Another I liked was of pink plaid taffeta with a full skirt—this was an afternoon dress which she wore to parties more formal than her Bridge Club. Mama's hair was bright auburn and long, falling to her hips as she brushed it until it shone. She piled it high and put in a little comb or hairpins here and there, until it stayed where she had piled it. She dusted her face with rice-powder; all the color in her face was her own and she couldn't have used more. Papa and Mama kissed us goodbye, and we watched them from the doorway as they left the house for the evening. After they left, we had a moment of feeling lost. In a wild sort of spree we could do as we wanted, but what did we want? We could and did stay up late; my brothers telephoned their girlfriends, teasing them and acting mysterious over the phone. Then our spirits lagged, and it was hard to keep up the pitch of excitement that had surged. We withdrew, Paul to his clarinet and I to my book; later Wendell usually read to me, put me to bed, heard my prayers and kissed me goodnight.

Our neighbors the Coles had come from England by way of Tasmania, 40° south of the equator, all the way to Montana, 40° north of the equator. Their eldest girl was named Tasmania for her birthplace. Raymond, their youngest child, and I (the youngest in my family) were friends. Since we were the older children on our block, Raymond and I chose our companions from the younger children for our games: Run-Sheep-Run, Hide and Seek, Anny High Over. The U.S. was at war and we played Huns and Allies; we must have made our game too real, because I was afraid to go home when I was called to supper. Raymond and I always vied for leadership, and although he was my most interesting companion, sometimes I sat on his chest and beat him. One day my mother called from the doorway, "Mary, get up off Raymond—you're getting too big for that!" And a difference was made in our play.

When the Coles had a pile of sand dumped in their back yard for construction work, the kids of the neighborhood came to play in the sandpile. We made a park with little stones and tips of shrubs for trees, but we needed the look of water; after trying pieces of glass for water surface we found that smashed glass produced the effect of water for our fountains, streams, and ponds. We had made a beautiful park and we stood up to admire it, calling to Raymond's mother, "Come and see!" She looked closely and began removing our smashed glass, and she sent us home although we promised not to smash glass any more.

After school, as I was the youngest and schooldays were shorter for me, I was the first one to reach home. I would race upstairs to the toilet, and as I sat my brothers arrived, raced upstairs and, standing in a row, peed into the bathtub. Then I went down to the cellar for an apple and a handful of peanuts from a hundred-pound bag that Papa had bought; I ate them raw, but Mama roasted them for the rest of the family. With my apple and my peanuts in my pocket I emerged on my back porch to survey the back yards and to find playmates. In autumn we played in the leaves. We marked out rooms with rows of heaped-up leaves, added halls and gardens, played at housekeeping and visited each other's house. Or we heaped a mountain of leaves to run and jump into, and for a few days when the frosts first came we walked to school through piles of gold and red.

Two factions among the kids on our block (perhaps from the two sides of the street) warred, with the red berries from mountain ash trees providing ammunition. We fought all the way home from school, and once when we got home Raymond and I captured Sylvia, who was perhaps two years old, from the other group. Armed with bayonets and swords from my brothers' belongings in the basement, the two of us marched out to defend our prisoner. We brandished our arms, and Sylvia's mother came forth to take Sylvia into the house. She sent us home, warning us not to play with real weapons again—and she was unarmed!

Next door there lived an old Norwegian couple, who owned a rug with great red roses woven into it. When the old woman baked flatbread on top of her big kitchen stove, she would call to Raymond and me. She buttered and sugared the hot flatbread, a piece for each of us, and we sat happily on her rug in her living room eating the fresh flatbread.

On the way to school in the winter-time, in the gloaming of winter-short days, I met farmers driving sledges loaded with wood. The low sledges had wooden runners, for the roads and streets were snow-covered all winter long. I would run and step on a runner, clinging to the sledge. Other children joined me, and we rode to school behind the half-frozen farmer and his powerful team of steaming horses. The horses liked the cold and the farmer talked to them: "Gee now, slow there girl, steady, steady." As we reached the school and hopped off we shouted our thanks, and he raised his arm in salute.

In winter my brothers took me with them to the coulée* with our dog Zeewag, trained by Paul to pull me on my sled. Paul went beside the sled on skis, sometimes letting one ski fly ahead of him, slipping his foot back into the ski-strap when he had caught up to it. At the coulée we unharnessed Zeewag, and Paul and I coasted down one side of the coulée and halfway up the other. We harnessed Zeewag again to pull the sled to the top. On other occasions our whole family went with our toboggan to the coulée, and we all piled on the toboggan to go flying down the steep side faster than the sled had gone and far up the other side of the coulée.

We waited eagerly for the ice to thicken on the skating pond; my brothers and their friends cleared the snow from the ice with a long-handled scraper, which they pulled or shoved over the ice, piling the snow at the edges of the pond where the edge-grasses grew and the ice was spongy and soft. In the center the ice was clear, and on the bottom bubbles moved in a sluggish current under the ice. I remember the skating pond at night, with a bonfire blazing near the path where we sat to lace on our skating-shoes or to clamp on our skates. Before I could balance myself alone on my skates, a brother or my father took me round and round the pond. The high-school girls and boys skated fast alone or circled the pond arm in arm almost dreamily, the boy holding the girl with his arm around her waist. As they skated near the fire they became bright and visible, but as they went on into the darkness they almost disappeared. On winter nights my brothers always ate supper fast, to hurry to the pond.

After school, for an hour or so before dark, Raymond and I played in the snow. We chose teams, built forts, and fought battles that lasted from day to day. At times the game was too bitter and we weren't easily

---

* A Montana word, meaning a cut, wash, or gully.

friends again. As I stepped out my front door, not thinking about the fighting, I'd be hit by a snowball and the battle would be on. I liked best to roll a snowball so big that I could not roll it anymore. I placed a smaller snowball on top, and then a third, and the sculpture work began. Or sometimes I made a dome out of a number of snowballs, with spaces between. I placed a lit candle inside the dome, and after I had gone home I could see, from the window of our house, my little snow-dome glowing and glimmering in the dark.

Before going to bed Papa always stepped outside the door, and sometimes I stepped out with him into the cold, sparkling Montana night. The Aurora Borealis sometimes lit the northern sky behind the mountains, and right at our door the snow sparkled, and we pointed to Orion, the Dipper and the North Star.

A great deal of the activity in our household went on in the basement. My parents sat before a box with electric light inside it, and against two holes in the box they held egg after egg; if the egg was clear, it was put in a crock of water-glass, a liquid which shut off the oxygen from the pores of the egg-shell and preserved the eggs. In winter I was sent to the basement, and from the row of big crocks I took sauerkraut or eggs, or from the big bags and barrels I took potatoes or apples, or I selected a jar of fruit for our dessert. I sat on the broad steps to the basement to watch my father and brothers skin the deer they brought home from the hunt, and it was also in the basement that Papa and I made new ammunition. He set out a blow-torch with the flame directed against a cast-iron pot full of lead and a ladle with a long handle to dip the lead when it was melted. The molds were laid out below the lead-pot, and we set out pans for the newly molded bullets. As the lead melted he dipped and poured it into a mold; a little hole at the end of the mold received the lead, and it flowed into the mold to make a dozen bullets at a time. When these cooled I spilled them from the opened mold and placed them in rows in the pans, and we melted grease and poured it into the pans to hold the bullets. On another evening I helped fill the shells. Pressing an empty shell against a device which released a measured amount of gunpowder into the shell, I then handed it to Papa, who operated a simple press that forced the new bullet into the shell casing.

Spring came all of a sudden. In March the Chinook wind blew, and we woke to the sound of running water; we knew the snow was melting, and we were suddenly too warm in bed. In the morning the snow was slush, and by afternoon the gutter in front of our house was running with swift water. I whittled a boat to launch it in the swift current, then I pursued it, for it carried the coffin of Ferdinand de Soto, who had asked that he be set adrift in the Mississippi river when he died. I thought of him and wondered if he had ever reached the sea.

When the Chinook wind blew we drove to the foothills to see the windflowers, the earliest flowers to bloom where the snow first leaves the ground. And in the early spring I wandered on the prairie behind our house, gathering the flowers that covered the ground with color. The farthest I walked was to the coulée, where the Indians encamped. Sometimes there was one teepee, sometimes several; these were Flathead Indians who had come to town to trade. The women sat on the ground working soft deerskin into moccasins or shirts. I went one year with my brothers to an Indian woman's teepee, and with some trepidation I gave her my foot to be measured. She made me a pair of beautifully beaded moccasins.

I had my own plot in the large family garden behind our house. When Papa gave me a red rose bush I planted it there, and when my pet rabbit died I buried him in a corner of my garden. Bergamot grew on his grave, and for years I thought that bergamot grew where rabbits were buried. Papa had rows of prize-winning gladioli, and Mama preferred roses in her part of the garden, but my brothers found garden work tedious. When they worked in the garden they pulled so many planted things along with weeds that Mama gave up asking them for help. Much of their time was spent in the forests hunting or fishing, but it was music that enchanted Paul. He unwillingly left his clarinet to go to school, and he raced up the stairs to practice when he entered the house; my childhood was accompanied by the sweet music of his clarinet.

When Paul was two years old he waded out in a flooded creek to an islet where his cat was stranded, and Mama had to rescue them both. Paul, my middle brother, had the redgold hair and strong Norman features of our maternal ancestors. In his outward boy-life he teamed with Noel in a boys' world of hunting, trapping, and fishing—two boys' secret world—but in the house he withdrew into his music, with which he surrounded himself and held us out. If he was drawn into conversation, he had a flashing, wicked wit and merciless humor; he was mockingly handsome. Paul was a loner—I think even his friendship with Noel closed as they approached adulthood. As a fourteen-year-old, Paul wore knickerbockers, one pant-leg always hanging, with his hair over his eyes as he lay on the floor reading, oblivious to all of us. He trained our animals, demanding slavish obedience and the devotion of our dogs, and he could also betray the dog with cold cruelty. Paul asked one day, "Mary, may I take your dog with me hunting?" I said yes, but he never brought my dog home. I have always thought that Paul shot my dog; perhaps the dog was a nuisance to the rest of the family, I never knew for sure. But the child's intuition is believed by the child, and I believed that Paul killed my dog.

What was it in Paul, what was the betrayal in his own young life that isolated him and alienated him? My mother did not reject either Paul or Wendell, they were her favorites; but Paul was never open to friendship from me. I found him closed at the time I first remember him, by the time I began talking. He looked on, perhaps never really very aware that I was there. Paul was intent on music as a career, but Papa did not see that Paul could support himself with music; he always thought of Paul's music as an avocation.

In the community, any prank was attributed to my brothers Paul and Noel ("those Colby boys"). My brothers tell of ringing front doorbells on Halloween until the irate householder burst from his door, to fall headlong because my brothers had removed the wooden steps from his porch. They tell of putting a buggy or a wagon on the roof of a man's own shed, of ringing the church bell until the preacher ran out of his parsonage, of way-laying the high-school principal and beating him up. My brothers, especially Paul, were outlaws. They got into nearly serious trouble: they ran away, they vandalized cottages at resort places, they had accidents, they got into escapades which required all the help our father could muster. In the outside world which seemed so mysterious to me, Papa had the strength which made our family a fortress against that world, a fortress to which we could retreat to recuperate for another attempt on the world outside the family. The home was a place so safe that by the time I was older, I assumed the world, too, would be a safe place for me.

Noel, youngest of the three boys, was charming—handsome not in the classic style that was Paul's but with a high, proudly-held head and bearing. He stood near Mama as she worked in the kitchen and talked to her, or when she was doing fancy-work he was so interested that she promised him the embroidery would be his one day. Noel charmed his teachers, his girlfriends—he was in a sense defeated by his charm, because he depended on it until he found himself at an age and with pride grown so strong that he was unable to pursue what he really wanted. Perhaps he never tried very hard to find what it was that he really did want. He grew cynical. He tried and failed in the great world outside; he was always uneasy, ready to feel he was being used for his intelligence or his charm. He never broke through these feelings to be his own man, with mature confidence in his own ability to live a life of the mind, and his mind gave him no peace. He had wanted to go to Annapolis, but my father's politics prevented his appointment in the year he graduated from high school, so he joined the Marines as a substitute for Annapolis. Noel served three years in Nicaragua during the intervention by the U.S. in that country; he came home malarial and thin, but to me he was a romantic figure. I was in love with everything about him—his uniform, the Spanish he spoke, his gaunt and meager body. It was a long time before he regained normal weight; when he recovered he worked for a while driving a taxi in San Francisco, then on the Pilot boat, the same old Bluenose Fisherman that still serves, now with reduced sails and a larger motor. The boat stayed a week at a time out near the Light-Ship waiting for the incoming ships to take pilots, until all the pilots were gone ashore and the pilot-ship came in to be replenished. I tell about these jobs because anything that touched Noel touched me. My father felt he had to find a way for the three brothers to continue in their lives, as they did not go ahead for themselves, and Noel gladly came home to Grants Pass when my father urged him to return. Perhaps it was too early in the history of education in the West to have thought of college for them, but I do not think such an idea was discussed. It would be a little strange not to think of college, because Mama had left Kalispell to go back east to a teachers' college and Papa had attended a business college. I think Noel did not know how one went to college, or what careers were open to him. When I was of an age to leave high school, I would not easily have found my way to college if the County Agent had not been vigilant to find me and to make it easy for me to get there. Noel did not find such help at the moment he needed it, and no male in our family line had taken the path to higher learning. The paths the two families had pursued had been agriculture and business, and the revolt of my brothers was to reject business or farming for lumbering, trucking, or the cutting of Christmas trees.

Wendell, Mama's first child, was bound to her as long as she lived; either she never let him go, or he never left her. Wendell stood outside the close relationship of his two younger brothers, yet "those Colby boys" included him although he never participated in their wild pranks or their adolescent anarchy. Wendell has clung to blood relationships. Mama broke up his marriages, and Wendell returned each time to live with her, until she died, when he remarried his wife Al, whose children eventually provided him with grandchildren. Wendell loves children and buys bicycles for his grand-nephews, just as he had bought me my first bike when I was nine and he was twenty-one, with the money he earned on his first job. Although Al divorced Wendell a second time, he still keeps a bond with all the young relatives.

I had a favorite cup and saucer from which I drank my morning chocolate. Once Wendell came into the kitchen, grumpy and not yet awake, and complained that I was not dressed as he wanted me to dress (I was adolescent and probably my skirts were too short). I only remember that I turned my full cup upside down, smashing it on the table, then stood up and left the kitchen. I knew that Wendell loved me; what I did not understand was that he wanted me to remain his little sister forever.

Wendell now comes to visit at Christmastime, when his Christmas trees are all sold. At seventy-nine, Wendell is a happy man. I sometimes ponder his happiness—is it that he is the best survivor of those Colby boys?

Mama enters my memory where she is necessary: to cook, run the house, care for me, rock me to sleep, sing to me. She seemed a part of myself at my earliest time. Energetic, lively, cheerful, strong, she was very active in her own house and in her own town. She sang professionally and practiced her music every day. She entertained her club members in our house. With her family of four children and with only a young farm girl to help her with the housework, she worked hard. She did all the baking, washing, ironing, mending, and sewing, as well as hunting with my father and brothers. I was probably with her more often than I was with my father, but my memories of her are less fond, for while my father never failed me, she often did.

Saturday was baking day and our pantry held loaves of freshly baked bread, cakes, and pies; and the cookie jar was replenished for the following week. When Mama baked she moved around our pantry confidently, in a swift smooth rhythm. These were life-long rituals from the earliest years of her life on the farm, transferred to her own kitchen in Kalispell. Rhythms from ancient times still held everywhere in the weekly order of household work; Monday was washday and all down the block washed clothes hung out to dry in the back yards. If I visited Raymond's house on Tuesday, his Mum would be ironing just as my Mama was ironing.

Mama had had enough of farms, and animals, and outdoor work. She had spent her childhood, one of fourteen children, living in a log cabin. I probably can't know what such a life was like, but below my mother's surface exuberance I know she felt deprived, and she wanted to make up for the deprivations. It seemed to me that she drove herself to take extra jobs; when she had a job that took her away from home, she organized the household and we shifted around a little to allow her to leave the house. When she sold the old black kitchen range and had an automatic electric stove installed, she would put our supper into its waterless slow cooker, set the timer, and when she came home at night supper was cooked. She seldom complained, and she was always pleased to be working. She and her sister sang at churches, funerals, lodge ceremonies and other social affairs; she also did office work at the County Courthouse. I think it likely that she felt compelled to be busy, and did not know how to slacken her pace, to reflect and to think.

Sunday was a day of rituals also. On Sunday mornings my parents lay abed, and I woke in the same room in my crib. When they began to stir I asked, "Can I come into your bed?" My brother Noel then poked his head around the doorpost and asked, "Can I come in too?" This day was the most carefree of the whole week; we all delighted in the free day ahead of us. After breakfast we sat a long time at table, taking turns choosing a Bible story for my father to read. I always chose Daniel in the Lion's Den or the story of Shadrack, Meshack, and Abednego: "Then Nebuchadnezzar came to the opening of the white-hot furnace and called to Shadrack, Meshack, and Abednego: 'Servants of the most high God, come out,' and Shadrack, Meshack, and Abednego came out."

Papa preferred to read a Psalm: "Yea, though I walk through the valley of the shadow of death, I will fear no evil . . ." In the evenings he read aloud from other books, and he asked each of us to take a turn at the reading. I can't remember learning to read, but I must have learned while Papa read aloud, pointing out the letters and then the sounds to me.

Papa lived his life at a different pace than did Mama; he went more slowly, and liked to walk, to talk, to read. Papa spent long hours at work, but he seemed to enjoy being wherever he was at the time that he was there. I felt that he was really with me when we were together, and whatever we did, he seemed to prefer doing it at that moment more than any other activity. I am convinced that he loved me entirely, and my brothers feel the same way about his love for them.

By the time I went to school I was reading for myself, and I progressed from grade to grade uneventfully. At the Carnegie Grant Library, on my way to or from school, I returned books I had read and chose new ones to take home. Reading fairy stories and myths of different countries, I found myself, my brothers, my mother, my father in them; the stories could have been rewritten from all that I found around me.

Montana was so newly settled that children and Indians were the only natives. My teachers talked of back east just as my parents did; they came from the midwest, but for them as for my parents "back east" was the center of the continent. Young women who had attended teachers' colleges applied for jobs in the far west in the more newly settled states. These young women were alone, and Papa, who had also come west and was far from his family too, was concerned for them. My parents often invited our teachers to dinner, and we did not feel strange with the teachers—after they had been in our house they became friends. An exception was my two brothers' school principal, whom they hated; perhaps he had struck or beaten one of them, because Papa met with the school board and proposed that a rule be made that no teacher strike a child, and it was made a rule.

Whenever we went for a walk in the town, Mama was amused; she would say, "Mary doesn't pay much attention to my friends, but she talks to every dog she sees." An enormous bulldog was my special friend; he walked the streets with one of the few remaining Civil War veterans, and they both waited for me to come from school. The dog ran to meet me, and we rolled and tumbled on my lawn—he looked ferocious but was gentle. The old soldier told me stories as I examined his cane, and he explained where he had found each treasure embedded in the cane: engraved bits of silver, broken jewelry, shiny bits of glass he had found as he walked, and he had inset them in the cane from ferule to handle; it glittered with every hue that had caught his eye as he walked all day with his dog.

From a catalog Mama ordered long-sleeved and long-legged underwear for winter, which we put on as soon as it arrived. We felt snug and warm, and we looked ready for a tumbling act. But by spring we looked less elegant, and I always longed for the freedom and lightness of summer underwear and short socks, for slippers instead of buttoned or high-laced shoes. Part of the freedom of spring was the light feeling in my feet as I ran, as though I skimmed the earth.

Papa worked an early shift at times in the Post Office and went to bed at the same time I did. I crept in with him, and until I went to sleep I would go over with him the happenings of the day at school, or he told me a story; this was probably the only way to be alone together in our large family. We woke early, and I climbed over the rail of my crib and hurried to the warm kitchen, heated by the fire banked for the night; a flicker of red light glowed from the cracks around the stove lids on the stove. Papa shook down the ashes, put the sticks of wood on the coals, and soon the fire sent out lovely heat. The oven door was usually open, and sometimes bread was rising to be baked; we removed the bread, and I sat on the oven door to dress. Going to bed and getting up together on these cold mornings was the closest association I had with Papa, who seemed to give me all his attention as we talked with a gay kind of ease. I do not remember moments of the same degree of intimacy with Mama; but when she was with one of my brothers a charge in the air let me know that she enjoyed them in a way which was closed between her and me.

I loved dressing up. Raymond and I would buckle on swords we had whittled and go out to play at being Knights of the Round Table; Robin Hood was also a favorite hero, who robbed from the rich to give to the poor. When Mama sang "My Little Old Sod Shanty" or "Sweet Betsy from Pike," I imagined myself crossing the continent as my grandfather had done, walking from New York State to Montana after the Civil War. He had stopped in a tavern one night to find that Jesse James was spending the night there too; Grandfather went outside and buried his Army discharge pay beside a fence-post before he slept, but in the morning Jesse James was gone.

I made my own hoop-stick as a child, from a lath long enough to reach the ground from my hand, to which I fastened a cross-piece. I then removed from an old wheel the iron hoop which bound it. I would give the hoop a little push to start it, and then I ran touching my hoop lightly with my stick to slow it or guide it. It now seems like a very small pastime, but it was elegant. I rolled my hoop when I ran on errands for my mother and I rolled my hoop to school; I hung it on my coat-hook in the cloakroom and leaned the stick against the wall. In cities years later I saw children, accompanied by nursemaids, rolling large hoops with sticks—and I had thought it to be a forgotten pastime!

When Wendell bought me a bicycle with his pay I do not know which of us was more excited at its arrival. I got on the bike and Wendell pushed me for blocks, until he could run no more. "When you can carry a pail of water around the block on your bicycle without spilling it, you may go for the milk on your bicycle," Papa told me. (It was my chore to get our milk every evening from a household which still kept a cow in the town.) In summer Raymond and I rode our bicycles on the only paved street, racing and circling around the Courthouse and then riding to the dairy, where we bought five-cent ice cream cones and rode home *no-hands*, feeling expert and elegant.

MY BROTHERS' WANDERINGS

1917–1925

Two brothers were drafted into the army during the first World War, but Wendell was rejected because of an eye defect. Paul trained in Minnesota the year of the influenza epidemic, and without winter clothing he nearly died of pneumonia after the flu, so he was sent home. In Kalispell, Mama volunteered as a nurse; whole families were laid low by the flu, and many died in the massive epidemic. In the streets people wore gauze masks; funerals were held every day. Fortunately, in my family Paul was the only one who had the flu.

> *Work and pray*
> *Live on hay*
> *There'll be pie*
> *In the sky*
> *When you die.*

The adventures of my brothers were the first stirrings I felt of the world outside Kalispell. When they first went away, I was the little sister left at home. The war and the following economic crisis threw many men out of work, some of whom became hoboes, "riding the rods" under box cars on the railroad, looking for work in all parts of the country or following the harvesting of crops. It was also their spirit of adventure which led my two brothers to roam. Some of the wanderers they met were trade union organizers, "Wobblies," or International Workers of the World (I.W.W.)—all part of a movement that introduced industrial unionism into the mines, the lumber industry, and the maritime industry of the western states. My brothers brought home boys who, like themselves, were wandering far from home. One, Luther Keene, a boy from bluegrass country in Kentucky, had a different speech than I had ever heard before. My father urged him to go home, promising to help him to get his own mule if he went home.

When my brothers turned up at home once in a while, my mother deloused them and gave them clean clothes before they came into the house. They seemed strangers to me, bearded and with a new vocabulary, new songs, restlessness, and dissatisfaction. In summer they drifted off again to find temporary jobs as fire lookouts on lonely mountaintops or as crop harvesters. They neither went away nor came home in a decisive way.

Wendell was working in a bank in Seattle and Paul was wandering when Papa, Mama, and I moved to Seattle. My brothers' wanderings and their jobs away from Montana probably decided my parents on this move; or the move may have been made because Papa received an inheritance and could invest in a business in Seattle, an importing firm dealing with the Orient. He dealt with Chinese merchants; one time he took me along to present one of them with a bunch of lilacs, which were blooming in profusion in our yard.

Seattle had foreign ships in the harbor, and there were distinct foreign groups in the population: Chinese in Chinatown and a large Scandinavian district in Ballard, across the lake. For the first time I saw stores with foreign products, ten-cent stores with counters over which to pore, a Farmers' Market. I heard Chinese, Swedish, and Russian spoken; the Swedes and Russians had come as lumber workers, and eventually their women came to join these men in Seattle. An occasional copra ship from Papeete tied up at the waterfront. To me all was wonderful, a glimpse of the world beyond all I had so far seen. In the middle of the school year, we moved to a large rambling house on Lake Washington; it was across town from my school, and Papa took me several times on the streetcar to teach me the route and to make sure I could cross streets safely by myself. I found the streetcar an adventure, and learned the whole Seattle system. I can't remember that we owned a car in Seattle, we all used the streetcars.

I was growing up; once, at his place of business, Papa said to me, "Choose all the dolls you want," and I chose thirty-five dolls. But because I no longer played with dolls, when I looked at them they seemed to accuse me of abandoning my childhood.

I walked Seattle's hills, going downtown by myself on Saturday morning to take my piano lesson, walking in the Farmers' Market where farmers sold their vegetables and fishermen their fish. I walked on the waterfront streets too, where I found a flea circus; Seattle was a city on the sea with ships and fish boats tied up at the waterfront. I loved to smell the coffee, spices and fish—to me exotic smells; one of these odors will still bring me memories of Seattle. I was in love with my first city.

The lamplighter came along at sundown with his small ladder on one shoulder and the lighter in his hand. He stopped at a light pole, leaned his ladder against the pole, stepped up to open the little door in the lamp, turned on the gas and lit the lamp. The light had a greenish glow and the evening ritual, the lighting of the lamps, was lovely.

Rich, older matrons went about the city in small electric cars with a stick control for steering; the lady sat back on her seat enclosed in glass, gliding quietly along on her errands. An occasional elegant carriage appeared, drawn by a pair of matched horses, and big department stores used a delivery service with electric trucks which glided to a stop at the curb and quietly started on again. The milkman delivered milk, his bottles making a characteristic klonk-klank noise as he ran with them to the door. Each milk company had its delivery wagon, and in the early morning the heavy hooves of the horses clopped by; the horse knew the house of a customer and stopped without command. Early morning also meant the sound of the morning newspaper landing with a thud on the front door as the delivery boy threw it expertly without leaving his bicycle.

On a visit to one of my father's friends near Seattle, his two boys and I roamed the wide beach by their house. I had never been on a seashore before with driftwood and small scurrying crabs, some of which I took home in my pocket. The boys and I smoked pith-filled reeds, and when we returned to the house on the beach at the base of the cliff we had dinner. Papa had to have bread with his meal in order to enjoy the meal, and I remember the discussion about such different customs—this was a German family with German ways. Perhaps I remember these small details because shortly after our visit a landslide covered their house, and they were killed.

My father dealt with a fireworks manufacturer named Mr. Hitt; I thought him a sort of wizard, like the Wizard of Oz, so Papa promised we would go to see the display of fireworks designed by Mr. Hitt for Seattle's Fourth of July celebration. We arrived early and sat on a hillside with a clear view. First rockets and fireballs, then larger, more complicated rockets exploded higher and higher, and revolving Catherine wheels sent out streamers of fire of different colors. I lay back on the grass to watch every star, every spark—they seemed to have always one more. Gasps and sighs passed through the throng of night-watchers and hung in the air with the showers of stars until it seemed we could bear no more. We waited, dazzled, and then trailed along behind the homeward-bound crowd.

My friend Russel and I went black-berrying on late summer days. Seattle had more vacant lots than it had houses in its outskirts, and we explored woods, canyons, brooks, and cliffs. The city was lovely with snow-covered mountains off in the distance. We came home at sundown scratched and sunburned, but with our pails full of berries.

On my way to school one day my dog was run over and killed; a passerby called the Humane Society to come for him, and I went to school sobbing. I would not tell the teacher what had happened, I would not say that he was dead—I could not yet accept his death.

On Saturdays my mother and I met Papa downtown, where we went to vaudeville shows which had a variety of entertainment: magicians, tumblers, adagio dancers, singers. I liked the dancers best and thought of becoming a dancer, but Papa said, "It is no kind of life for you." In Kalispell I had seen only Chautauqua-circuit performers and an occasional opera or an acting company, so vaudeville in Seattle was the first I had seen of a real stage, with lights and a full orchestra in the pit to accompany the performers. I practiced dancing by myself, and once when Wendell and I were at home alone on a summer evening I asked him to watch me dance. I danced in the garden; it was my only performance.

Papa was not pleased with his partners in the import business in Seattle, so he sold his share and traveled down the coast to find a place to start a new business. He chose Grants Pass, Oregon, because a new dam was being built on the Rogue river, and the dam indicated that agriculture would develop from the abundant water for irrigation. He also had in mind that his three sons were wandering and that my uncle and aunt and their four children were his responsibility—wherever we went, they soon came too. My brothers were relieved to be called back by my father to help in the new store; they came home, never to go far from my mother or that region. Eventually they took to the forests for their livelihood and to hunting and fishing for their recreation.

For my brothers, coming home was a return to a life they understood. The Marines, the Army, and the city had been confining and stultifying experiences; freedom meant roaming the woods with a gun or a fishpole. Wendell vowed, "After working in a bank, never again will I work at anything that requires that I look through a window at the world." Not one of my brothers ever entered a factory to work. They feel still, at their advanced ages, that the city is the enemy—when they travel they drive a car or a truck, and they detour around cities. But when my family moved to Grants Pass I was twelve years old, and almost at once I began to save money to escape; my own direction was set by the family move from Montana to Seattle, my first city, which I loved. My mother was an example of this first movement away from the farm life which had been the only way for a large proportion of the population. Her yearnings for town and city life had behind them the consciousness that she was a farm girl, and a feeling of inferiority to townspeople lay under her seeming confidence. She was never sure that her dress, her style, her manner were the ones which gave her equal status in the town or city. While she felt comfortable in the greater anonymity of Seattle, she didn't have the easy emergence into the community that had been hers by right in Kalispell, where she was a native daughter. In the back of her mind, I think, was a vision of riding into town on a wagon with thirteen siblings, well-fed but certainly not looking like town children. In Seattle she had found it more fashionable to be thin, and she became thin. She was quick to observe, to learn, to adapt.

In Grants Pass, a few blocks down "A" Street, I found a building not much larger than a big schoolroom—the library of the town. There were so few books that I started at one end of a shelf and read everything I could of any possible interest, from Maeterlinck to Sax Rohmer; I re-read my Bible and our other books that I already knew well. My father bought me a puppy to keep me company, and I built a doghouse for him, even finding shingles for the roof. He was my first companion in this town which even for dogs was different from other towns; if dogs ate of the dead salmon that came floating down the river after spawning, they died. Soon the little house in the back yard stood empty.

Papa met Ruth, a girl near my own age who worked in the lodge-hall next door to his store, and invited her to meet me. Ruth took me with her to the river to teach me to swim. The Rogue is wide and deep, and near the bridge at the city park a swim-float was moored out in the river. I could swim, but not against such a current; I practiced, and when Ruth thought I swam well enough we walked upstream to a gradual bank from which we could reach the swim-float if we struck out strongly for the opposite side of the river. It was not a safe swimming place, but we used it during the summers, when heat is intense in Oregon. It was out on the swim-float that a boy pinched me on the nipple and then dove into the water—I had not been aware that I had breasts.

When school began, Ruth and I entered the old red-brick school building up a flight of steep steps to a first-story hall which ran through to a flight of steps on the other side of the building. No light entered the central hall except that from the two entrance doors at either end. The floor was black splintery wood, oiled each day by the janitor with an oil that reeked through the hallway. Stairways at either end of the hall led to the second story. Windows of classrooms were above our heads when we were seated. One room on the second floor was larger than the others, and it was used for gymnastic exercises or for pronouncements by Miss Crane, the principal and English teacher. The desks were scarred with generations of carvings of students' initials and those of their first loves. Miss Crane is the only teacher I remember from that year—Miss Crane, hated yet loved by all the kids for her ugliness, her temper, her red wig. Her distinction lay in being the worst possible teacher I could imagine. She shouted, she threw ink-pots, she hit with a ruler; she could have been the Red Queen in *Alice in Wonderland*.

A boy named Jack McArthur gave me a valentine in eighth grade; probably I received other valentines, but this was a declaration of serious love that I was not able to accept. Yet he persisted in assuming that I was his girlfriend, and since the other boys assumed it too, I did not find boyfriends later in high school. Jack had the first crystal radio in the town, and he invited me to his home to listen to it. His home may have been the first I had been in with a worker father; Jack's father was an engineer on the railroad, and he had a comfortable home with a secure way of life in this town where there was poverty, but the ways of the house were not ways to which I was accustomed. They seemed to be living in a stasis, to be going nowhere—although the radio and the railroad were symbols to me of the outside world and of travel.

One day Jack came running through the town to find me. He had been to my house, and he came to the library as the next most likely place for me to be. Breathless, he had run from the improvised airport at the edge of town, where he had a job as watchman of the airplane for a barnstormer who was offering rides for five dollars to daring townspeople. Jack's payment was to be a ride in the airplane, and he gave me the ride. No one was at home to ask permission, so we ran all the way back to the airfield, I climbed into the seat, and the owner took me up. The plane was small and open, the air rushed by, the motor worked hard and lifted us. Labor ceased and the plane seemed held by air. I leaned over the side to see the whole valley as I had never seen it before: the pass through the mountains from the north, the river winding through the valley from mountains on one side to mountains on the other, and endless mountains reaching in all directions away from the valley. I saw my house in miniature; the whole town lay like a map of itself. My aunt and uncle (with whom my brothers and I were taking our meals while our parents were out of town) evinced considerable consternation when I came to dinner bursting with the story of my airplane ride. But my brothers took the news calmly, and my aunt's family gradually calmed.

As I was packing for a hiking trip with some girls that year, I asked my mother to cut my long hair, thinking that she would object to cutting it. She picked up the scissors, cut my hair and turned back to whatever she had been doing. My parents were preoccupied with my father's health, and I think they were not very much aware of me that summer. Margaret, the girl to whom I felt closest, and I went for long walks and talks in the hills, sometimes riding her horse Babe. Margaret was not the favorite child of her mother, and as we talked we tried to understand our mothers and ourselves. Margaret had a fine contralto voice that filled the church on Sundays when she sang solos in the choir. Like many others, she felt she must keep a connection with her established family back east, too, but I had no one back east; my grandmother Colby had moved to California, and I had not been old enough when we left Montana to keep friends there as my brothers had done.

I made friends with the girl who lived across the street, the daughter of the train dispatcher, a gentle and sweet-natured man who played his piano after work and sang to himself as he played. Dorothy and her mother, on the other hand, were nervous, irritable, and unpredictable. But I needed a hiking companion, and Dorothy loved to hike, as did her boyfriend. She was never ready when I called for her in the mornings to walk to school, and I waited for her while her mother toasted a slice of bread over the coals in the wood stove. Dorothy came downstairs sleepy-eyed, took her toast, and we walked the mile to school. I wore what nearly every freshman girl wore to school, a short skirt, a heavy sweater, and boots with socks turned down over their tops just below my knees; it was almost a uniform. On rainy days I wore unbuckled galoshes and a "slicker" raincoat. On our way to school we stopped in to wait for a friend whose older sister was dressing, and I watched, fascinated, as she taped her nipples flat before putting on a tight, flat brassiere. She then slipped over her head a straight unshaped dress that almost touched at her hips and fell not quite to her knees. This was the way the older girls dressed, and the term used to describe them was Flappers.

For only one year the Thomases lived across the street from us; Mrs. Thomas made friends with me, and I joined the Campfire Girls group that she organized. Since Mr. Thomas came to town only on weekends from the lumber camp he managed, she was lonely and planned to adopt babies if her husband could be persuaded. She invited the druggist's daughter and the banker's daughter to join the Campfire Girls group, and as a result the group was divided from the start. Perhaps their families formed a society in the town of which I knew nothing—in any case, the group did not last long, but Mrs. Thomas and I remained friends. She asked me to spend the summer with her at the lumber camp when the snow left the mountains and my school year was finished. The house at the lumber camp was a cabin built "board and batten" style on the edge of the clearing for the mill. The back of the house was against the forest, which I loved, but I also felt strange and isolated to be away from the town. I had no library to take refuge in, no place to drop in and talk as I did in several households in Grants Pass. Mr. Thomas was a boyish shy man who called me "Swede"; I did not understand why he called me that—perhaps it was because of my light-colored hair. Clearly he meant to be affectionate, but he did not talk much to me or to his wife. He was a busy man who spent most of his time at the lumber-mill office. The Thomases had decided to adopt babies, so the mission was accomplished with me for their trial child. I started to menstruate while I was with them; I was so startled and disturbed that I had to go home immediately. My mother was not at home, but a sister-in-law explained in an off-hand way that comforted me and created a bond for me with her.

My brothers had all married in the same year, choosing girls not a great deal older than I was. Wendell married Helen, a girl from Montana whom he had met in the bank in Seattle where they were both working. She came to Grants Pass to marry him; Mama made wedding clothes for her and Papa had a little house built for them up the street from our house. We all helped to prepare the little house for them, but Helen was not happy. She went away after three months, and Wendell came home.

Noel met Emma, a young school teacher, at a country dance very soon after he came to Grants Pass, and they married almost at once. I came bursting into my bedroom one day and found them making love—my brother's penis was large, and I felt a virgin's shock at beholding an erection.

There was little to do in this town. I was accepted and sang for a while with a singing club. When a group in the town put on a production of *The Mikado*, I sang in the chorus. My ancient history teacher had studied with Breasted, the archaeologist at the University of Chicago who had returned from the dig of Tutankhamen's tomb; she was filled with enthusiasm over the new "finds" in Egypt. Since she loved what she was teaching I loved it too, and I found it the only subject taught with enthusiasm in my three years of high school.

I was thirteen years old, and my friends my age were joining churches. I said to myself, "I will read the Bible, and I will decide if I believe in God.

If I believe in God I will decide if I should join a church, and I will then decide what church I will join." Pressure from the churches was strong on the young people in the town, and the ones who had already joined had a special aura for a little while. I read my Bible every night when I was by myself, pondering to find if I did believe in a supernatural God and in heaven as an otherworldly place. I could not make myself believe in the way the church people apparently expected belief, but I did believe in the Bible, which I loved; it seemed to me probable that it had been written in real times by real people. My brothers were outspoken unbelievers, but my parents never proselytized. Papa's belief was clearly an acceptance of the Old Testament God; when he read the Song of Songs or a Psalm it seemed to me to be love poetry. I loved Papa's quiet voice and his deep calm acceptance of the world as a sufficient place for us to be.

I soon knew all the country around Grants Pass from hiking with Dorothy and her boyfriend Russel. We hiked down a trail which followed the Rogue River all the way to Ilahe, an Indian trading post. The Rogue rushed along beside us, between high banks and with a swift current. Toward the end of each day Russel stopped to fish for trout for our supper, while Dorothy and I hiked on to choose a camping spot, where we cut fir-tips for our bed and built the fire. When Russel came with the trout we broiled them over the coals. Next day we boarded the mail-boat, a small launch which met us at Ilahe, and in a few hours we were at Gold Beach on the ocean. Noel met us to drive us home, and we camped out one more night with Noel where the highway turned to go inland to Grants Pass; we bought large Dungeness crabs and had a feast around our campfire.

In our second year of high school Russel, Dorothy and I built a canoe; we all shared the expense, and Russel did most of the work. The canoe had a frame of thin strips of wood over which he stretched canvas and painted it several times. It was a good canoe, and we used it for a whole season, shooting the small rapids near Grants Pass and exploring the river below the town.

Noel's wife Emma was a fiery, pretty, very bright young woman with no outlook except getting ahead in a material way. Like other hill-people, she was fiercely jealous and easily offended. It took very little to excite

Emma, she felt she had to be independent, and she never really believed that Noel loved her. I think he did love her, and he was hurt in his male pride when she could turn in petty anger against him and "get even" by sex with other men. I went once with Noel and Emma to look at a house for sale. The house was littered with old papers and in disrepair, but they bought it and soon filled it with new chairs and embroidered pillows. Still, there was no attempt at beauty—I doubt if such an idea entered Emma's head—but she was pleased with her home. The work she did and the money she earned gave Emma the strength to feel she was equal to the townspeople; she continued to teach at one country school or another after she was married. She also continued her teacher training, taking courses and examinations to increase her qualifications. I was with her at one of these examinations, and I took it too. Although I had not finished high school, I passed the exam easily, and I taught her school for her one day. That same day I drove her Model T for the first time—the kids in the school helped me through the day, and my only mishap was stepping on the wrong pedal while turning the Model T and backing it into a ditch.

Paul and Wendell had a successful dance band, and they put great energy into organizing dances outside the town on Saturday nights. During a pause in the dancing, a hearty supper was served, prepared by the women of our family and of the other band members' families, after which the dancing resumed. Parents brought their children, who went to sleep on top of piles of coats or in corners. When the dance was over, at three or four in the morning, the dancers straggled to find children, coats and partners to make the long drive home. There was violence at these dances, where all the emotions of the week at work or at home found expression in fighting, drinking, or sex. It was a lively and rough evening. My brothers got the contract to play for dances every night at the County Fair, at a time in which they were responsible for me because my father was ill and our parents were away, and they took me with them early to the fairground. But they did not need me, and I wandered through the Fair by myself. I liked the stables with the race-horses and the families who lived with their horses in the stable; they were gathered around a little fire singing to a guitar, "He was the people's favorite, the little boy in green," a ballad of a boy jockey who was killed in a racing accident. I drifted through the arcades and exhibits, then back to the dance. Early in the evening, before the men were drunk, fighting, or asleep, I danced with whoever asked me. Every other dance was a square dance with a caller; at first I did not know how to dance, but I soon learned. In one square dance I was whirled about and one of my slippers flew clear across the dance floor and into a corner. I liked square dancing best, as dancing with a partner who smelled of boot-leg liquor was no great delight.

Noel had the shoe department of my father's big general store, and I could have what I chose of stockings and shoes. In Grants Pass the working girls, especially waitresses, bought new shoes and stockings every Saturday—I suppose some status was attached to new shoes every week. Noel stocked the store with the most extreme dancing slippers, high heels, colored and lace stockings. I didn't like high heels but I wore colored stockings and took one pair of each color. Mama protested when she noticed me taking so many stockings, but my loyal brother Noel only smiled a little and handed them to me.

My parents were away that year because Papa was to have exploratory surgery in order to diagnose some alarming symptoms. Papa and Mama were staying at a friend's house, where Papa was convalescing after the surgery, when he sent for me, and I went on the bus by myself. I sat with him, and he held my hand while he told me, "I may not get well, Mary dear," but I did not really understand what he was saying to me.

With only a year to live, Papa was preoccupied with the store; he planned for it to provide for us all. He was in a race with his death, and in the fall of my fifteenth year he was less and less able to go from the house. Finally he could no longer move about, and the last few days he was in a coma. One night I was called down to find my family gathered around his bed. I was uncomfortable, because I could not find my father in the wasted form gasping for breath. He was alone with his death, and his death left each of us alone too. He was buried from a church he had never entered in life. I had a hard time realizing that he was dead; I could not make the connections between his death, the funeral, and the father I had known.

Before my father died I felt myself a part of a family of six; with his death very suddenly I was alone. We were not a united family after he died, and I struggled with this new way of being. We also stepped down in class; I faced these changes without time to adjust to them. I knew I had to get away from my mother and earn my own living at once. I was willing, even eager, to do this—the only obstacle was my age. I felt a desperate loneliness for my father; I couldn't bear his absence and was pressed to realize his spirit in myself. All my young life, it now seemed, I had been vigilantly avoiding the trap that was Grants Pass, and I now looked for a way into the world. I considered losing myself in wilderness, but no answers came from running away into nothing; I lay beside a spring in the forest with only a bird or squirrel to see me lying there, or I climbed to a hilltop in order to look out at mountains. I pondered a way into the world, into a peopled world. Almost immediately after my father's death I took a lover from this outside world, an adult man who was not a Grants Pass man.

Mama did not entirely accept my brothers' wives; probably she felt robbed of her sons as she had been robbed of her husband by death. I found that she and I could not live under the same roof. My mother did not want me, and I wondered if she had ever loved me. I remember her pride and my embarrassment when she mentioned my appearance when I was present, as though I were an attribute of hers. She may have been proud of me, but she was uncomfortable with an adolescent girl and could not bear to have me near her. Perhaps our love for each other failed at the same time. Her needs were great for male attention, but I was old enough to be receiving male attention also, and I had to move away from the house that had been my home. Her guilt increased as mine began, to continue until she died—guilt that I did not love her with that love which means life itself when one is very young.

Noel was concerned for me and asked me to live with him, his wife Emma, and their little son. But still no one discussed with me what I would do when I finished high school; we were still shut in ourselves with the shock of Papa's death. My adult brothers seemed bewildered boys still, who made no further moves to progress past the point they had reached in high school. They were not rooted in themselves as my father had been, and I think they have not been happy men.

My brother Noel persuaded my mother to give me the use of the family car after Papa died, since she did not drive. She complained a little because the gasoline I used cost her money, because I would not spend my savings for any purpose except to get away from Grants Pass. I loved driving; it was liberation and solitude. I was part of the generation that took the automobile for its own—a high school kid could put together a jalopy from old car parts, and could then pick up walking students to drive them to school on the way through town. Each of us in my family had a car; our driveway was always full, and I knew before I entered the house who was visiting.

Lack of trust among girls, lack of a tradition of trust, and secrecy about sex were total in my high school. I took no one into my confidence except Noel's wife Emma, and I went to her only if I needed something I couldn't get for myself or if I didn't yet understand something about sex. I puzzled out my relationships, forming attitudes and an ethic for myself. Noel talked to me in the idle hours when we were together in the shoe department, where I worked after school and on weekends. He had the most influence with me, and I can trace some of my attitudes directly to those he had worked out for himself. I remember his philosophy of self-love most distinctly, and I made it my own: that one must love oneself the most in order to love others and in order to survive.

In eighth grade one of the teachers put a row of books, "for the girls when they have finished their work," on her desk (no books for boys!). These books were of the birds-and-bees variety of sex information, and what I remember from them was probably not printed there at all. I used this reading in forming my early attitudes; the books seemed to say that boys, if sexually aroused and not satisfied, would suffer indescribably, so I determined never to "pet." How could I deal with a half-dead boy if I aroused him without satisfying him? "Petting" was the form that girls used in the 1920s to contain their sexual behavior. In the back seat of an automobile, the girl's struggle was to prevent penetration by the boy's penis, while the boy's manly obligation was to use any method short of rape to accomplish just that. No "nice" girl ever went the "whole way," but boys boasted of their prowess whether they had been successful or not. Many methods of arriving at orgasm were invented or experimented with, but I did not hear them frankly discussed among the girls I knew. I saw the struggles going on outside the dance place on Saturday night, at favorite parking places where lovers climbed into the back seat to struggle. This was the form of courtship in Grants Pass: the boy pleading "Aw, come on," and the flushed and struggling girl finding no safe, satisfying or honorable outcome to the courtship. It was the only form, and it was dangerous and ruinous for the girl. There was no birth control; pregnancy meant marriage, probably to the first boy a girl had ever gone out with, or it meant abortion. Abortions were available in all categories, from low-cost up to legal abortions with doctors conferring and performing the abortion "for the sake of the woman's health." This latter was for rich married women only. Still, I decided in favor of sex for myself, but only sex which was not a trap. I felt appreciated by very few, really only by Noel. I suppose he discussed me with Emma and that she took care of me and advised me with his full consent. Noel assumed, I think, that any healthy young person would enjoy sex, but he did worry that I might marry badly and ruin the rest of my life. I was influenced by the attitudes I found in the town, but I rejected the "morality" of Grants Pass. Of the different standards I set for myself the most important was my determination to get away from Grants Pass, which held for me the greatest danger I could conceive: to be trapped in a meaningless life with birth and death in a biological repetition, without serious thought or a search for life with more meaning. Moreover, I had lived in the trust and confidence and love of two men, my father and my brother Noel; I was not open to love that was less than theirs.

Sex in Grants Pass was permissive; the veneer of strict puritanism was not more than a surface ethic which the church people tried to enforce in a lumber town full of lumberjacks and country people. Dance places and amusement halls were full to overflowing one night of the week. Prohibition incited lawlessness and added an air of secrecy and license, an air of drunkenness, to sex. Sexual activity went on all around me, among all ages of the population. Across from our house on Saturday afternoons we watched the wife polish the new car for the weekend, and when she finished the husband got in the car to drive it away for his own spree. She seemed unconscious of his purpose, and no one told her.

I enjoyed Emma's little son Pete, a two-year-old who had never had his hair cut and spoke little, but when he did I was charmed by him. As I was driving him in the car one day and we were crossing the railroad tracks he talked of "tin-trees." "Show me a tin-tree," I said to him. He pointed to the signal posts with their changing signal-arms. "Tin-trees," he said.

Emma said to me one day, "Mary, would you take Pete to have his hair cut?" He was small and frightened, but we stood by each other; Pete didn't cry, and I was proud of him—he looked manly with his shorn head and his slender little neck. He was the first young child I had known, and we loved each other.

On my block in Kalispell I had been in and out of every house on the block and knew, at least intuitively, the ways of parents and children. By the time I was ten years old we had moved to Seattle and then to Grants Pass, a small town which differed greatly from Kalispell, Montana. On my block in Grants Pass was one household that was a remnant of a farm, with a cow and chickens, kept by an old couple so helpless and filthy that they were in disrepute. I visited them occasionally to buy eggs, which my mother thought was a kindness, and she was not afraid the eggs would be contaminated by the dirty farm. The farm-woman was old, hunched, and hobbling; old machinery lay neglected, the doors of the barn and sheds hung at angles, and utensils were scattered about the porch, kitchen, and yard. Chickens wandered in and out of the house, and the cow was led each day to a field at some distance. Probably the farmer had sold bits and pieces of his land as the town grew until his farm was untenable, unviable, and unproductive. All the rest of the houses on our block had been recently built by newcomers. Our friends the Whorleys from Los Angeles lived at the end of the street, while next to them two families of Osage Indians from Oklahoma had bought large pieces of land and lived a strange half-Indian, half-town existence. They were oil-rich, and each person in the family old enough to drive had a late-model car. Mr. Whorley saw one of the little boys one day, sawing through the legs of the new grand piano. The two older children of the families were a handsome, dark, reserved and intelligent eighteen-year-old boy and a sixteen-year-old girl so beautiful it was breathtaking. They each drove a new sports car, dressed elegantly and formed an elite of themselves, the only dark-skinned people in the area; their beauty almost burned the town. They lived in a home in which old ways were more dominant than new ways. The older women looked like women on a reservation, with loose dresses and braids. The father, head of both families, was a somewhat heavy, dark-skinned man who was very dignified. The family made no friends in the town. The boy and the girl, with all their elegance, carried alone the weight of being different in the little town so full of prejudice that my family, too, was ostracized for being from Montana and Seattle—we were called "foreigners." These Indians were only tolerated because they were rich. Why the father picked Grants Pass for their home was mysterious to me; perhaps he had seen so much discrimination that he saw no difference between one town and another, or perhaps even more discrimination had existed in Oklahoma. At any rate, they stayed, and the children lived fairly normal lives with the other young people of the town.

There was little chance to know neighbors well; almost all the old families knew each other, but we were the newcomers. I was the only one in our family to find haven in houses not my own. I made friends with Prudence, the daughter of a grocery store owner. Prudence was a polio victim, hopelessly crippled and confined to a wheelchair, but she was intelligent and eager to be friends with me. I took her out in her wheelchair and we talked; as she was several years older than I, she was full of quirky information and thought. Other friends, the Voorhees, were of Dutch extraction and had come from New York. Mr. Voorhees ran the town's only newspaper while his household was run by his cousin, Miss Benedict. This family was well educated and interesting, their attitudes were open, they welcomed me and I dropped in at their home often. They took me with them on picnics and excursions. After my father died I went often to these two homes; they accepted me so simply that I found security and stability with them. My family did not talk about a wide range of topics or show me a way out into the world, and these friends helped me decide to go to college. But it was the County Agent, Jessie Griswold, who in precise and practical terms convinced me that I could go to college and that I could support myself there. The Voorhees advised me to go to the University instead of the Agricultural College, not realizing how little I was able to deal with the more sophisticated city people who attended the University.

What was the character of Grants Pass? The greatest number of the residents of this town 400 miles from a city mined or worked in the lumber industry or farmed; most of them were not interested in enriching their lives in other ways. The library had its pitiful few books, and the school had no library at all. The town's inhospitable attitude toward all newcomers closed it to new ideas as well, and the itinerant agricultural work-force drifted through. It was a one-street town settled by forty-niners who had come over the Rogue River trail from Gold Beach on the coast, hunting for gold. The attitudes reflected in the schools were southern attitudes—a Ku Klux Klan organization existed, and Catholics were not welcome; Negroes were not permitted to stay overnight. Prospectors searched, and when one gold strike was made every shovel, every pan, and all equipment for panning gold was sold out in the town and we would see men bending over streams washing the gravel. Always a little gold was in the pan, but usually so little that a day's work barely paid a day's wages. Today the search for gold continues in southern Oregon, but volcanic activity and earthquakes have broken the veins of gold, preventing large quantities from being found in one place. Settlers from the hill country of Missouri and Kentucky had come to this valley; they loved the hills, guns, hunting, fishing, and searching for gold. One-room schoolhouses with a local teacher like Emma taught the three R's. The children at the school ran from age six to sixteen; the usual progression was to go on to high school in town, but this meant that the student had to be supported while in town or had to get to town each day, and so those not intent on an education had only to continue at the local school until they passed the age of sixteen, when attendance was no longer legally required. Children in the country were needed on the farms, and if they reached the age for dating and marriage before they had been introduced to town life they usually preferred to stay at home; they married a neighbor and continued the old way of life, fishing, hunting, and farming the meager hill-country soil. For the woman, childbearing and housework became her whole future life. Country people were suspicious of townspeople, and townspeople were suspicious of outsiders. The fears and angers resulting from these unresolved and misunderstood differences were not surmounted, and the results were petty destructive ways. "Foreigners" tended to choose "foreigners" for friends, townspeople usually chose townspeople, and few country people had a view of a world larger than their farm and the surrounding forests. My family aroused great suspicion; I think we were somehow shocking to the sober business people after Papa died.

Mama and Paul invested in one get-rich-quick scheme after another. They were gleeful, imaginative and unsuccessful so far as getting rich was concerned, but with each new scheme they hoped anew that they would emerge suddenly rich. Grants Pass was already, in 1921, a highway town based on automobiles, and the buildings were strung out on both sides of Main Street. In Southern Oregon there is a wet season with months of rain, and overnight the country turns as green as a rainforest; in late spring the dry season comes and everything turns brown—the land that is not irrigated turns dry, and summer is hot. An irrigation dam was being built when my father chose this valley, but even with irrigation agriculture did not develop very much, although almost anything will grow in the rich soil of the valley bottom.

Papa's preoccupation with his impending death and his responsibility to provide for us after his death did not allow me to find the world outside with him and through his ideas. I never saw his family again after his death; that tie was broken. I studied and worked during the following summer, passed the examinations, and applied for acceptance to the University. I made some clothes to take with me to Eugene in the fall. My brothers had to explain to my mother that, although my father's will left her all the assets of his estate, she still had a responsibility to me and should help to pay my expenses at college.

At Eugene I was given a place to live in a small apartment with three other girls. No jobs were offered, and I did not know how to look for one. I was invited to a sorority dinner as a possible member, but I was uncomfortable with the sorority girls, with their bourgeois tastes and needs. Early marriage to the boy most likely to enter bourgeois life seemed their first concern. I settled into dormitory life with a senior student named Onslow, a cool intelligent girl, a sophomore named Sally from Portland who became my friend, and Katherine, a rancher's daughter from eastern Oregon who was an aggressive bully of a girl—she wore my clothes without asking and trod rough-shod as though she were too large for apartment living. Girls in the dormitory or in class did not speak to other girls if they were walking with a boy.

I do not know how I met the boy who became my friend. He was a mathematician, a senior honor student, a tall shy boy from Marshfield who told me of the beauty of the marshes. I wondered at a life in the marshes, with plank-walks laid over outcroppings to marshy islands. I began writing dreamy romantic prose of green watery country. There was a fairy-tale quality to knowing him—perhaps he lived in a fantasy. We went for walks at night in the hills around Eugene, and we peered into houses where people were sitting, reading by their fires. One night he brought a revolver, which we shot once to see if the people in their snug houses took note, but no one even looked up. He had a younger sister whom he loved, and we bought her a book about marsh birds.

Because my father died of cancer, I said that I wanted to be a doctor, but the first term I had a "D" for chemistry. The instructor looked me up to tell me that he thought it was his fault, that I had not understood that the first semester's work required memorizing the tables of symbols and quantities. I could have memorized them, but it seemed to me stupid to be memorizing at a university. Chemistry was without interest for me, and the "D" discouraged me further. I left the university at Christmastime; my boyfriend wrote to invite me to the Senior Prom, and I went back to go to the dance with him. He had not yet kissed me, and my needs were for a lover, but I think he was a virgin. He asked me to marry him; this offer to marry surprised me, and I said "Yes" just as girls in novels say "Yes" if asked to marry; but I did not intend to marry, certainly not at age sixteen, nor with this boy. I had to write and tell him I could not marry him, and I never heard from him again. At home I worked, saved more money, and planned to go to the Agricultural College next fall in Corvallis. Meanwhile, a new boy had come to town at the moment I had come home, and although we were both of high school age we were both out of school. This boy had been a lightweight boxer, and intellectually he was of no interest to me, but I went out with him and kept the relationship for the sex. I was glad not to have to think about him very much, although I think he gossiped about me in the town.

While I was dating this boy, Noel asked me to go for a drive, and as we drove along he asked, "Mary, you don't intend to marry that boy, do you?

I was shocked and said "No," firmly.

As he turned the car to go home, Noel said, "That's all I wanted to know."

I didn't know what freedom and independence meant for me, but I was at an adequate age for sex, which I accepted as I needed when it was offered. Sex provided only a momentary fulfillment, and I did not find any way through my first relationships out of the trap I was in. I found instead that sex itself was a need, and it formed part of a greater need for a larger world, but it did not give me an identity. As I reached the age of sixteen, I saw in Grants Pass that sexual relationships were for the most part made and lived with diffidence. And I too entered into relationships with no ties and no expectations that they would solve anything.

On Monday morning, of course, we all met on Main street or at school in our roles of wife, teacher, husband, banker, student, businessman, preacher, etc., but underneath this veneer the couplings went on, perhaps in a freer manner than in communities that have more to occupy them. Only two of my girlfriends seemed not to be engaged in sexual encounters. I have heard this small-town sex life described as circular sex.

LOVE & ESCAPE

1926–1927

I n the fall of 1926 I entered the Agricultural College at Corvallis. At the first assembly a speaker told of Mussolini and his Blackshirts' march on Rome, the first political event of which I had been made aware. At the second assembly Carl Sandburg sang and read his famous poem, "The fog / came / on little cat feet." He sang "My Little Old Sod Shanty," a song my mother had sung, and for the first time I heard this song and others as songs of my country, of the West. Hearing Sandburg read and sing I gained respect for my derivations, my roots in the United States.

Jack Lyons, a young English professor who had taken his degree at Berkeley the year before, loved poetry, and in his class he introduced us to contemporary verse. I don't think any of us in his class had known that poetry was being written in our times. He read poems of Vachel Lindsay, Millay, Dickinson, Cummings, Jeffers, Stephens, Pound, Eliot and others. He was in love with poetry, and he talked to us and asked us to write; he was eager that we too find poetry. I wrote, my first attempts since trying to write the poetry of my friend's marshes. I wrote poems of my father's death and of the forests I loved.

George Oppen sat in the front row, directly in front of me, and after a month or so Jack Lyons introduced us to each other. One day when I was sitting on the library steps George asked me to go out with him that evening, and I agreed. He came for me in his roommate's Model T Ford, and we drove out into the country, sat and talked, made love, and talked until morning. The moon made such a white light—we could almost see colors, it was so bright—and in the low spots the fog came up toward morning, forming a lake. George has written:

THE FORMS OF LOVE

Parked in the fields
All night
So many years ago,
We saw
A lake beside us
When the moon rose.
I remember

Leaving that ancient car
Together. I remember
Standing in the white grass
Beside it. We groped
Our way together
Downhill in the bright
Incredible light

Beginning to wonder
Whether it could be lake
Or fog
We saw, our heads
Ringing under the stars we walked
To where it would have wet our feet
Had it been water

We talked as I had never talked before, an outpouring. When George said, "I am Jewish," I thought, The Bible! Jews! "That's good," I said, and we went on to tell as much of ourselves as we could in that first night.

When we returned in the morning, many heads were thrust from the windows of my dormitory, watching us. I went inside, and someone told me to go to see the Dean of Women. I was expelled from college for coming in past the dormitory curfew. I collected my belongings and spent my last night at college with Nellie, a remarkable girl and my friend from Jack Lyons' poetry group. I took the bus home.

I found George Oppen and poetry at one moment, but the college expelled me and suspended George as a result of our meeting. Choice may not have been apparent to someone outside our situation, but what happened to us, our joined lives, seems to us both choice and inevitability. Once we found that we shared the same vision, our response to each other was to stay together, but it certainly was not easy for me to get away from Grants Pass. My brothers heard my story without comment, and I went back to work in my family's store, bewildered at how fast I had been removed from college and the life I had begun to see for myself there. Looking back now, I see that it was not necessary to have been expelled; I would only have needed an adequate pretext to stay out all night. But I did not make that choice.

Mama passed through Corvallis a little while after I had departed. She told the Dean that the Dean had interfered with my education, and that the Dean exceeded her responsibility in expelling me. I was surprised when Mama reported her conference; I had supposed, when she had made difficulties about giving me money, that she did not want me to go to college. I heard my family disapprove the strict rules, the curfew for girls and not for boys at the college, and I benefited from their strength. In what they took as a defeat for me, my family closed ranks around me; and for a few months I lived again in my mother's house.

George arrived in Grants Pass in a torrent of rain in his roommate's Model T. When he stopped in a garage in the center of town and got out of the car, the man said to him, "What hotel are you going to?"

George replied, "That one across the street."

But the man said, "It's run by Catholics."

George went to it anyway, and then he made his way to our house to meet my mother and brothers of whom he'd heard on our first night together. Brave young man to come into our stronghold! George and I went out in the rain in the Model T. South of Grants Pass we passed the Rogue River dam; the rain was now nearly a cloudburst, and the water flooding over the dam was dramatic. The dam-gates were lowered to release the pressure of the water, and the force of trees and floating debris swept the banks clean of stumps, trees and small buildings. We stopped at a place marked "Tourist Cabins"; inside our cabin was a little stove, and while George built the fire I bought crackers and cheese and toasted them on the stove. Talking together, it became clear that all we needed was to stay together, and we could do the things we wanted to do: go out into the world together, discover the world, and become whatever was in store for us to be. The comfort of our first bed, our first fire, our first home were all in that little cabin, at the time of the Rogue's first flood.

We started back to Grants Pass on the road that followed the river. When we came to a high spot before the town we parked the car and walked to the bridge, where we stood and watched the water creep higher and higher, to the roadway of the bridge. Chicken coops, pots and pans, even trees were held against the bridge, adding to the weight of the water. We turned to look at our car, which we had left on high ground; the sheriff who was standing with us turned too to see his car, left on the roadway, disappear as the water closed over it. We waited until the water stopped rising and we could cross the bridge safely; as we entered my mother's house I turned off the kerosene lamp Mama had left burning for us. George went into my room and I went upstairs to sleep. Mama must have awakened at our homecoming—she went to the mantel and burned her fingers on the still-hot lamp!

The boy with whom I had broken off before I went away to Corvallis met George and me as we walked home after dark the next evening. He had some high-school toughs with him, who held me and beat George, blacking his eyes. When we finally got home Mama and I did what we could for George's eyes; next day my brothers came to the house and said, after seeing us holding hands, "If Mary wants him," and went away. Eleven years later, on a visit to Grants Pass, an old lady came up to me on the street. "Please," she said, "can my boy come home?" My brothers had said to the boy who had beaten George, "Leave town and never come back."

George went home to San Francisco and went to work in one of his father's theaters. I continued to work in my family's store, saving money to leave again. This time I planned to go to San Francisco to enter nurse's training. George and I wrote frequently, and finally Nellie, who had moved to Berkeley, invited me to come to Berkeley to live with her. I discussed the idea with my brothers and mother, but my mother opposed my going. When I went for my trunk I found it on the front porch, and the door closed; I left without seeing her. At a bus station in northern California I met a salesman who sold shoes to my brother, who persuaded me to return for my mother's permission. Back I went again to Grants Pass; it took many attempts to leave that town.

I had decided against marriage. I considered the marriages of my three brothers to be disastrous traps into which they had fallen. My mother remarried and divorced several times after my father's death, and I was shocked and shocked again at her choices. I accepted the necessity of earning my own living, which did not seem difficult, and when I met George I was prepared to simply step out of the life I had been living the day before and to live my life with George. My plans for myself had offered no solution to the problem of loneliness and the possibility of being unloved; George and I would be complete, a mated pair, with the strength of our intelligences, our passions, and our sensibilities multiplied by living our lives together. If I had consented to live in Grants Pass, of course my life would have continued; but I had glimpsed a different reality, a different vision of what is possible. A world in which I would find conversation, ideas, poetry, peers—this I am sure did not exist for me in Grants Pass.

Intuition operated in each one of us within my family while we lived together, but we were not articulate in discussions or analyses. An expanded discussion that began to get too serious caused restless movements and uncomfortable embarrassment. The one who was not initiating the discussion would invariably rise to escape—I still find myself going to the sink and turning on the water, or leaving the room. Now I can deliberately return and face the discussion, but years passed before I learned that such depths or heights were not going to destroy me. My family's conversations were gossipy, and judgments were made based on acute observation of all that went on around us. My mother and Paul, especially, were wickedly witty and hilarious in their judgments of the townspeople of Grants Pass who had rejected us. My sisters-in-law were not admitted equally into the tight group of my mother and brothers; when my sisters-in-law were present, I don't think the ribald and scathing wit was quite so sharp. Mama did not trust a female to the same degree that she trusted her husband and sons. Even I made her uncomfortable; she was afraid of me, and she had more than a little apprehension that I felt superior to her and intended to achieve a life that was outside her concept of a life.

Within the family we did not dwell on each other's foibles; our little ways were known and tolerated, and mentioned only in anger or when necessary. Like a primitive tribal defense of territory, my family closed ranks and presented a united attitude to any threat from the outside world. Criticism within the family ceased when any one of us was threatened; no one asked me why I had so willfully got myself expelled from college.

I do not think my life would have followed the same paths if Papa had not died when I was fifteen years old. My family's judgments were, in some degree, judgments that bolstered our ebbing class position after Papa's death; I cannot place such attitudes within the family before his death. While he was alive more discussion took place, reasons for things were made clear, more ideas were proposed to circumvent the unfriendly manners of our fellow citizens in Grants Pass. For instance, Papa had begun to invite acquaintances from Montana, from Seattle, and from among his mother's friends in Los Angeles, where he regularly visited; he invited them with the express purpose of getting them to come and live in Grants Pass. The Whorleys, loyal friends of my mother and brothers, came to Grants Pass because of my father's urging, and I even discerned what I thought were plans for a marriage between me and the Whorleys' son, but both he and I viewed this match-making with wariness and amusement. Our family would have been less notorious in the town had Papa lived; he probably would have eventually become a leading citizen. But Mama and Paul became the harum-scarum leaders of the remnant of our family, while Noel and I withdrew in reserve and watched. Paul was anarchic and destructive, perhaps by his own choice, and Mama would grow nearly hysterical with pent-up emotions which she expressed to Paul in zany schemes to get rich quickly: a turkey farm, a gold mine, a lily plantation, and her several brief marriages. I never knew any of her husbands, and not one of them was ever part of the intimacy she maintained with my brothers.

This was the atmosphere to which I returned and in which I worked two more months. Then, with my mother's permission and three hundred dollars in the bank, I set off for San Francisco. When I got off the train at the Berkeley station there was no one to meet me; George was waiting in

Oakland. I went to Nellie's house, where George found me, and I moved into George's San Francisco hotel room, but I was not registered in the hotel, and one day the manager knocked on the door and told me I must leave. I had been writing, and I was sitting in a sea of paper. From the hotel we went up to Myrto's on Telegraph Hill; Myrto ran a restaurant at the top of Union Street, and she also befriended all artists. She gave us the garret above the restaurant, where we were not disturbed, even by the police raids, which periodically searched the restaurant for liquor. These were Prohibition times, and Myrto would come running up the stairs to hide the liquor under our bed.

George and I were both writing, and George was also attending a prep school in Oakland in order to enroll in the university at Berkeley in the fall. We dined in one or another of the many Italian restaurants in North Beach; Prohibition had not changed the habits of the Italian community, and we were always served red wine with dinner. After dinner someone from the family would bring out an accordion to play for the guests, often for only George and me. The first time I was not sure George could dance, but he looked at me, we stood up, we took one step together, and we danced. These small restaurants had a floor perhaps as large as a table top, but whenever we could make the opportunity, in our first years together, we danced. Later in the San Francisco night, George and I wandered over the city, walking through the tunnel down by the fishing pier and out to the Golden Gate. We also went swimming with friends from Telegraph Hill; we swam naked from the little beach beside the Sausalito Ferry pier below the Ghirardelli Factory. George and I were happy to be together—it was a delight to make love or just to talk with friends or with each other.

George got up at the last possible minute in the mornings to run to catch the ferry to Oakland. I stood at the top of the hill to watch him run down the wooden stairs to the Embarcadero and all the way to the Ferry building. Later in the morning I attended Heald's business school; nurse's training was no longer a consideration since George and I had decided to live together and to write, but I felt I had to gain skills to support myself.

Most of the land on top of Telegraph Hill was vacant and grassy, dotted with shacks or houses where young people lived; poets, artists and writers lived among the Italian householders with their gardens and goats and chicken. One of these, a friend of ours and a poet from Texas, was also an expert book thief—his greatest exploit was picking up a rare edition of Edna St. Vincent Millay's poetry at the entrance of a bookstore, then selling it at the exit of the same store. I also liked Market Street in San Francisco; I had found in my first experience in a city that I liked being with people in crowds, and there were so many people, never quite touching, on crowded Market Street.

I had arrived in July, and at the end of August Miss Lawlor, George's father's secretary, told George that his parents were expected home soon. A woman was legally of age at eighteen, but a man was not, and we were sure that their plans for George did not include me or poetry. We decided to hitchhike to New York. George's friend Don, who owned the Model T, drove us to Riverside, and while he sat in the car and waited we got our first ride and were driven away. We were continually given rides, meals and money; we were offered work and we were asked to stay. It was a friendly world we found from the first step we took together. *Generous* describes the world we found when we stepped out into it together.

We were in search of an esthetic within which to live, and we were looking for it in our own American roots, in our own country. We had learned at college that poetry was being written in our own times, and that in order for us to write it was not necessary for us to ground ourselves in the academic; the ground we needed was the roads we were traveling. As we were new, so we had new roots, and we knew little of our own country. Hitchhiking became more than flight from a powerful family— our discoveries themselves became an esthetic and a disclosure. The people we met, as various and as accidentally met as thumbing a ride could make them, became the clue to our finding roots; we gained confidence that this country was ours in a sense which we hadn't known under our parents' roofs. The sense was not only a patriotic but also a personal one, for as people generally accepted us, we felt comfortable and at home in our country. I have never felt so at home in any other land.

There are endless stories to recount. Two men with a great Dane in the back seat picked us up once. They were on their way to water their new date-palm orchard in the desert. It was August, and as we watched the great Dane run in circles on the desert under the full moon, the men opened the sluice-gate to let irrigation water run into their orchard before we slept on the back seat of the car.

When three men going across the border to gamble picked us up, we went along with them to a gambling place in Mexicali, where one of them handed me a stack of silver dollars. I had never gambled; I stood and laid down dollars as the croupier picked them up.

We were picked up by a young man in a Model 'T' who ran narcotics into Los Angeles from Mexico in a fast car; he was on a return trip now in an inconspicuous car, and he took us through deserted Indian country, where Indians were moving with dignity on the desert. We saw Indians going to market dressed in velvet blouses with gauzy scarves blowing in the wind, the braves and young girls riding horseback, the women and children walking. We passed through lead and copper mining districts in desperately poor country; it was only a glimpse and we felt we had to come back again sometime. George was sleeping when the young man said to me, "Sister, you two better get married—you are crossing State lines, and they may pick up your boyfriend on the Mann Act [white slavery] and you will be left waiting on the jailhouse steps."

Often we were told to move on. There were many young people, boys and men roaming the roads of the country. The terms had changed since my brothers' wanderings, from "riding the rails" to "hitchhiking" and from "hobo" to "hitchhiker," and our traveling was all by automobiles on the highway. We met no other girl on the road, nor any couples like us. I was not asked for sex; we must have been traveling in an aura of innocence, perhaps because we were so innocently in love. We sneaked into a YMCA where our driver had rented a room for one person! We slept in odd corners, and we washed up in gas station restrooms; we ate when we had money or when someone gave us a meal.

At one spot where we had been let out, we were desperate for a ride. The Sheriff said, "You can't thumb rides in this town. We need bean-pickers, and if I see you again I'll take you to the bean-pickers camp." We did not want to pick beans, especially under a Sheriff's threat, so we stopped a car full with a family of Mexicans, and the little abuelita in the front seat rearranged the children and said to us, "Pase, por favor."

Tired and sleepy and with only a dollar in George's pocket, we asked for a room in a run-down hotel. We noted that the bed had only one sheet, but we slept soundly, and in the morning we talked in the doorway with a black girl in red silk stockings, who was as young as we were. She asked, "Have you any money?" and she insisted that we take a dollar for breakfast. Another time a traveling salesman who picked us up paid for a room for us. People took care of us; they worried about what would happen when we left them.

One night, very late, we were still on the highway and very sleepy, and in the moonlight we stumbled into a little building beside the road. In the morning we found that we had slept in an abandoned chicken house. We brushed ourselves off and walked into Tucson—not the Tucson of today with irrigation and green fields, but a poor desert town.

Although I had a strong conviction that my relationship with George was not an affair of the State, the threat of imprisonment on the road frightened us, so we went to be married in Dallas. A girl we met gave me her purple velvet dress, her boyfriend gave us a pint of gin. George wore his college roommate's baggy plus-fours, but we did not drink the gin. We bought a ten-cent ring and went to the ugly red sandstone courthouse that still stands in Dallas. We gave my name, Mary Colby, and the name George was using, "David Verdi," because he was fleeing from his father. The judge mumbled along, and after he had finished George fished the ring out of his pocket.

"Oh," said the judge, "that's an entirely different ceremony."

"But we are married, aren't we?" said George. "Suppose I put the ring away."

"Do that," said the judge.

Our Texas friend from Telegraph Hill had given us a letter to the poet laureate of Texas, Jan Isbelle Fortune. We found her in a small house with her husband and her three children. She invited us to sleep on her living-room floor and made us welcome. Her husband, hinting that he could give us jobs, explained to George several times that he was the foreman in the National Biscuit factory, but neither of us had thought of that kind of work, and a factory was entirely outside our experience. We did not respond to his restrained offers, but went downtown to look for jobs. We asked for a meal in return for dishwashing, and the man said, addressing George, "I know, I know, your family threw you out for marrying a girl who isn't Jewish. What is your family name? Oh yes, I think I know your grandfather. I will have jobs for you if you come back tomorrow to eat Rosh Hashanah dinner with us."

"What is Rosh Hashanah?" I asked George as we walked away from the restaurant.

"I know it is a religious holiday, but I don't know the ritual," said George. We went back the next day and ate with the family of the restaurant owner, who had plans for our future. He offered help to a fellow Jew as unquestioningly as if George was related to him; he accepted me too, nor did his wife or brother-in-law demur.

His plan was for George to work in the brother-in-law's factory. He said, "You can do bookkeeping, of course, and you can learn cutting. Mary can go to work hemming handkerchiefs—she knows how to sew, of course."

I was afraid George might lose a finger in the electric cutting machine, which cut through fifty or sixty thicknesses of cloth at one time, but I went to work in the brother-in-law's handkerchief factory (for of course I could sew), and I was soon earning the three dollars a day that he had assured me I would earn. George found a job in a theater doing the same kind of work he had done in his father's theaters. The clothing industry was just starting in Dallas, and had we followed their plans, who knows? We might be Neiman-Marcus today.

George and I were both writing all through these times. Jan Fortune suggested that we try to sell some of our work, so we sent out two poems each to *Holland's Farm Journal*, a Texas paper. We each received a check for twenty-five dollars. A slip of paper in the envelope for me said, "Payment for two poems concerning Death." George, when I asked him, remembered one of my poems—

> *After I am dead*
> *and you wonder*
> *where I am and you see*
> *the dark blue wood-smoke*
> *in dark green evergreens*

climbing over their tops
and disappearing perhaps you will know
where I am
but I think not

I stopped writing. We were deeply immersed in ourselves during these fast-crowding experiences. The time and the urge to write did not come again to me until I was working on translations of St. John of the Cross in 1971 or 1972. I have quite often translated poems I wanted to read from the original French or Spanish. The St. John translation was so poor in every version I could find that I began to make what I called "transpositions." From that I began to write again; my readings in the prophets brought me back to a search for my father, who had read Sirach, Ezekiel, the Psalms, the Song of Songs, and other parts of the Bible to me. It was as though pent-up emotions were waiting to be released—I wasn't aware of all I remembered until I tapped at the door and memories came flooding in. Apparently nothing is forgotten, but all is waiting to be called forth; I think I have reached a safe age from which to release these memories which have troubled me over the years. Perhaps they would not have been released for the asking when I was younger.

We rented an apartment in Dallas and moved away from Jan's house, but we were still close to her and we especially loved her intense and lovely little girl, Jan Isbelle, a long-legged child of ten or so.

I was not well and could not work. Someone, probably Jan, told the Salvation Army to come and help us, for two ladies in uniform came to our door and brushed by George when he protested, "But we're not religious." The ladies left a large basket of food and came later with another, which was welcome, as we had paid our rent but had no money for food. I was pregnant, and Jan took me to have an abortion, but still I did not get well, and she was frightened. She wrote to George's father, who sent her money which she used to take me to her doctor. It was very nearly Christmas, and a friend of George's father wrote that we must come home, both of us. Jan outfitted me with black lace nightgowns, black underclothes, all that she would like to have had for herself, and she bought us tickets to San Francisco. I enjoyed the trip as much as I had enjoyed that first train-trip when I was five years old. As the train pulled in and slowed to a stop in Los Angeles, a feminine version of George's face appeared on the other side of the window. It was Libby, George's older sister. We walked and talked with her and her husband until the train left for the overnight trip to San Francisco. We had not anticipated the intensity of their curiosity about me. Libby telephoned her father after she left us, and while we were nearing San Francisco they were talking about whether they would allow us to remain together. Although their power over us was real, we did not consent to it, but we did have fears, and I dreamed. I had dreams even before we fled San Francisco the first time; in one dream, there was a contest between George's father and me. George and I were on a merry-go-round, and if I caught the ring when we stopped I could have George; his father stood and watched.

The family had discussed an annulment before they saw me. After they saw me they schemed to use me to trap George, and to use luxury and wealth to trap me. George was to enter his father's business; we were to live in a house they had already chosen for us, with Erich and Adele, old household servants. In this house across the street from the Mark Hopkins Hotel on Nob Hill, which we had not even seen, we were to live in their style and to move in their sphere of society, in their city. I supposed it was a natural, normal parental attitude, especially as we were very young; we both assumed all this was a gift. George's stepmother, Seville, took me to buy clothes; I was still wearing the clothes I had worn when I left Grants Pass, a dark blue overcoat, a ribbon for my hair, and flat-heeled shoes. I loved my big, warm overcoat because it had served as blanket at night and had stood me in good stead in our hitchhiking, keeping me warm in the cold Texas winter winds; I wore a ribbon to tie back my long straight hair, and with my flat-heeled shoes I was dressed very much as June, George's nine-year-old sister, was dressed when I first saw her beside the door of their apartment. She was attending a convent, and her eyes were big, waiting to catch her first glimpse of "the painted 'hoor' Buddy had run off with."

Seville had selected a complete wardrobe from a description of me by Miss Lawlor, the secretary. We went to the store, and I tried on beautiful dresses, coats, underclothes, and shoes. Next we went to a hairdresser, who taught me to comb and dress my hair. Seville bought me a hairpiece, similar to one my mother had, which she had called a "rat."

"When you come to visit me," said Seville, "wear your girdle and always wear gloves and see that Buddy has his nails manicured." I got through the day and joined George at the hotel room which his father had engaged for us. George had spent a day similar to mine, and that evening we were to be dressed in new clothes to meet the parents' friends and relations. We telephoned Nellie and Jack in our first free moment and told them, "Come over tomorrow and see all the clothes we've been given." When they came we were wildly gay; we tried on the clothes and found there were plenty for them and for us, too. We dressed in the new clothes and went out for a 50-cent meal in North Beach to celebrate being together again.

George agreed to go to work in one of his father's theaters. "Not to learn the business, but because you ask me to do it," George explained to his father. "We do not intend to stay in San Francisco. We do not accept this plan for our lives." George worked evenings at the theater, and Seville asked me to spend the evenings at their house. I wandered about, watching the bridge game and listening to their conversation—these ways were not our ways.

My father-in-law went with us when we rented a studio on Montgomery Street, a very beautiful room two stories high, with a balcony where we slept. Later he sent us overstuffed leather furniture. It was strange letting someone decide for us what to work at, where to live, what clothes to wear, even the way to spend our evenings; he was shaping our lives in the shape of his life. We were patient and we complied for a while to please him, but George protested often that we were not going to stay. I seemed to be floating in a nightmare which was made seductive and silken, as when George's father took me to buy jewelry and gave me George's mother's ring. They assumed I would be persuaded, and that I would hold George to this life of luxury and comfort.

We thought the hotel room and the clothes were gifts, but the manager explained to us that we owed for the room and for the many things that had been sent *collect* to us. George said, "I am sure my father will take care of all that," and we moved out. But we were still removed from our

Berkeley friends, and I wandered in the evenings in Seville's drawing-room in a strange limbo. I remember reading Lewis and Clark's reports of discoveries in the Northwest, Stevenson's *Travels with a Donkey*, and Doughty's *Arabia Deserta*–all travel documents.

(In Cambridge, England, in 1972, our host Jeremy Prynne said one evening, "I have a key to the rare bookroom in our library—would you like to visit it?" He walked directly to a cupboard, unlocked and reverently took out in both hands a box, and unwrapping the contents carefully laid before us Charles Doughty's tiny notebook, handsewn, with his list of words in Arabic and his medicine kit. All of it could have been placed in a cigar box, and nothing Prynne could have shown me would have pleased me more.)

Seville's day began with breakfast in bed, brought to her by her maid at nine-thirty. At ten the masseur arrived to give her a massage. She then discussed with her maid the clothes she would wear that day. She returned to bed to conduct the business of the house: dinner invitations, engagements of all sorts arranged by telephone, interviews with the cook and housekeeper concerning the dinner that would be served to a full table of guests almost every night, and a talk with the gardener if necessary; any number of household affairs were taken care of from her bed, before she set out for the day. At eleven the chauffeur appeared at the door, and Seville was driven to the clothing stores, to I. Magnin or to Ransohoffs, or to a hairdresser. Clothing which had been delivered to her the day before was returned if Seville had decided against it. In the stores Seville's personal saleslady came forward to greet her and show her first the new arrivals from Paris. At one o'clock Seville usually met her friend Germaine, and they lunched in an expensive restaurant. They were greeted by the head waiter, who suggested food, and a great discussion took place because Germaine and Seville were always on a diet. After lunch they went to their afternoon bridge game (for a brief time the game was Mah Jong). They played these games quite well, as they gambled to make the game more intense. At five Seville returned home to rest, bathe, and dress in evening clothes for dinner and for the bridge party which followed. Here the talk was of the stock market and of their investments. Seville was the daughter of a paint manufacturer who also manufactured linoleum, and

Seville's stock in her father's company provided a large part of her income. All her friends dealt in stocks and bonds, and this discussion interested them perhaps more than any other; the subject was never far from their minds.

In Seville and George's father's house the latest books on the bestseller list were always lying about, because their bookseller sent over any books he thought might interest them. Literary talk was not entirely absent, and George's father was sensitive and intelligent; it was just that literature was not taken seriously in the household. George's outspoken desire to be a poet and writer was taken lightly as a youthful aberration from which he would recover with maturity. George and I, with our marriage, introduced a factor to be dealt with so suddenly that our plans and desires were not taken into consideration; their attitude was that we would settle into their social set with relief and gratitude at being rescued from our way of life. Our brief concern with college and education was to them also an aberration, a diversion from the career of business, to be cast aside as we got down to serious aspects of life: bridge, the stock market, business, shopping, and a child or two. George's younger sister was entirely loved and valued and I understood their treatment of us as I watched their treatment of this girl when she later tried to leave home, get an education and break away from her parents' patterns.

We were constantly searching—searching in our travels, in our pursuit of friends and in our conversation concerning all that we saw and felt about the world. We were searching for a way to avoid the trap that our class backgrounds held for us if we relented in our attempts to escape from them. We understood from our experiences while hitchhiking that in the United States we were not required to remain in the class into which we were born. We wanted to see a great deal of the world, and the education of which we talked for ourselves was to leave our class and learn our life by throwing ourselves into it.

Soon I went to work in the Alexandria theater where George was working. One day the manager did not come to work and George was told, "From now on you will be the manager."

Next day George went to see the manager, who had been fired from the job. "I do not want your job," George told him.

"Oh, yeah!" replied the unbelieving manager.

We went to see George's father and explained once more that we meant what we had said about not staying in San Francisco. "Don't you like it here?" asked his father.

I burst out, "No, no, it is not our life we are living here, it is yours—your friends, your business, your bridge parties and dinner parties and I don't like your way of life."

He went out, slamming the door in anger or in tears. I know now that we must have seemed to him vulnerable and too young to be out in a world of which he knew nothing. I think now that he was afraid for us. But we had found people out in the larger world to be open and friendly to us wherever we had been; his life did not hold for us this wealth of people of all classes that we wanted to know. I think we felt the world was ours, and that it was not his to give to us.

Young George and Mary, or George and Mary now—so long as it is George *and* Mary it is life as I have known and lived it, as we have known and lived it. The young people now come to visit, to talk, and they seem happy just to look at us, survivors. Perhaps they are strengthened by a view of us which represents fifty years together in a fully lived life. This achievement, be it luck or choice, has been inevitable.

FIRST TRAVELS

1928–1929

We packed our two suitcases, leaving the other acquisitions to Nellie and Jack in Berkeley, and left town in an agitated frame of mind from our quarrel with George's father. We had now grown even more wary of those who tried to control us. In Portland we sold our car, asking a friend to hold the money for us while we continued eastward, hitchhiking. We headed for the Midwest, meeting and talking with other young people on the road as we hitchhiked. We rode with businessmen, salesmen, and one young couple with an infant whose car had flat tire after flat tire, which we repaired for them.

The Midwest meant to us not only the geographical center of our country, but a center for the poetry which was being written everywhere, which meant that a literature was being written out of our times. We carried with us Conrad Aiken's *Anthology of Poetry*, and in Chicago we thought of Sandburg and of Sherwood Anderson, whose writings colored the landscape as surely as the landscape shaped and colored their writing. These were the times into which we emerged.

We arrived at Detroit, on wide and lovely Lake St. Clair. The wind was free and George could sail, and when we examined our road map we saw that we could sail to New York. We sent for the money from the sale of our car and found a cat-boat, which a young man sold us together with an old outboard motor and an old gasoline stove. Our first sail, which was a short turn out of the harbor and back in again, frightened me—I had not known that the boat would heel over in the wind. Our cat-boat was a wide, low-sided boat with one mast set in the very eye of her bows. Her only sail was an almost rectangular gaff-rig sail; she was very simple to handle and had ample room for us to lie full-length beside her centerboard to sleep. She was slow to windward but fast before the wind, and with her centerboard up we could paddle close inshore—but most important, the wind was free.

We sailed down Lake St. Clair and down the river into Lake Erie. Storms, which are dramatic and beautiful on the lakes, came up suddenly on hot days; a bank of black cloud would arrive swiftly, and we kept a sharp lookout for these short but violent storms. When one hit us, we took down our sail and sat out the storm. We swam if the day was too hot, trailing a rope behind the boat for safety; we drank the lake water, which was clear and clean. These were the times of the Volstead Act, or Prohibition, and a Coast Guard cutter was tied up in every harbor mouth to chase rum-runners, who ran liquor into the United States from Canada at night. We found that if we tied up beside the Coast Guard boat and made friends with the cook he would usually feed us. At eveningtime we tried to be in a harbor, for after a day's sailing we were eager to walk and explore and talk to whomever we met. The river-mouths were the harbors, and the industrial towns had a quayside with facilities for loading and unloading the ships that plied the waters from Chicago to Buffalo. Canada was across the lake, with its many towns along its shores. Traffic in grain and ores as well as passengers moved on the lake, an inland sea 240 miles long and over fifty miles wide. Sailboats were fast disappearing by 1928; only old-timers were still interested in sailing, and it seemed to us the right time for the canal trip.

(The barge canal is no longer open all the way across New York State. Now, such a trip would have to be made through the St. Lawrence waterway to Montreal and the Atlantic Ocean, and the big ships and tankers would not give a twenty-foot sailboat a tow.)

As we drew near the end of Lake Erie we watched for the entrance to the Erie Canal. I didn't know what to expect, but I had imagined a marquee or a large sign over the entrance under which we would sail into the canal. Instead, we found ourselves drawn into an increasing current, and in a sweep of excitement George yelled through the foggy mist created by the falls, "Throw the anchor, we're near the falls!" We paddled over to the lakeside, and after collecting ourselves a little we sailed back along the edge of the lake, out of the current, and examined the lake side until we found the unmarked entrance to the canal. Unnoted, we entered and began the long locking process. We had sailed this far on our trip with only the road map we had used for hitchhiking as guide!

Lake Erie is 570 feet above the sea, and the system of locks took us daily nearer to the Hudson River. At each lock we tied up at the side of the canal until there was room for us to go through with a barge. We took great care that our boat not be crushed or scraped in the lowering water and current, for when the water is released it lowers suddenly. We lowered lock by lock. Along the way we made friends with bargemen, and we often hitched a ride behind a barge. We found that the cook was always glad to be invited to sit with us on our little boat to escape the heat and vibration of the big steel barge. The cooks who rode with us were Scandinavian, and they showed us snapshots of their families in Sweden or Norway, where women in 1928 were dressed in styles my grandmothers had worn; these cooks also fed us—soup and coffee was the usual handout. Family-owned barges also plied the canal, with the family aboard and the children playing about the decks. Special schools at each end of the canal allowed the children of the bargemen to keep up with their schoolwork.

We tied up at night to a wide place in the canal and went for a walk to stretch our legs and to see what was on the other side of the high banks of the canal. We walked on paths that the horses had used in earlier days, when the barges were horse-drawn. We reached the end of the Erie Canal at Albany, which is on the Hudson River, and across the river in Renssalaer we found a small boat yard where we had our boat hauled out for a paint job. George remembers asking the man there what the lines which lift the boom were called—he had forgotten the word between ages five and twenty.

"Toppinglifts," the man replied scornfully.

We scraped our boat's sides and her almost-flat bottom, painted her topsides black (they had been white) and her bottom with copper paint for the salt water of the Atlantic Ocean, and left her while we went to look at Albany, the capital city of New York State. While we were away from our boat someone scrawled on our new paint, and the job had to be done again.

We left the canal at Albany to go down the Hudson River to New York City. The lovely Hudson River, held between its high cliffs, is a clear, fast-flowing deep river, widening in only a few spots. In one such spot, just above the city of Nyack, we anchored near the shore in shallow water. In the middle of the night we were suddenly thrown on the boat's side, and George found himself in the water, holding the boat up to keep her from broaching. The Albany nightboat had passed by, going full speed, and water, which had been drawn from beneath us, came back with a rush. George knocked off the hatch-cover, which had been firmly built into the boat, when he left the cabin precipitately, and we never did find it. As we neared the city (at that time there was no George Washington Bridge) we found we had gone faster than we had reckoned, probably because the tide was stronger nearer to the sea. We were in New York City, and the white walls at the tops of the cliffs were the apartment houses of the Bronx and upper Manhattan. George suddenly called, "Throw the anchor, my Aunt Agnes lives up there." I threw the anchor into the river at Seventy-ninth Street—where the yacht basin is today. We climbed the steel stair and bridge built over the railway tracks to Riverside Drive, but Aunt Agnes didn't live there anymore, and the doorman suggested that years had passed since she had left. We were dressed as we had dressed all summer on the boat: I was wearing a middy blouse and skirt, and George wore white pants, given him by one of the Coast Guard cooks, which were too large. We walked among the conservatively-dressed population of the city, and I stared in wonder at the skyscrapers, which in 1928 were unique to New York City. I rode my first double-decker bus. We found no places to sit and rest, no vacant lots as in most cities where one could sit undisturbed. We were told to move on whenever we sat on steps or beside statues or on curbstones; when we sat in hotel lobbies we were told to go away because we were not dressed in New York City style.

We called on Aunt Elsie and Uncle Tracy, both of whom were very kind and good to us. Aunt Elsie took me to buy some New York clothes; in 1928 a black coat with a large light fur collar, a hat that pulled down over the ears, high-heeled shoes, and a dress loose above and tight around the hips made nearly a uniform on Fifth Avenue. For men the style was equally rigid: a black hat or Derby, a black overcoat with a velvet collar, and black shoes with a dark suit.

Old friends of George's father and mother invited us to dinner parties, where we were accepted and treated with respect, as young adults who knew what they wanted and knew what they thought. We were exhilarated by New York City, which was the cultural center of our country—not a political-cultural center as Paris was to France, but for us the center where young people congregated to exchange ideas in writing, painting, sculpture, all the arts. In New York City standards were set and professional levels were achieved; if talent was recognized in New York, the rest of the country at some time also gave recognition. We had not felt in San Francisco that we knew the people who were writing and thinking and searching for what was new, and we went to New York searching for those people, for a circle of peers. We had the conviction that the works of artists and writers had to be new, or there was no point to the effort. We were undoubtedly lucky, for we found almost at once, and seemingly without impediment, friends who had these concerns too, and who understood us and accepted us as friends.

Uncle Tracy took us to the theater, but theater was past its day of greatness and the ideas were not fresh. Moreover, our western childhood contained almost nothing of the tradition of the legitimate stage. We didn't respect it as did those who were closer to their European background, nor did we like opera; but we saw the Ballet Jooss troupe dance "The Green Table," a political satire, and found it brilliant and clever.

We found an apartment in Minetta Lane in Greenwich Village, but it turned out to be a dark hole, and noisy—bottles were thrown down our entry-way at night, which disturbed our sleep. We spent the rest of the winter in the Madison Square Hotel, taking our meals in the surrounding Syrian, Armenian, and Lebanese restaurants.

George had a letter of recommendation to the editor of the *New York Sun,* and on the first day after we had found a room and clothed ourselves conventionally, he took the letter and went to ask the editor for a job. The editor was kind and interested, and said, "Suppose I call my advertising manager and ask him to take you with him on his rounds— perhaps you will see something of his work and you will know better what job you want."

George set out with the advertising manager; they took the subway, which was crowded, and at Sixty-eighth Street, where there are two stair-way exits from the subway, the advertising manager took one stairway and George took the other. George finally gave up trying to find his man in the crowd and came home. "I can't go back, I'd feel too foolish," he said. Instead he took a job as a switchboard operator in the brokerage house in which Uncle Rob was interested. George disconnected customers, made wrong connections, and caused general consternation the first day on his job, but he soon got the hang of it. It was also his job to run out for coffee and sandwiches, and he was soon being asked for tips on the stock market. These were the days just before the stock-market crash of 1929; stenographers were asking for tips from elevator boys, and George, being from inside the office, presumably had much hotter tips.

I was reading Marcel Proust, sinking deep into his memories and awakening to intuitive knowledge of my own; more than I had known before I read him and learned to trust my intuitions. As I read Proust and Henry James I became conscious of Europe and of a cultured life in a society I had not glimpsed from my western childhood. I found that my understanding increased as I read, and that I had my own knowing ways. If I knew how to exercise them, I knew more about the people around me, and I brought to this intellectual life of New York my background, with knowledge of people in a small town, intimately known. I found that upon entering a room, if I were observant and made myself sensitive to the people in that room, I could know almost at once more than I had thought possible without spending a long time with them accumulating the knowledge. Henry James opened the world around me by making the life of Europe and his society an example for me of a way to think and analyze; to find meaning in the social world around, to penetrate and understand it and to value the contribution of the U.S.

I also discovered Virginia Woolf's novels, just appearing in 1928; her writing meant to me the flash of insight while a leaf falls, the knowledge of complex relations that comes in a moment of understanding. Her feminine mind was close to mine—my thought too brought me sudden realizations of life being lived in complexity while a moment of time passes. Her novels are always about what life is, about how death coming in life to a loved friend is impossible to separate from one's own life. I learned that love does not die with death, "that love is simple but people are not simple." Virginia herself found in her writing what life meant to her, and reading her works I found a little more of what life meant to me.

Once, invited to a party to which we had to walk the length of Manhattan because we had no money, we paused at a bookshop and leafed through more books of poetry than we had ever found in one place before. This was the Gotham Book Mart, and George was reading Pound's *Exile 3*, which had the first section of "Poem beginning 'The,'" by Louis Zukofsky. At the party Mary Wright said to George, "Oh, you are a poet, you must meet our friend Zukofsky."

George said, "He wrote 'Poem beginning "The."'"

Mary said, "You are the only one in the world who knows it."

Louis introduced us to Charles Reznikoff's poetry, and then to Reznikoff himself, whom we returned to visit often. Charles' job was writing definitions for a law-book company, and across the table from him every day sat another man trained in law who also worked there. Every day they faced each other, and beginning with A they worked through all the definitions of law until they came to Z, keeping the definitions up to date. The company was at the Brooklyn end of Manhattan Bridge, and often we met Charles after work to go for a walk with him. Along the way we stopped to eat; Charles was a connoisseur of cafeterias, and we ate the best muffins in town at one cafeteria, walked further to find the best chicken, and ate Beecake at the Automat. Or we met Charles at the President Cafeteria near Grand Central Station, and after supper we walked as far as George and I felt like walking.

One day when we were in her house, Charles' wife Marie Syrkin told of her teaching at Textile High School in Manhattan. Marie was very fond of Shelley's "Indian Serenade," but she was afraid of the reception a love poem would have among the teenage boys from the poor districts of Manhattan. She decided to read it nevertheless, and as she stood there before the class reading the poem, a hand in the back row began waving as she finished the lines, "Oh lift me from the grass / I die! I faint! I fail!" She raised her eyes, and still affected by the poem, she said to the boy, "Yes?"

"What's wrong with that Indian?" he wanted to know.

Charles walked all the way home most evenings. We went to his apartment on Friday evenings—I don't remember that he invited us, maybe he found us knocking at his door week after week and took us in. While we were visiting Charles ran out to fetch ice cream and cream soda. Years later, when we called on Charles, I asked, "Charles, why don't you buy us ice cream and cream soda as you always did when we were young and came to call?"

"It's strange," said Charles, "I never had cream soda before that, nor since!"

Charles was a hard man to compliment. He outmaneuvered our attempts to tell him what his poetry meant to us, and countered with anecdotes about his father's millinery business or how he, when he lived at his sister's house which was identical to all the others on the street in Brooklyn, couldn't find the house because she had removed the rocking chair by which he identified it. He had walked all the way back to the corner store and telephoned her, and she put the rocker back on the porch so Charles could find his way home. Such stories belittled Charles, and many times they were ironic. In later years George said to Charles, "Your poems have been with me through the war, during all my adult life."

Charles replied, "George, I'm sure we all do the best we can and George, I think that's all any of us can do."

In the basement of his sister's house Charles kept his printing press. It was a small press, and yet it was a big, very heavy piece of machinery. He set a few lines of type each evening, just as he tried to write at least a line or two of poetry at the end of his day of work. He was generous with the books he printed—if we showed interest he immediately gave us a copy.

We were riding along in our car one day, Charles in the front seat with George, and we stopped at a light somewhere in Brooklyn. When a passerby stepped forward to ask directions, Charles thought a moment and said, "You go . . . no, not that way, first you go down this street as far as where the statue used to be—" The light had changed, and the cars behind us were honking their horns, so we moved off, wondering if the passerby ever found his destination. For Charles, each street carried memories; he had lived only briefly in other places, and New York and Brooklyn were his home. In his sixties some thirty years later, when he was ill, Charles went to the doctor, who said as he was recovering, "Do you get enough exercise?"

"I walk," said Charles.

"Well, I think you should be sure you walk enough to get adequate exercise. How far do you walk?"

"Oh, ten to twenty miles a day," answered Charles.

We went exploring New York with our friends Mary and Russel Wright, through the East Side of the city where lines of drying clothes festooned the area-ways and backyards of the tenements. Fruit stands and vegetable stands and wagons drawn by horses were piled with heaps of color created by oranges, lettuce, tomatoes, and watermelons. Russel wept at the color. Women leaned with their elbows on pillows at their window sills, idly gazing at the street scene, or shouting at children in the street, or engaging in conversation with a next-door neighbor, window to window. Everything seemed to be going on at once; men hurried across streets pushing loaded racks of clothing, and boys carried bundles of cut cloth to be sewed at home for bosses, who sent out the cut pieces and later collected the finished garments. Sweatshops in every block hummed with their machines, and small industry crowded in among the workers in the neighborhoods where they lived.

At Coney Island we went into the hall of mirrors and laughed at ourselves, then as we stepped out onto the promenade, a blast of air raised Mary's skirts above her head; her arms went up too, and she was a pretty flower, a half-naked shrieking girl. We rode the giant Ferris Wheel which lifted us up above the city and the sea, and when our car reached the top, high above the surrounding city, a system of rails started the car in a slide of its own as the rest of the wheels stood still, and rocked us in a violent pendulum motion before it came to an abrupt stop. Russel bellowed, and we screamed; Russel's voice rose above the noise of the holiday makers, "GET US OUT OF HERE!" The Ferris Wheel made a half-revolution, without any stops, brought us to the platform and let us out.

We took Mary and Russel sailing on the Hudson before we laid our cat-boat up for the winter, and we found that our boat, so roomy for two during the previous summer, was crowded with four. On our return to the mooring, I lost my balance in excitement and misjudgment, and in what seemed to be slow-motion comedy I fell in a forward somersault into the water. I seemed to see myself fall, and I clambered out in chagrin. There was no way to be adequately myself while, soaking wet in a new red sweater and skirt, I entered the hotel lobby and dripped up in the elevator to change clothes. Zukofsky went with us to strip our boat for laying her up at the end of summer. I took off the sail and tied it into a bundle, Louis continuing to talk. I started up the steel stairway to Riverside Drive, with Louis right behind me; George followed with his burden, up the stairs, across the tracks, and up the next flight of stairs. Louis gallantly protested, "Mary, let me carry it, Mary please." Near the top I turned and handed him the sail—he staggered and went down a few steps before he landed against the railing to recover himself. I gathered the bundle again in my arms and dragged it to the top of the stairs.

George and I were western kids. Although there was much that New Yorkers knew which we did not know of the arts, the theater, Europe, and the ins and outs of their city, they did not know the forests of Montana or of Oregon, the swift flowing rivers and the mountains. Nor did they know the life of hitchhiking and of sailing across half the country with almost no money. We had our own strengths and knowledge, and I think in our friendships the differences were part of our fascination for each other. Mary Wright's family had been friends of George's parents from their time in New York as a young couple; aunts, cousins, and friends formed a closely knit and intermarried group, from which Mary was the first and George the second to have married outside the tight circle.

In Aunt Helen's drawing room during that winter, directly before the elections, I remember a discussion; I would be old enough to vote the following year, but I was not interested in their talk. The election that year was between the Californian, Herbert Hoover, and Al Smith, the Tammany Hall man who was then mayor of New York City, a colorful man with what seemed to me to be no substance, no ideas, and no indication that he was anything but a Tammany Hall man. Herbert Hoover represented the most conservative views possible on running the country, and in that election year the issues were vital; the country was threatened by depression, and neither Hoover's ideas nor Smith's ideas seemed to consider the people or the needs of the country as we had observed them in our hitchhiking. But we held ourselves aloof and did not enter the conversation at Aunt Helen's party. Afterwards, as always, we burst into talk with each other as soon as we left her house, but preferred our other concerns, and left politics until later.

Aunt Elsie took me to lunch one day to ask me if we intended to have children. I thought it was none of her affair and said no, but I did not have any kind of birth control and we had gotten no advice from doctors we had asked. She took me to the birth control clinic the next day, and I never had to have another abortion. I wrote to Nellie and to my sister-in-law Julia, who had so many children, and told them they must find birth control clinics at once. Nellie replied in high glee, with cartoons, but Julia could not arrange getting from Oregon wilderness to a San Francisco birth control clinic, and she had one more child. At that time there were only eleven states that allowed even doctors to give birth control information.

Snow in Central Park in December seemed a return to my Montana childhood; it drifted down in a silence in which we walked in a white world with lit-up Manhattan instead of the Rocky Mountains meeting my eyes when I raised them. But we felt trapped in the tightly-built city as the winter wore on. We lived in a steam-heated room, warmer than any room in the west, and the air was a strange dry heated air which smelled the same in every building when one stepped inside out of the cold of the streets. We didn't yet know the subway system, and we got off at stations at random just to see what was above ground. Once we stuck our heads out into a cemetery, another time we were on clay fields with standing pools of water, and once we were among gigantic identical apartment buildings in the Bronx, block after block. When I walked in neighborhoods near our hotel on Twenty-fourth Street in Manhattan, each direction took me to a neighborhood intact in its national origins, with corner stores and markets reflecting the culture of the people and the country from which they came. Most of these people did not know the United States beyond the subway system. It was strange to be looking on at this tense New York City life, which was just as American as was life in Montana or Oregon or San Francisco.

In the following months we met more friends through Mary and Russel Wright and Louis Zukofsky—writers, musicians, poets, composers. One of them, Tibor Serly, was custodian of Bartok's papers and music. Serly, who played with the Philadelphia Symphony Orchestra, tried to interest the conductor, Stokowski, in both Bartok's music and his own. Stokowski was reluctant, but we did hear one piece by Bartok performed in Philadelphia, performed over the objections of the musicians, who found this music of our times too difficult, too new.

Russel Wright had wanted to continue with his first love, stage design, but his marriage to Mary made earning money imperative. He turned to industrial designing of objects for household use, and he became well known as the designer of "Russel Wright" dishes, which modern young couples bought when they set up their first homes. Mary and Russel planned their house, designing their furniture. They clung to possessions, but we wanted to travel. We had left college, and our education now meant looking at and thinking about the world we were in.

In April George was twenty-one, and his uncles Robert and Tracy Rothfeld sent him a case of fine port wine and insisted that George's father relinquish his guardianship and leave us free to do as we wanted with our lives. I don't think we were sufficiently aware of the Rothfelds' attitude at the time, but I see now that they were protecting our interests. We decided to live our lives within as small a budget as possible so that the inheritance George received would continue to have this meaning: to free us from meaningless work, so that we would not have to follow a profession as William Carlos Williams did or try to seek political power as Pound later did, or do tedious work, as Reznikoff did at the law book company. We agreed that we would work when necessary to augment this income, and as it turned out George did most of the money-earning work.

When Zukofsky's school year was finished we drove to Quebec with him and one of his students, Jerry, who had never been out of New York City. Louis sat in front, his head down, poring over the map and pointing out the window. "The White Mountains, the Green Mountains—this is *Vermont*."

Looking at the sunset, Louis said, "Why should I praise it, I had nothing to do with it."

Jerry, trying to contain his youthful excitement, said, "I wonder if they dance the same way here as in Yonkers?"

We stopped and walked along a stream by a meadow with cows; these two from the city had never been near a real live cow. We stayed overnight in Quebec, where we practiced our French and drove slowly through the beautiful countryside.

When Louis left the city the following fall to teach at the University of Wisconsin, we also left New York. Louis, George and I agreed on a plan for publishing books: Louis would be the editor, arranging and getting the books for publication, while George and I would go to France in a year to set up a household and find a printer. We would see the books through the printing and ship them back to Louis, who would market them. The plan was to print paperback books, reasonable enough in price that students and others could buy them. At that time no paperback books existed. We would pay for the cost of the enterprise, and Louis would be paid $100 a month. Louis chose the name To Publishers—"to" in the sense of "to whom it may concern," as on a bill of lading, or as in usage before a verb to indicate the infinitive, "to publish." Louis had already prepared material for a special issue of *Poetry* magazine; Ezra Pound had insisted that Harriet Monroe allow Louis to edit one issue of the magazine. At first Louis had been reluctant, but at Harriet's insistence he provided the name "Objectivist." Louis said later in an interview:*

> . . . objectivism—I never used the word; I used the word "objec-
> tivist," and the only reason for using it was Harriet Monroe's
> insistence when I edited the "objectivist" number of *Poetry* . . .
> Well she told me, "You must have a movement." I said, "No,
> some of us are writing to say things simply so that they will affect
> us as new again."
> "Well give it a name."
> "All right, let's call it 'Objectivists.'" . . . I wouldn't do it today.

Of that group, appearing together for the first time in *Poetry*, very few did not achieve later recognition. Pound had served poetry in this way when he was in England before the First World War; Zukofsky, on home ground, was aware of the currents in poetry as it was being written in the 1920s and 1930s. Williams, Reznikoff, Oppen, Bunting, Rakosi, Niedecker, and Zukofsky himself have become known with the help of Pound and of Zukofsky; they owe a debt to both Pound and Zukofsky for bringing light

---

* *Contemporary Literature*, Spring 1969

to bear on their poetry at a time when they were struggling with lack of recognition. Louis was a great teacher as well—George has said many times, "I can never repay my debt to Zukofsky, he taught me everything."

Louis, four years older than George, was a prodigy and a remarkable friend. We spent so much time together that we very nearly lived together. When Louis came to our apartment on Columbia Heights in Brooklyn, he stayed late talking endlessly about poetry or any of the topics which young people discuss, and we laughed and teased. We loved each other.

We went once with Louis to visit his friends Kate and Ted and their two-year-old son Joe, who played Bach for himself on a little wind-up phonograph. Kate, a heavy matriarchal woman, was huge with her second child, soon to be born; Ted was teaching in a Staten Island high school, and they were living in a non-Jewish neighborhood near Ted's school. Louis, a bachelor and an elegant young man, moved between them with their old country culture and New York's intellectual life. Kate and Ted clung to Louis, who was precursor for them in areas where they still felt strange and isolated. George and I may have been their first experience of a couple with no experience of the ghetto. Kate behaved as though she was jealous of Louis' friendship with us; she was afraid, perhaps, that she would be abandoned by Louis, who indeed found them to be a heavy responsibility. He had brought us along to lighten the burden of that visit. Afterwards we went home first by train, then by ferry, and lastly by the subway to the hotel where we were living that winter. Next day Kate phoned me and said, "Mary, would you and George consider moving in with us, and would you take care of Joey when I go to the hospital?"

"I'll discuss it with George and I'll call you this evening," I promised. We were puzzled that Kate chose us—why us? She had not appeared to be at all comfortable with us in her house. George would have to commute to work, but I was tired of city streets, and it was nearly spring. We decided to say yes, so I called Kate and told her, "We'll move in; we'll share expenses until you have the baby."

The baby was delayed, and we were well acquainted but still strange to each other by the time Kate went to the hospital. The next day Kate's mother arrived, a nearly blind old-country woman who traveled alone about the city. Joe and I were having a simple time: I fed him, we went for walks, he played his records while I read, and I put him to bed at his usual times. I was honored that Kate had chosen me to care for her precious first-born. But Kate's mother, who observed the religious food-laws, brought her own food and touched no dish, fork, or knife in her daughter's house; she was suspicious of me and communicated antagonism by pulling Joe to her protectively. But Joe struggled away from her and came back to me, "Shiksa," the non-Jewish young woman.

When Ted came from the hospital he proudly announced, "Another boy!" He took his mother-in-law to the train to start her back to Manhattan—blind, fearful old woman, who survived in spite of the gentile world that surrounded her world of the ghetto. Ted, who had concurred in choosing me to care for their child, dismissed us as soon as he returned from the hospital, "Another boy!" The baby was born and he, Ted, needed us no longer, but Kate wasn't yet home and we were eating supper, Ted was very high with the birth of one more son. He began telling me in great detail how to accomplish each act of housework within the house that I had been doing, apparently satisfactorily, with Kate's approval. Ted was busily demonstrating how to dispose of garbage, wrapping it in newspaper, tying it with string. Somehow he had forgotten that it was Kate who had carried and given birth to the baby, also satisfactorily. Ted was filled with his own importance, his son, his sons! Males, like him! He became rounder and puffed with his own role—George and I were not audience enough. I was annoyed and wished to bring him back to some simplicity and awareness that he still needed me; that Kate was not yet home from the hospital and that I was going to be there with the first-born tomorrow when Ted went to work. I stood before him and not being able to break through his talk walked up to him and began unbuttoning his jacket, his vest, symbolically to strip him of his unbearable masculine take-over of the roles of two women on whom he was dependent.

Kate came home after ten days in the hospital, and the next day we left. "We want to be alone now with our new baby and Joe," she said. Louis later told us of another strange incident, when Joe was a few years older. As he played with the kids on the block, Kate watched him skate on borrowed skates. She stood with tears streaming, and as Joe skated up to where she stood, she patted his head and said, "Skate, Joey, skate, just like the Goyim."

Remembering that very young people, when they trust each other, throw away all guards to enter into each other's lives, I can try to recreate the relationship we had with Louis. We were all looking for an identity different from our families' identities, and we found strength in bonds of love and friendship such as we had with Louis, which gave our lives shape and intensity. Reaching for clarity of vision, we gave each other freely whatever the other could take from us, and this giving was our friendship.

Louis had an elegant accent in his spoken English; we three had different accents. My way of speech comes from my Montana birthplace, and it is clear, clipped, and very hard on all consonants. George speaks with an upper-class New York City accent, almost dropping R's in the middle of words and occasionally adding R's to the end of words. Our accents have been tempered over the years by living in different places. When I visited my family in Grants Pass after having been away for many years, both they and I were a little shocked—they by my changed accent and way of speech, and I by realizing how my speech must have once resembled theirs.

Louis had to choose his way of speaking English, as his family did not speak it, and his mother and sister never left the Bronx. I think Louis chose the accent of John Dewey; when Louis was at Columbia, Dewey was a leading figure and a great influence there. Students who graduated from Columbia in that period, in many cases, had what was recognized as a Columbia accent. In any case, Louis had beautiful speech, and he was a great mimic; he saw the Noh plays with a famous Japanese actor who toured the United States several times, and he delighted us with imitations of this actor. Louis was the center of a considerable circle, and we met and talked and visited within this group. Mary and Russel Wright and Louis remained our friends for many years; the others, if we met again, would no doubt interest us, but Louis was the best friend we had, and we both miss his friendship. In an interview in 1969 George stated, "I learned from Louis, as against romanticism or even the quaintness of the imagist position, the necessity for forming a poem properly, for achieving form. That's what 'objectivist' really means. There's been tremendous misunderstanding about that. People assume it means the psychologically objective in attitude. It actually means the objectification of the poem, the making an object of the poem . . . The other point for me, and I think for Louis, too, was the attempt to construct meaning, to construct a method of thought from the imagist intensity of vision. If no one were going to challenge me, I would say, 'a test of truth.' If I had to back it up I'd say anyway, 'a test of sincerity'—that there is a moment, an actual time, when you believe something to be true, and you construct a meaning from these moments of conviction."

In the same interview, George said, "I can name the poets who really have been of decisive importance to me—Charles Reznikoff and Zukofsky as a person, his conversation, not his poetry—although again as with Pound, while I can make an awful lot of objections to parts of A, the opening words, 'A / Round of fiddles playing Bach,' have rung in my ears for a long time and always will, I imagine. Reznikoff has been the most important to me, consciously at least. And otherwise this is what I have to explain—really Blake is more important to me than Williams, and several philosophers may be more important to me than Pound. The contemporary poets aren't the most important thing in my life, with the exception of those few things that really matter to me. Wyatt's poems and several Middle English poems, among other antiquities, mean more to me than any except one or two of the contemporary. It must be some habit of life that makes it seem to a young poet that all the other young poets are the major factors in his life. At any rate it's not true."

In the spring we sailed the cat-boat around Manhattan Island to Long Island Sound to New Rochelle harbor. There we rented a small house and lived in it with almost no furniture—I remember only the bed, a beautiful carved swan bed. We bought Zee-wag, a wire-haired fox terrier who accompanied us for several years. She was an over-eager dog, always falling off docks or out of windows, but she was so intelligent that, with sighs, grins, and facial expressions, she tried to talk.

Sailing on Long Island Sound was nearly ideal for our cat-boat. Winds and storms announce themselves with more advance warning than on the Great Lakes, and harbors are everywhere on both sides of the Sound. We sailed every weekend past the estates, villages, harbors, and beaches along the Long Island shore. I love to fish, and I prefer flounder to any other fish; at times we anchored over sandy bottom and caught a flounder for our supper. Once, sailing along, we looked over the side of the boat, and keeping pace beside us was a large head! It looked as though a black moon had fallen into the sea, and though we observed it all the time it stayed alongside, we could never believe what we saw or figure out what it was. We also sailed with big sailing ships, lumber-schooners bringing lumber from Maine. We sailed faster than they, but while we were alongside we talked to the crew, then came about and sailed with them again. Louis often came on weekends to sail and to talk.

When Aunt Helen and some of George's father's friends came by our house they showed their shock at its emptiness. We had the swan-bed, a new puppy and wooden boxes to sit on. We were changing class, and we did not have the kind of house, the symbol of class and of power, that Aunt Helen and her friends assumed we would have.

At the end of summer we walked away from the cat-boat, which we left moored in New Rochelle harbor. In 1963, Jim Weil of the Elizabeth Press came to visit us on Henry Street in Brooklyn. "I'd like to see New Rochelle; I'll return your visit," said George, who wanted to remind himself of this village and harbor near the house where he was born. The train passed large apartment buildings that George did not remember, but the station was the same familiar building. Jim Weil's address in hand, George started walking, and after several blocks he asked directions. He was told, "Oh, you had better go back to the station and get a taxi." In the taxi he was driven on winding roads for several miles.

"Can this be New Rochelle?" George asked Jim. "I lived in a house on the water, near the harbor, in a small village."

Jim replied, "What village, what harbor?"

In 1929 George, Zee-wag and I took ship for California. We shipped second class and found ourselves among our own age group, young people who were going to California to attend the University or to look for jobs. The crew of our ship, the *Virginia*, was British, and we made friends with the men who came on deck in the evenings to flirt, sing and talk with us; nights were warm, and we slept on deck when our cabins below grew too hot. I remember one young passenger who strode toward us, arm extended, and said, "My name is Cone, c-o-n-e," so that we would not for a moment mistake him for a Jew. As always on ship travel, the passengers were removed from their previous lives and felt suddenly free, and during the ten-day trip romances flourished.

We made a stop in Havana, and with several hours to spend we asked a young taxi-driver to take us to his favorite places and show us Havana. He was not an expert driver, and he was impressed with the difficult and different gear-shift of his Dodge. When time was growing short for us to return to our ship, George suggested, "Perhaps I had better do the driving." Our taxi man, who was no older than we, agreed, as he was no longer in a condition to be driving at all; but he was concerned about the mysteries of the gearshift. George demonstrated that he could master the shift, and we arrived back at our ship just as the gang-plank was being taken up.

We wanted to spend a year in San Francisco writing and assimilating our New York experience and getting together the money for the To Publishers venture. The house we rented in Belvedere was built over the water, and we soon had a boat moored out in front of the house. We sailed in the bay and up the Sacramento River, but the sailing did not compare with the trip on Lake Erie or the small-boat sailing on Long Island Sound.

George's older sister Libby rented a house near ours on the beach in Belvedere, where she and her two little girls spent a few days each week.

Libby came from a time far back, from the times of rich young women of a previous generation, in which a girl prepared to marry and then to live within the marriage as though everything she was to be was decided at the moment of the wedding. Parents, even grandparents had nodded wisely and approved Libby's first marriage.

Libby's mother had described Libby, "A satanic child, difficult, unmanageable." I would have said, "Lost, lonely, tragic." I could say satanic too, but it is enough now to say that she was always that same child.

Libby tried to get from her younger brother what she needed from the world "Out There," a world she never entered. He, who was two years younger, could not tell her from superior experience what she wanted to know about men and boys, and her infatuations embarrassed him. He could not help her because he, too, was isolated. Libby attended a convent school. He went to a boys' military academy, and the information he could have given her would not have been acceptable to her; he could have told her that the boys in his school dreamed of catching a glimpse of a bared breast, but that her cleverly contrived and memorized conversation in preparation for meeting a man probably would not aid her in arousing his sexual interest. She tried with bright colors, high heels, a long cigarette holder—but she was on the outside looking in, circling an imagined world, an imagined life, with herself at its center, conversation flowing around her clever remarks, and her quotation of poetry and her epigrams holding a circle of men spell-bound. She quoted:

> *I cried for madder music and for stronger wine,*
> *But when the feast is finished and the lamps expire,*
> *Then falls thy shadow, Cynara! the night is thine;*
> *And I am desolate and sick for an old passion,*
>   *Yea hungry for the lips of my desire:*
> *I have been faithful to thee, Cynara, in my fashion.*

She gleaned from the romantic poets of the turn of the century: Dowson, Oscar Wilde, Swinburne. She tried to create a style of life to fit the year 1930, and she imagined a passionate and beautiful life, a semblance from her reading.

Libby had no mother, not even an aunt who was her model. How was she to know what to be? She married straight out of boarding school, and her children were born before she had time to learn what she wanted from life; by the time she was nineteen she was a mother, a wife with a husband much older than she was, and keeper of a large household with servants. George remembers the title and one line of one of Libby's poems: "*Come into my Parlor* / I live on a sheet of glass." The poem accurately expresses her feelings; Libby was the spider waiting for the males, exposed and living transparently. Was she beautiful? Her brother says, "To me Libby did not seem beautiful, she was too intent on others' eyes on her, she was always searching her mirror with agonized eyes." Her love for her brother and for her father was faithful and childlike, but Libby never achieved self-love, and so her love for anyone else was also wanting. As a child she had only her father and her brother. Her father, who was a well-loved man, was her model. Libby sought by conquest and daring the love of men, but no man loved her with a love that nurtured her, and no woman really loved Libby except her daughter Andy.

I entered this family when I was eighteen. Libby would have liked to be my friend—I know it now, but at the time I was a stranger, a newcomer, a new young wife. Libby would drop in (we lived in two little houses built out over the water), and for her this was a second house, to which she came on weekends with a maid to cook and to care for the children. Our house was full on weekends with friends from the university—Nellie and her friends from the department of anthropology and Jack who invited his associates. Our friends and favorite teachers filled our lives as well as our house.

From our porch we climbed down the ladder to the rowboat to row down Raccoon Straits to search for the oysters which grew on the rocks and which we ate as soon as we found them. A curious young sea lion swam along behind us, keeping a distance but traveling with us, slowly sinking from sight when we slowed or stopped. We rowed home—Dorothy, who was from Crete, was going to cook our meal, and Nellie and I were going to learn by watching her. We had asked Libby to go with us on this expedition in the rowboat, but Libby declined our invitation; we had not included any men, and she did not know how to talk to us, or how to enter this friendship of women.

George and I loved boats and the water, as did Libby, but in such different ways that boats and the sea were not a bond between us. Libby, afraid that she might not appear graceful or beautiful in case a man might see her, always consulted her mirror, and she became so lost in gazing deep into her own eyes that by the time she was ready to go we were already out upon the water.

George, Jack, and a friend of Jack's who was a professor in the department of psychology were discussing Jack's work—he was running laboratory rats in mazes and had been finding that the rats apparently improved their abilities to run mazes and that a heritage of improved learning ability seemed to be in their offspring. We all discussed the possible consequences if this were true—we all entered the discussion. These weekends were busy, happy and interesting. After our meal, when it was dark and our neighbors had turned out their light, we swam naked from our porch, returning to dry ourselves in the warmth of our fireplace.

I sometimes saw Libby standing in our doorway looking on, her clothes too provocative, her bathing suit too daring. She wondered at our youthful spirits, she who had no experience of exuberant living. Wistful, lonely, she looked on at us as an eight-year-old might have looked at us, but when she entered conversation with one of the young men it was with epigrams and shocking statements, and the young man was stopped speech-less, surprised at this *femme fatale* talking to a college kid, embarrassed for her. The next time I looked for her she would be gone. Libby was bewildered by our talk and by our enthusiasm for learning to cook; our discussion seemed to her to concern men's work or servants' tasks. Where were the clever epigrams, the romance, the glamor which formed Libby's imagined world?

Libby's children woke from their nap, and in the quiet of the house they crept downstairs, climbed down the ladder, and swam to our porch, and climbed up our ladder amid surprised welcoming cries and laughter. Every weekend they escaped the nursemaid and their mother; they loved to be with the young people in our house who picked them up, whirled them about and teased them a little to make them laugh and talk. But Libby, who did not know how to enter our youthful, high-spirited life, could not allow her children to enter it without her, and they were quietly removed as soon as it was discovered that they were gone from their house. I looked at the younger little girl sometimes and thought, "When I have a child I want her to be like Andy; I feel that Andy should have been mine."

George and I sometimes set off for a walk in the hills to gather mushrooms; after I had filled my bag we sat on a hill to look out over the bay to San Francisco, and when we returned to our house we had a feast of mushrooms. Or sometimes we drove to the city for a meal in North Beach in one of the speakeasies where we could dance after dinner as we had danced when I first came down from Oregon two years before. (Libby seldom joined us in these undertakings.) Or we sailed; we did not ask anyone to sail with us because we sailed to be just two together.

Now it is clear to me that I was with good reason afraid of being engulfed in Libby's family, and that although poor Libby was no danger to me, if I had accepted her into an intimate place in my life I would have been drawn into the family. My identity was other than to become like Libby, with only marriage and a couple of children for a whole life. Once, returning from a long sailing trip, as we approached Belvedere we saw Libby, who swam marvelously, swimming toward us a mile out, to meet us and welcome us home. She wooed us, and we wooed her children. When Libby asked me, "Would you make me a yellow dress like yours?" I sat down at once to my sewing machine to make it for her; and when we began to talk of going away she asked me, "Will you give me your kitchen curtains, the ones with the red embroidered dots?"

When we prepared to leave Belvedere at the end of summer Libby came out to the street to watch us packing our car, and in the confusion and our busy-ness the children crept into the back of our car and hid. Andy, the littler one, was discovered, and her mother laughingly dragged her out, but Andy clung to our legs, trying not to cry, and Libby had to pull her away and hold her. We said our goodbyes and drove away. After a few miles of driving, the older little girl suddenly stood up in the back of the car, laughing but challenging us with blazing eyes, and sadly we turned and drove back with her to abandon her.

We traveled between Belvedere and Berkeley to spend time with our friends; Nellie and Jack were finishing their degree work at the university. On weekends our house was full, and we found after a few weeks that we could not invite so many people because we could not pay the grocery bills and also save money for the books that we were going to France to publish. We also found that anywhere in California was too close to George's family for us to live our lives. We were still finding it hard to break away from our families and we returned as though we were not sufficient in ourselves; George's father and sister influenced the way we lived in California, and we were trapped into a semblance of their lives. Although we had left San Francisco several times, we found we were still in the process of leaving home. Leaving is not easy; the first time I saw Grants Pass I was thirteen years old, and I decided then to leave, but it took at least five tries before I could go and not feel the need to return. In downtown San Francisco there is a little bar with a sign over the entrance, "WE ARE ITCHING TO GET AWAY FROM PORTLAND OREGON." I like to sit in that bar sometimes and reflect that it was hard for me, too, to get away from Oregon. George and I were fully agreed on staying together, on being independent, and on pursuing our own lives without following his family's pattern, and yet we returned to San Francisco; but each time it was less home to us, and each time it was easier to leave again.

With Nellie and Jack we went up the estuary to the Oakland flats, where many old schooners from the Alaska fishing fleet were tided out. A few sailing ships still came into San Francisco, but most of the fleet was retired, and the ships were sitting in the mud, side by side. In a forest of masts we clambered over bulwarks from ship to ship, hunting for a life-boat that was in good condition; Jack wanted to buy one and convert her to a sailing boat. He picked one with THIRTY PERSONS written on her bows. He named her the *Thirty Persons*, brought her around to Belvedere and set up shop on the beach next to our house; he came over on weekends to work on her.

Jack and Nellie had many friends, and we met them all. Jack Lyons, our beloved teacher from Corvallis, was also in Berkeley often.

Entwhistle, a neighbor lad in love with our boat, the *Thelma*, sailed with us for a few days. The trade wind blows several hours a day, and we reeled along south, down the California coast, past nearly-bare hills which roll back from the sea to high mountains behind. In the rainy season these same low hills turn brilliant green; I love these hills, and my heart grows tight when I see them again after a long absence. Few harbors were to be found, but many small beaches stretched along the northern California coast—small pockets of sand shone out where hills came down or where a stream or river debouched. We noted the fog settling in, a wall that slowly enveloped us. As we approached the land, Entwhistle asked, "How are we going to find the buoy in this fog?" Although we had laid out our course on the chart, estimating any current that we knew of or had read of in the Pacific current-book, and although we had tried to vary our steering equally on each side of the point on the compass we had set for ourselves, how were we to be sure we had not by-passed the buoy? It was important to find it, for by its number, color and shape it was to tell us where we were on the coast and what our next course was to be. I was forward on the bowsprit, peering into the fog; it seemed to me that we were in a circle of not more than a hundred feet of visibility. When the wind is carrying the sound away from the boat it is nearly impossible to catch the sound of the bell buoy, but just as we were getting very tense and knew we were near the coast, I saw the bell. I shouted to George, "Veer off to leeward, there's the buoy!"

We grazed it, and the impact even removed a little varnish from the rail; I shouted, "We found it! We hit it!"

This sort of thing has happened to us quite a few times. Despite the fallibility of a sailboat and the impossibility of steering a straight course, despite currents, fog or nighttime, we still find our way. George and I both have good vision, which is a great help; I can see after dark, but George usually makes out the numbers on the buoys before I do. Such abilities become valuable when sailing small boats. Binoculars are of little use, as the boat is moving in all directions, bouncing on the waves or sliding up and down. We always test our compass and make sure it will be as accurate as possible, but there are currents that change with the tides and with the winds. We seem to have an uncanny luck.

We spent the first night in Santa Cruz, which is not a protected harbor. An arm of mountain forms the north point of Monterey Bay, ensuring shelter from the north, and a pier is built out into the water at the town of Santa Cruz, but there is no protection from the winds from other directions and no end to the constant swell of the Pacific, day in and day out year round. We anchored off the pier and went ashore to stretch our legs a little before returning to sleep aboard the boat.

No weather-watch in 1929 aided seafarers, nor did we have a radio. We watched the weather ourselves, and in somewhat increased wind we sailed south the next day, the wind quartering off our stern; we had no intention of stopping until we reached Santa Barbara, but off Piedras Blancas, with the neighbor boy steering, the wind caught our sail on its lee, and boom! she jibed. The helmsman was so horrified at what he had done that he jibed her back again, and the sail ripped. With the mainsail parted, the shreds quickly wrapped themselves around every stay and became an entangled mass—in fact, a terrible mess. We continued sailing on the jib and jigger sails. George prepared to go up the mast in the bos'n's chair to clear the sail so that we could get it down on deck. We limped into San Simeon and anchored, where we found only a slight indentation in the coast, not a harbor at all. A pier had been built there for the Hearst ranch above this spot on the coast; Hearst's castle was being constructed from numbered blocks of stone from an ancient European castle which had been dismantled and shipped to this forlorn spot on the California coast. To land at the pier, George rowed alongside and held the skiff off the pier in the huge swell until a good moment came for me to jump, rope in hand, to the pier. We ordered a new sail, sent our young neighbor lad home on the bus, and settled down to two weeks of waiting. Every morning, as the wind came up, we could feel the vibrations of our anchor as it slid over the sand bottom; we would start the motor, move up near the pier again and let the anchor go again, waiting awhile to see that it held before we left the boat to go for a daily walk, usually to the park surrounding the castle where many kinds of imported grazing animals roamed the hillsides.

Our sail arrived; we rigged the boat with the dazzling white sail and continued south to Point Conception, which is one of the most westward points of the continent at latitude 34° where a weather break occurs. The weather is much warmer south of Point Conception, and Santa Barbara has a mild climate compared to that of San Francisco. We moored safely in front of the yacht club beside the breakwater, with a very large yacht, almost a breakwater in itself, alongside us to seaward. Outside the breakwater a great bed of kelp stilled the waves and decreased the swell that entered the harbor. We appreciated being in such an anchorage after our two weeks of insecurity in San Simeon. The Yacht Club members welcomed us, and we brought the *Thelma* into the Yacht Club pier to take on fresh water; we sloshed the decks to wash off the salt with which the boat was covered. Two wide bunks were in the main cabin, and we kept extra gear in the two narrow bunks forward in the peak. In her lockers were two long black over-coats such as my father had worn in Montana years before, which buttoned from chin to ankle; we laughed at these coats, but except when we were in harbors, we wore them the whole way down and back up the coast—I don't remember that we even took them off when we went below.

We were eager to sail to the islands which lie out in front of Santa Barbara. With the same prevailing winds, but with a blue sea and without the driving towering waves of the northern California coast, we sailed around the eastward end of the islands and skirted the wooded shore, watching for the break in the rocks that was the entrance to the harbor on Santa Cruz Island. We were sailing in when—boom! and again boom!—someone started shooting a cannon at us. We turned, but as we sailed out we realized from the shouts of our new Yacht Club acquaintances that they were firing a salute of welcome! We sailed back in and anchored to spend the evening with everyone on one boat; we had supper, and then in the warm night with a light shining on the sail, we collected the flying fish that hurtled themselves at the sail and landed on deck. Next morning the other boats sailed back to Santa Barbara, and we were left alone in the small harbor.

Living on Santa Cruz Island were three people: Hjalmar, Paul and Marie. These two Swedes and the American wife of one of them had lived on the mainland, but an earthquake took their living place, and they had decided to come to the island. Sheep roamed wild, fish were plentiful, and they had a garden, but most important to the two men was the beer they brewed, which was essential to their sense of well-being. In 1929 the brewing of beer was illegal, but Paul and Hjalmar had to have their beer. Once, as Paul rowed out to greet us in the morning, he said, "Now take me, this morning I've only had five beers." They drank so fast they couldn't keep up with themselves; it was new beer, which we sampled and didn't like.

On the upper beach in the sand banks we found Indian beads, pieces of pottery, and a few arrowheads. In times past the neighboring mainland Indians had come to the island to catch and dry fish for winter food.

The two men were sailors from their childhood in Sweden. As one of them hauled our anchor, the other had the mainsail up, and with George at the wheel of the *Thelma* we were sailing. Marie and I sat, talked or made coffee; George and I were like guests on our own boat. We knew that no matter what winds blew, all was going to go smoothly on the *Thelma* with competent hands to do the work.

Hjalmar and Paul went hunting for a wild sheep, and they brought us the hind quarter as a parting gift. We hung the meat forward in the coolest place in the boat and used it as fast as we could.

Back in Santa Barbara we invited a young Scotsman we met at the Yacht Club to sail part way up the coast with us. He was a fine sailor, and we were glad to have him with us, for the *Thelma* was too big for us to sail alone—the sails and the anchor were too heavy, and in bad weather we grew tired. Our Scots friend described to us a boat he had recently owned, on which he had taken his little boy sailing with him. Bowling along in a fresh breeze, his son had fallen overboard; alone in the boat, he brought her around and, while keeping his eye on his son in the rough water, sailed by the spot where the boy was. Before the child went under, he swept him with one arm out of the water and into the boat—an incredible feat. Afterwards he sold his boat and sailed only occasionally on other people's boats. At San Luis Obispo, our next stopping-place, our Scots friend took the bus home.

On the pier in the harbor at San Luis Obispo a man lent us a big crab net. With two hauls of the net we had several big crabs, all we could eat for that day and the next. The next stop was Morro Bay, after that San Simeon again, then the big hop to Monterey Bay. We found a small bight, a hole-in-the-wall on Point Lobos; we were following the sailing directions in the Coast Pilot book, with its dire warnings of the dangers in such narrow entrances. The craggy rocks all looked the same from seaward, and it was hard to see just where to enter the small harbor. George climbed the mast, and with his added height above the water he conned us in, shouting to me the way to steer. It was indeed a narrow entrance to a very small cove, but once in we were completely protected from storms and from all but the ocean swell, which reaches everywhere. A small building on the steep bank of the cove, once a whaling station, was now a cannery. The only boats were a small motorboat and two rowboats, which the motorboat towed out each day with Japanese divers, two to each boat. Each diver looked at the sea bottom through a glass-bottomed box pressed against the water surface, and when he saw abalones he dived; with the tire-iron in his hand he pried the abalone from the rocks. Toward the end of each work day the motorboat tooted once for each hundred abalones pried from the sea bottom, as it came into harbor.

George and I have spent hundreds of days on the water, in boats ranging from twelve feet in length to the *Thelma's* forty-two feet. The isolation, with our world at times a twenty-foot enclosure of fog in which we are complete in ourselves, is a repeated experience from which we absorb meaning. We have spent hours silently, returning from these absences refreshed and knowing ourselves and each other more deeply. This experience is one which holds our world together for us.

As our year in Belvedere drew to a close and we were preparing to take ship for France, Kenneth Rexroth paid us visit. He had recently come from Chicago, and he probably looked us up because he was in correspondence with Louis; it was but a brief encounter.

With Nellie and Jack we had an intimate relationship, one that can probably not be found in full adulthood. We were intimate, more intimate even than most siblings, because we chose to be together and all four of us threw ourselves into the friendship. We had a great deal to learn from one another, and my friendship with Nellie is the only one in which I have not kept the reserves that block such intimacy. Our ideas were open and shared with each other; it was a relationship based on mutual admiration and trust. Nellie and I had a wealth of knowledge to share inside our friendship, which reached its peak of understanding while George and I were in Belvedere and Nellie and Jack were in Berkeley. As years passed and we didn't see each other often, we finally stopped writing to each other and drew apart. In 1939 I went to visit them; they were living in a restored New England farmhouse; Jack was teaching at a nearby renowned college, and Nellie, who had become a social worker in the 1930s, was working for the Red Cross in a disaster area. Although we never admitted the break in our friendship, the very ways we had severally arrived at the places where we found ourselves by 1939 describe that break. George and I had become leftists, and had functioned as organizers of the unemployed; Nellie and Jack had climbed the academic ladder with care and circumspection.

In 1967, when George won the Pulitzer Prize, Nellie looked us up in San Francisco. We tried to bridge the years, but there was a stiffness. She said, "We never laughed again like we laughed together, the four of us." It was true, our laughter never again had the same abandon; it had been the laughter of a time when we just wanted to laugh out of the sheer joy of life and our first independence, an independence that leaned on the strength of four. We supported each other in our wildest dreams and opinions. After Nellie's visit in 1967 we sent notes back and forth, meaningless formalities, until I wrote, "Let's break through or stop writing." Nellie sent the following letter and poem:

NOV. 11, 1971

Dear Mary:

It's been a long time since I talked with anyone. Mostly I try to cover up what I think. I'm tired of thinking but I can't stop and I know how I feel but I don't expect anyone to see with the same brutality and acceptance. I don't really want people to know me but to wear dark glasses and watch as if being too aware will increase the capacity for being hurt. So a superficial discussion of the routes we take isn't really non-revealing. We learn to read gestures of movement.

. . . In short I can't tell you how I think or what I think. I'm enclosing a couple of things put down today that perhaps will show my involvement. I'm sure they have no meaning for anyone else.

NAIVETÉ

When the news came
we rushed to the street
grabbing the aluminum dishpan
and an agate spoon
we joined the crowd
marching down the streetcar tracks
on Columbia Ave.

Banging the pan
Seeing the blue flakes fall from
the spoon
pushing, shoving, laughing
Celebrating
the Armistice

We went home
on back streets and paths
shortcuts from school

routes unthinking
like Uncle Charlie lying dead in a doorway
beaten and robbed for his pension check
from the Great War

or
my mother opening the door to a stranger
pointing to me
an Alien child full of dumb savagery

Rigor Mortis

How could I tell you
Death is a friend
Coming in peace
The struggle is in the meeting
And Could I shield you from this
with my caring
so that you knew, thinking of that
and the ice cooling your blood gently.

And I'm mailing this before second thought—

Nellie

It was a poem written directly out of our twenty-year-old lives, a poem such as she had been writing when our lives were intertwined. But it would be hopeless to try to recapture that relationship; in its time and in its place, it is perfect.

Alice Conklin Colby, my mother   *Ora Colby, my father*

Mary Oppen, Kalispell, Montana, 1917

George Oppen, New Rochelle,
New York, 1914

Mary Oppen, Corvallis, 1926

Mary and George Oppen, San Francisco, 1928

William Carlos Williams, at our house to discuss publishing, Brooklyn, 1933

Mary Oppen, 1936

Mary and George Oppen, San Francisco, 1929

Charles Reznikoff, New York, 1934

George, Mary, and Linda Oppen, 1942

Mary and George Oppen, Long Island Sound, 1936

George and Linda Oppen, Mexico, 1956

Linda and George Oppen,
Detroit, 1942

George Oppen, France, 1943

David Ignatow, George Oppen, and
Harvey Shapiro, Long Island, 1970

Mary Oppen, Mexico, 1957

Mary and George Oppen, 1951

Mary Oppen, George Oppen, and Charles Reznikoff, San Francisco

George and Mary Oppen, Little Deer Isle, Maine
(photo taken by Rachel Blau DuPlessis)

George and Mary Oppen, San Francisco, 1977

FRANCE

1929–1932

W e were eager to travel, to have a view of our own country from a distance and from another culture. Many American writers, poets and artists were living in Europe, and we wanted to visit those who especially interested us. In 1929 Europe was already full of American students, and it was very late in that hejira. While British artists at the same or at a slightly earlier time were drawn to Germany, our antipathy to Germans and things German, even before Hitler, governed our travels; we chose France, and briefly Italy. We were in a narrow stream influenced by Pound, by Eliot, and by the Impressionist painters.

With our dog Zee-wag we embarked on a small French freighter from San Francisco, destination Le Havre, a thirty-day trip. As our ship passed through the sea it removed us from the continent as though it were a planet, and we touched back occasionally to see if it was still there. We stopped in at Nicaragua on the day of a great earthquake, and a mother with her children came aboard to take the only places vacant on the ship. We spent hours each day in our cabin; George worked at poetry, and I sketched and worked with watercolors. George wrote me a Valentine:

he de dark
handsome

young man has

for her
de fair

maiden Uh

present,
de darling

We read, strolled on deck, and talked with other passengers. Once we descended into the hold with another young couple who wanted to establish their status with us by giving us a view of their Cadillac, which they had brought along to drive across France to Cannes.

We had planned this time in France to be for as long as we liked, in order to paint, write, and continue the conversation we had been seeking before we met and now were pursuing together. We wanted time to "look, gape, gawk, to dawdle"—to try to comprehend what was before our eyes. We wanted to talk with the people we were seeing for the first time, and we wanted to find what France had to offer two young Americans. The United States at this time was a place in which one did much better not to admit being an artist or poet or writer, especially if one believed in oneself. We did believe in ourselves, and we believed in each other, but we could not yet demonstrate our work because we had done very little. Writers, poets, and artists who were important to us were not yet recognized in the United States, and we needed to find our generation, to meet the poets and artists of our times and to find a way of life in which the poetry we felt within us could come out of our lives.

We arrived in Le Havre, and as we watched the other passengers stream to the boat-train for Paris, we hung back. We said, "Let's not rush to Paris; let's stay overnight in Le Havre and see France—not only Paris."

We needed time, so we decided not to travel by train or automobile, or even by bicycle, but we and our dog could not conveniently walk and carry our belongings. A horse! Looking out our hotel window the morning after our arrival we saw that here we could travel with a horse. We told our taxi-man, whom we'd met when we left the boat, "We want to buy a horse and cart."

He drove us to the nearby countryside, where his brother, an Algerian banana merchant who took bananas from ships as they arrived from Central America and peddled them in the streets of Le Havre, had a horse he would sell to us. The horse was Pom-Pon, a beautiful slender "Anglo-Arab," half-Arabian half-English thoroughbred gelding, steel-gray dappled and accustomed to the wagon he pulled daily. A cart and saddle were included in the bargaining, at which our taxi-man and his brother were much more expert than we, but we were delighted with the horse and with our plan for travel. Pom-Pon was ours, the cart and saddle too. We and Zee-wag started back to the city, driving our horse and cart. In her fox-terrier excitement Zee-wag fell from the cart, and our own cart-wheel passed over her and left her screaming and unable to move. We gathered her up, but her back seemed broken and her hind legs paralyzed. We found a veterinarian and undertook his plan for her recovery; massage, careful exercise and time, he said, would recover for her the use of her legs.

We launched into the life of France. We drove out in our cart to explore the narrow streets of Le Havre, and we and Pom-Pon soon learned to know each other. At first he would not give us his hooves to be cleaned, but his manners were perfect, except that he loved too much— bananas, babies, and young women particularly. If an unwary banana-eater came near, Pom-Pon yearned toward the banana; when a woman with babe in arms came near, we had to dash out of the cafe or restaurant to hold his head and keep him from nipping. Pom-Pon was frightened when the cartwheels scraped corner curbs, and we had to reassure him on very sharp turns or up steep streets.

We started on our travels. We planned to cross France, to stop briefly in Paris, and then to search for a place to live, work at writing and painting, and establish our publishing venture. We were in pursuit of a style of life for ourselves, for we did not yet see ourselves in the perspective of our own culture or of our own country's history; we were searching for some-thing more than a life of "making a killing," as my mother said. The United States we had just left was rich, with an affluence of new cars and talk of the stock market. We wanted a way of life that allowed us to paint, write, think, and converse in friendship with those who were on our same path.

We traveled thirty or forty kilometers a day, stopping over a day and a night after every five days of travel, for Pom-Pon needed to rest and to eat more than he had time for while traveling. The slow progress suited us, and we found the long stop-overs a time for talking to people, wandering, and observing. Pom-Pon's needs gave us a long lunch-time too. We unharnessed him beside the road, gave him his hay and threw down straw for him to stale; he was such a polite little horse that in harness he was inhibited. He munched his hay and switched his tail in contentment. We found hotels with a courtyard and a stable for horses, family-run hotels with very good meals. These were our stopping-places all across France; they bustled with activity on market day, but on other days they were quiet, with few people in the dining room. I learned to speak French with words I needed in the market, for the horse and for our hotels. I think if I spoke French now it still would come out of me with words from this time: *vétérinaire, écurie, ménage, paille, avoine.* Our room in the hotel usually overlooked either the street near the market or the courtyard of the hotel. We drank our breakfast bowl of hot milk flavored with chicory, we ate our baguette of French bread with fresh butter and we talked with the hotel keepers each morning. On market day we observed the busy life that went on in a market town. A farmer brought his produce to market by horse-drawn cart, and the horse had to be stabled and made comfortable before the farmer could attend the market. Meanwhile, the farm woman was already in the market with the produce—fruits, vegetables, cheeses, eggs, or any of the many products so perfectly grown in France. The men drank a glass of wine together before going to market, or they bargained together over animals to be bought or sold. We harnessed our Pom-Pon and made our way out of the town.

The style of the houses and churches, even the costumes of the people changed with each region. The land that was farmed lay outside the villages, and the streets of a village lay between high walls; but it was behind their own walls that the villagers really lived. They went to the fields each day, taking the animals with them, and they drove the animals home each night to their household in the village, with its courtyards and outbuildings in which they carried on the many tasks that make the careful life of peasant farmers in France. At the center of each village were always the same shops: the *tabac* that sold matches and tobacco, a *boucherie* with a red flag flying on butchering day, and a *boulangerie* with the ovens visible behind the store counter where we bought our daily bread, as did every family in France. There was also a bistro, a place where men dropped in for an early morning drink of white wine or for beer and conversation at day's end. The market town nearby and the need of almost every farmer to go to town on market day, either to buy or to sell, made other shops unnecessary in the villages. Always there was the Church. The women did the church duties, going to early morning Mass and stopping in briefly if they passed the church during the day. When the farm woman went with the farmer to the market town, she had her own stall; she arranged her produce so beautifully that it always seemed to me a sacrilege to take a bunch of radishes, but she would quickly rearrange the remaining bunches. She also bought provisions to take home at the end of the day. Food shops in the towns were like playstores or jewel boxes; there was a shop for each type of food, little shops in a row on the narrow streets— *Charcuterie, Fromagerie, Laiterie, Patisserie.* In the villages the man did the errands and helped out in busy moments, but the woman ran the store, kept house, fed the family and maintained a lively conversation with her customers. The men had more free time when they were in the town; they sat sometimes in a bar and talked loudly with friends over a glass of beer.

Unlike the United States, class differences were not reflected in comforts. Quite rich townspeople did not yet have flush-plumbing or electric appliances. As we accommodated to these lacks, we began to define a style of life different from our life at home. We now lived out-of-doors as did the people among whom we were living; we were to be observed as much as they were. In our hotel room we bathed from a water pitcher and a bowl and dressed hurriedly, or hopped into bed between coarse-woven, pure linen sheets and covered ourselves with the big red down comforter with which every bed was provided.

In Rouen we passed under the Horlogerie to find a hotel. While Pom-Pon rested, we explored the streets of the town. A small row of houses of ancient red brick, built with blackened cross-timbers, had been preserved from a much earlier time in Rouen; these houses were tiny, but so perfect that each was a work of art. As we explored, wondered, and talked, we began to learn about the people who had been here before us. In wash-houses along the streams and rivers of France women knelt with sleeves rolled up and sweaters buttoned, their knees on a board, and pounded the laundry with big paddles, commenting on all that they saw. Women of artisan and peasant class lived more out-of-doors than did women of similar class in the United States, and they lived more in comradeship with one another; there was more of a sisterhood than we had seen at home. These women worked in the fields, took care of the cows, geese, and chickens and shared the work of house and garden; women in the United States rarely have shared in the heavy outdoor field-work of farm life. We have put European ways behind us so fast that the changes are hard to understand. At first in France we were shocked, and then we began to understand that the old ways had qualities that some of the newer ways in America have lost. The market was a place set aside at the heart of the town, or sometimes it lay outside the ramparts of towns that had been walled. Climbing to the tops of walls which remained, we tried to imagine the life of earlier times—the castle high and safe, the smaller houses below, and the hovels and huts of the very poor at the outskirts. We realized that here in Europe the class into which one was born was accepted as inevitable, by the lower as well as by the upper class. We found it hard to penetrate and to understand this acceptance of a limit beyond which aspirations were not to rise.

We stopped along the rivers at small hotels which were empty during the week but thronged on Sunday with people from the towns and cities. We seemed strange to them, and they puzzled over us. Why had we left home? Did we have family? Why were we here? We found that we were the first United States citizens these small townspeople had met; to a Frenchman in 1930 it was difficult to think of life apart from France, and they could not understand our eagerness to find out about their lives, or about France. A few who knew us long enough to grasp our purpose furthered our search by showing themselves, their ideas and beliefs—these few were, in most cases, radicals.

As we drew near to Paris we passed villas of concrete decorated with rustic boughs and branches of molded concrete, with names like "Mon Rêve," or "Sans Souci." On weekends Parisians crowded every road leading out to the many river and forest resorts, to beautiful villages or old châteaux, to ponds and roadside taverns with gardens, bowers, and a dance place with music or a pavilion for the Sunday band concert. Everyone turned out, and vehicles were as varied as people's fortunes; in automobiles, motorcycles, or bicycles, some with a third wheel and sidecar into which a family crowded with baskets of lunch, everyone went off for a day in the country. In the United States we had felt crowded if there was another family nearby when we picnicked, but here there was a joyful air of a carefree day in the country, with sports and games. Boules was the pastime of the older men, and a court for boules was swept and rolled and kept in perfect condition in back of every bar, restaurant, and tavern in the country. Lovers strolled in woods not very similar to our western forests, but enchanting, intimate forests of deciduous trees. Corot painted their shimmering light—the play of sun through moving leaves.

On the rivers there were always beautiful pulling boats, which we called St. Lawrence skiffs. They were built of thin cedar planks over steamed and bent oak ribs and had a seat around their hourglass sterns. They pulled easily with long light sweeps. We would row upstream, pull into the wake of a passing barge, and with our skiff's bow held against the stern of the barge, sit and talk with the bargeman and his family until we reached a lock, where we would turn back to row or drift down the current to our hotel.

We reached Paris, and we did not know how to find a stable for Pom-Pon. George asked a pedestrian, a solid-looking citizen, "How would you suggest I go about finding a stable for the horse?"

"Oh," he replied, "I'd go to the Café de la Paix and say to the busboy, 'Boy, stable my horse.'"

And we did. The stable was a riding school on the edge of the Bois de Boulogne where we rented for Pom-Pon a stall larger than our hotel room. The straw was changed in his stall every day.

We were budgeting ourselves to 25 francs a day. If we exceeded 25 francs we spent less the following days until we had regained our budget. In the afternoons we went for a drive with Pom-Pon in the Bois de Boulogne, where we saw a few horse-drawn carriages; there were many horseback riders on the bridle paths, and the Bois was beautiful.

In the Louvre we wandered through galleries hung solidly with pictures; we found the French Primitives, and we loved the Pietà of Avignon so much that we came every day to see it. There was also a portrait of a lady with a banner in her fingers: DE QUOILQUE NON VEDE. YO MY RECORDE. The paintings carried deep sincerity, as though they expressed their times to me in a later time. I copied the lady with the motto of her patient remembering in egg tempera on a polished gesso panel. The arts of Paris were a splendid education, before our eyes each day there was as much to be absorbed as we could carry away. Each day there was more to see all around us, in the streets and cafes as well as on the walls of museums and galleries. We discovered the still lifes of Chardin and the landscapes of Claude de Lorraine, whose paintings opened up out of the seventeenth-century discovery of the New World and of science; and here we were, two children of that new world come to find the meaning, the new light cast on time before us by the opening of the human spirit into art. There was not at this time the opportunity to see such wealth of art in the United States as we found in Paris.

We stayed perhaps two weeks before we took Pom-Pon, rested and gay and ready to travel, on the road south. We found on our way down the Rhône valley the Romanesque art of early Christian-Roman Gaul. This art has a force, a simplicity and sincerity and strength of conviction that made for me a deep root in art; it nurtured me.

We reached Marseilles and began to look for a place to stop. George's parents were soon going home from France to San Francisco, and we had agreed to live near Cannes to welcome my little sister-in-law on her vacations from school. We looked for a house outside Le Beausset, in Var, which is a mountainous district with hills down to the Mediterranean. The climate is hot in summer with winds from Africa, and in winter it is cold and rainy. There were empty houses in the vineyards, and we wanted to rent one of these houses. I wanted to paint, George wanted to write, and we planned to live for a while in this place and publish the books. We stopped at the only hotel in Le Beausset and found that the hotel owner and the town butcher were eager to help us; the women ran the businesses and the two men had time to help us find a house. In the community, a grape-growing district with a cooperative, the Vinicole, to press the grapes, it was a problem to rent an empty house on land that was in production. No one had thought of such a thing. The butcher and the hotel owner took us from one land-owner to another in the butcher's little car, which he drove like a madman; the land-owner would purse his lips, expel air explosively in puzzlement and disbelief and refuse to rent his house. At last the butcher thought of a land-owner who had visited New York, and in Ollioules, in a house surrounded by the terraces that grow flowers for the perfumes of France, we found our landlord. He understood us; I think he was amused by us. We rented his empty farmhouse in the vineyards of Le Beausset. He recommended Mme Sicard, who looked after his house for him, to care for us. Our house, built of plaster and stone, glowing with golden color, had a small courtyard to the south, and the sloping valley floor was planted with grapes. We became a center of interest for the whole village of Le Beausset.

Mme Sicard came every day to care for us; she cleaned the house, polished the red tile floors until they shone and washed our clothes. She brought us a little gift, a candle-snuffer. She asked for an "osaydar," and we didn't understand what it was that she wanted; but one day in a hardware store in Toulon I saw an *O'Cedar* mop. "Osaydar!" I exclaimed, and I went into the shop and bought it for Mme Sicard. She may have wanted one for years—for her it was a helping hand which made the task of keeping red tile floors much easier.

We had a toilet put in this centuries-old farmhouse before we knew that the water supply was seasonal. Villagers came to see this marvel on their way to work, to hunt or to gather herbs in the mountains, or a peasant shouted, "Ça va?" across the grapes as he passed.

On the surrounding hilltops stood remains of medieval fortified towns. We drove with Pom-Pon as close as we could, then we walked to explore the ruins, which were usually empty. Sometimes we came across poverty-stricken peasants who lived without paying rent in and among the rubble of these ruins. From these old towns we could see over the surrounding countryside, and we tried to imagine the life when peasants descended each day to work in the fields and returned each night up the long steep climb to spend the night behind the walls. Life must have seemed very hazardous. Far in the distance we saw the Mediterranean, where on hot days at the end of summer we went with Pom-Pon to bathe in the sea. We found that Pom-Pon loved to swim, and we unsaddled him and rode him bareback. It is a great sensation to ride a swimming horse and feel his stertorous breathing and the tremendous surges as he strikes out strongly with all four legs. We found a small village called Cassis, where we drank the local wine; it was a delicate wine that could not travel, and we savored it. We were out of doors most days; occasionally we saddled Pom-Pon and made an excursion back into the mountains, which were different underfoot than they had seemed from our house in the valley. Each flower was fragrant, each shrub and almost every growing thing aromatic. Small birds I did not recognize twittered and rustled in the bushes. Pom-Pon scrambled up the steep paths, which always led to huts which were owned by someone who used them only a few days out of the year, when the hunter carried a bird cage with him from home to hang in the trees near his hut; the bird was always of the same kind as that which he was hunting, and served as a decoy.

We puzzled at their customs as they puzzled at ours. Discussion must have taken place in every house in the village concerning the strange young Americans who had come to live in their valley. They welcomed us, and wherever we were invited we made a visit. We drank the little sweet drink offered us after the proper conversational formalities, and we stayed until what seemed to us the completion of the visit, during which more drinks were offered. When these visits were repaid we found that the correct way to pay a call is to leave as soon as the first drink is finished. We had behaved rather like Drag-Your-Tail-Feathers, the Indian Chief, who used to stay all day when he visited my father in Big Fork, Montana. But we watched the life around us and learned the ways of the village. In the vineyards, open shelters or a small house covered with a trellis of grapes made a leafy, shady retreat where workers and horses rested through the heat of the day. Tools and supplies were kept in the unoccupied houses, and we began to understand the need the peasants had for the houses that stood empty. Peasants arrived at the fields from Le Beausset every morning, hoe on shoulder. The white stallion who drew the water-cart for the village brought water to the vineyards for the spray-tanks, filled with a copper solution, with which the peasants sprayed the grapes, turning the vineyards a ghostly gray. The little white stallion and Pom-Pon the slender tall Anglo-Arab, were friends who whinnied across the fields to each other. Once in a while the stallion escaped as he was being unharnessed in the village; he galloped, tail and mane and harness flying, down the hill, past the Vinicole, and straight up the road to our place. Over the fence or through Pom-Pon's stable window they nuzzled, caressed, and nibbled each other's necks in delight.

As spring drew near, the peasants prepared for the blessing of the animals and for the annual race, to be held on a track plowed around the circular grove of trees left intact on the valley floor a short way from the Vinicole. This grove may have always been sacred—it still had a Virgin in her own little shrine at the entrance, where some goddess may have stood earlier. Pom-Pon was specially invited to the race, as our neighbors were eager to see him run. Heavy draft horses, mules, and Pom-Pon's love, the white stallion, were beribboned, and hooves were varnished while flowers were braided into manes. We polished and braided Pom-Pon too, and George rode him in procession with all the animals of the village to be blessed. Children and women led or carried the small animals as the procession went past the church, the priest flicking a few drops of water to bless the animals for the year to come. We went along to the grove in the procession to determine this year's champion in the race. Pom-Pon won the race, and George was given the prize, a halter big enough for the largest Percheron. All the riders from the race went through the village riding on a wagon, to receive the drinks that were brought out for the horsemen. After the festivities, George and I and our blessed Pom-Pon, now the champion of the village, trudged home.

Our friends the hotel-keeper and the town butcher had duties to their wives and to their businesses, but they were not occupied full-time. The butcher went to market to bring back meat; after he carried it in to hang on the big hook inside the entrance, he was free. The butcher's wife was storekeeper and kept the house in back of the store. The hotel-owner, too, was free after brief duties in the hotel each day. The two of them escaped in the butcher's little car to pursue other interests, and once in a while we were invited too. It is likely that they only meant to invite George, but I didn't think of that, and I always went along on these expeditions. The hotel-keeper questioned us about our politics, and we replied that we hadn't any, or to speak more accurately, that our political concerns didn't yet go beyond a very narrow circle of hunting for the nooks and crannies of our society in which we might live as artist and poet. Our hotel-keeper friend took us to Toulon to see the Tom Mooney room that had just been completed in the Labor Temple; in 1916, at a

Preparedness Day Parade in San Francisco, ten people had been killed and forty injured by an explosion of a bomb, and Tom Mooney had been framed and convicted. George and I had heard his name, but we had not realized the meaning of the case. The election of Governor Olson in 1939 was to result in a full pardon, but this came only after a world-wide campaign of workers to free Tom Mooney, a cause célèbre; it was people like our new friends here in Le Beausset who created sufficient awareness among peoples of the world to exonerate Tom Mooney.

Depression and poverty were heavy in France in 1931. In this valley of grapes and wine not one cow supplied milk for the children; after weaning, children drank water with a little wine poured into it. Town water supplies all over France were labeled "potable" or "non-potable," and the only safe water to drink was boiled water or bottled water. "Tisanes," or herb teas, were drunk, for which the herbs were usually gathered by old women who roamed the hills and roadsides. We observed them as we passed in our cart; these women carried the age-old knowledge of the medicinal and edible qualities of herbs and mushrooms, and they lived their lives in the same place and pattern as had their mothers before them. Their way of life dated back as far as anyone knew, and probably forever before that.

Mme Sicard prescribed and brewed tea for our stomach-aches and back-aches and to relieve muscular pain. "Cupping" was also a common remedy; George caught a cold, and a man came with little glass cups, which he heated and applied to George's back in the area where the congestion seemed to be. Long after George had recovered, he bore the round marks of the cups, which, with their vacuum, had made blood collect in bruise marks. Mme Sicard taught us to save orange peels and fragrant blossoms of flowers to put in bottles of Eau de Vie that were left as gifts when callers came to visit. In time these infusions made the liqueurs so loved in this part of France. By wintertime we were settled in our farmhouse; rains came, and the winds blew cold from the Alpes-Maritimes, just behind us to the sea. In daytime when the sun shone and we were out-of-doors it was warm and fine, but the house was so cold that our bones ached. We bought carpet-slippers with thick soles, and pattens which stood outside the door, to step into when we went outdoors. We bought the only heating stove we could find in Toulon; it was so small that someone had to stand beside it to feed it, at first with little slivers of wood and then with coal, and our floors were never warm. We learned to live out-of-doors. I was painting, learning to use oil paints and watercolors. I sketched our plane trees in our courtyard and our house with its courtyard and its structures around the well, work-places that had been built during years and years of use; the colors and structure of our house were beautiful.

The weekly movie in Le Beausset was usually a film of Chaplin— "Charlot" to the French. They loved him, and we did too; we saw his films again and again that winter.

My accent when I speak French reflects the language I learned caring for Pom-Pon and living near Marseilles. I picked up the Marseillaise accent, which is notoriously ludicrous in France, and my beginnings in Montana, the far north, added the clipped harsh consonants of most northerners to my speech. More than once someone has said, "You speak French very well, Madame, but where did you get the Chinese accent?"

During that winter we published *An "Objectivist" Anthology*, William Carlos Williams' *Novelette*, and Pound's *ABC of Reading*; these paperback books were intended to be sold at low cost in the United States. We wanted to make poetry and other types of literature, that could not find a publisher, available at least to poets and to their own circle, for we had to search to find the writing of our own times. We made frequent trips to Toulon to the printer. The books were printed in English, but they were typeset by non-English-speaking French printers. We read proof after proof, each time finding more mistakes. In Toulon, after we finished our business at the printer's shop, we ordered a cup of champagne, six oysters on the half-shell, and half a loaf of French bread at a quayside cafe; usually we ordered another cup of champagne and six more oysters. We then found our Pom-Pon and climbed into the cart while we could still walk, and Pom-Pon took us safely home to Le Beausset.

When we shipped the books of To Publishers from France to Louis in New York, he found that he could only get the books by paying a duty. Customs declared them to be magazines, not books, but a loophole existed—if we wrapped them in bundles of twenty-five or less they could come in duty-free. This entailed numerous trips by us and by

Louis to the Post Office. Louis hated to carry bundles, and he lived in a rented room, where storing the books was another problem. Charles Reznikoff stored them in his sister's house, in the basement where he had his press, until his sister sold the house. Charles then gave each author his own books.

In 1929, at the age of twenty-one, neither of us understood anything of business, and neither did Louis. It is perhaps surprising that we actually did get books printed. Financially we had taken on too big a burden; we could not support ourselves, Louis, and the printing and publishing of the books unless at least a small amount of money came back to us. And no money came back to us. The book-sellers called the paperbacks "magazines" and would not give them shelf room. When we returned to New York from Paris in 1933, George went from store to store, leaving books on consignment, but the return was negligible. Later, at almost the same moment that George and I terminated To Publishers, James Laughlin founded New Directions. Since then he has continued to publish fine books through the many years, and he deserves the credit for carrying the burden of running a business in the interest of publishing poetry.

As the second winter approached we decided to go back to Paris; we had completed a year of life in the French countryside, and our only regret was that we had to sell Pom-Pon. Sadly we watched him go up our lane, past the Vinicole and out of our lives. Before going to Paris we went to Rapallo to visit Ezra Pound. We took rooms on the promenade, at a distance from Pound's pension where he lived with Dorothy. Across the harbor lived Marian Bunting with Basil and their two children. Dorothy invited us to the tea-dance after our arrival; Pound asked me to dance, and, gravely, we danced. Dorothy always seemed diffident, reserved and remote. I met her always in the pension living or dining room, while George met Pound upstairs in his study; or we both walked with Pound on the promenade.

Marian was lonely, and she seized on me, another American woman, to share her loneliness and her problems, but I was too much younger than Marian to do more than listen. Her family insisted she leave Bunting, give up her poet, but she found it hard to obey them. We rented bicycles together, took them on the bus to the top of the mountains behind Rapallo and came down on them—a breathtaking trip through the forests of cork, chestnut, and pine trees.

Walking with us on the waterfront, Ezra pointed with a grand gesture of his cape and his cane in the wrong direction and said, "From there came the Greek ships." He was telling us, "Read, study the languages, read the poets in their own tongues."

Our message to him would have been just as clear: "You are too far away from your own roots." But we were twenty and Pound was forty, and respect for him as a poet forbade our telling him that we lacked respect for his politics and that he should go home.

He asked us, "What do 'girlfriend,' 'boyfriend' mean?" New words were entering the language, and he didn't hear them from the tongues of those who were giving them their meanings. We would have said to him, "Go home."

Back in Paris, we settled in a hotel on the Quai des Augustins, a fourth-floor large room, with windows from floor to ceiling looking out over the Seine near the Pont St. Michel. We carried with us a minute alcohol stove, a cooking pot and coffee; bread and food for Zee-wag we purchased each day, and we ate breakfast in our room. In the morning I woke and left George sleeping to attend my painting class. I painted from a model, which was not at all what I wanted, but I could not find my way alone to knowledge of the craft of painting. What I wanted to know was what paints to buy, how to mix them, what brushes to use, how to use gouache and watercolors, how to stretch canvas and what paper to use for water-colors. Instead I was standing in a crowded room, and the teacher made casual rounds. "You have made the nose too long, a sign of stupidity," he would say, and I wondered if he meant my stupidity or the model's.

When I returned at noon, George and I ate lunch, went to the museums or sat in a cafe, and had our dinner, after which I slept while George worked late into the night. We lived in that way for several years, a successful system for good sleepers.

Pound was generous; there was nothing he could do for us that he did not do. Hilaire Hiler, his friend, was experimenting with new techniques in order to publish a much-needed book on painting materials and painting techniques. Pound suggested to Hiler that I work with him, and Hiler invited me to come to his studio in the mornings, to test paints and papers and to try techniques demonstrated by artists whom Hiler invited to the studio. Dorothy Pound came up from Rapallo for one of these demonstrations of watercolor technique.

Pound also said to us, "Go visit Brancusi," and he gave us other addresses of his friends as well. We visited Brancusi at his studio, which opened on a garden with plants growing in the entrance way; it may once have been a stable and garden, but now it housed Brancusi and a great many of his sculptures. Brancusi was a bearded man so kindly and gentle that we felt welcome at once, although this was his "at home" day and many other visitors were there. He said to us, "Stay, after the others go." He had been to the United States, and he was impressed with the homestead law. I supposed it was still possible to take a grant of land from the government, but the idea startled me. I thought homesteads were of my grandfather's time, but to Brancusi free land meant democracy, freedom, generosity of spirit—it meant America. The sculptures which I liked best were the totems; many of them were hewn from log-like pillars with his adze. I especially liked the seats he made with the adze to fit the bottoms of his favorite visitors. He pointed to Ezra Pound's seat and said, "If you come to see me often, I will make you seats too."

We visited Rodin's studio, a museum preserving his statues in the place where he created them. Both Brancusi's and Rodin's statues spoke eloquently to us. Maillol's statue in the gardens of the Louvre is a woman floating up, balanced on the upper round of the hip in a Yoga position, floating like a lily on a pond; yet she is heavy with all her female weight, and the meaning is one of tremendous strength—floating up, an aspiration of physical as well as of spiritual being, a grace and gift, *herself*. Rodin was of the times immediately before our own (we were both born in 1908, Rodin died in 1917), and his sculptures seemed extravagantly emotional. The extravagances of nineteenth-century stricture hung over Rodin, and to express his freedom from those strictures he leaned heavily on emotion; but by this excess the way for Maillol was cleared. The distance of twenty years between himself and Maillol gave him the freedom to present, simply, his meaning.

We also visited Zadkine, whose sculptures we had studied at an exhibit. The sculptures were as much absences as they were presences in the stone; as one walked around one of his works, it seemed not entirely abstract, but more an abstraction of human shape. It became remarkable for design and form. Primitive African statues had this effect, but at the time Zadkine's works were startling. Zadkine received us cordially, and asked us, as had Brancusi, to wait, "after these damn people leave." He asked us to come again, plying us with cakes and tea.

Mont St. Michel and Chartres by Henry Adams was one of the books we had taken with us on shipboard. We visited Mont St. Michel and Chartres, staying overnight as we do on every trip we make to France, and the visit gave rise to many thoughts. The conditions of society condition the times of each artist, and each period is propelled by the fingers and the intellect of its time, which claw and climb . . . up? We say so, in the belief that humanity must have a purpose. By definition history is the record of times past, times no longer living, dead times. But for each fact gathered from that dead past how many facts were not recorded? Which ones are the key to understanding? We looked for understanding by immersing ourselves in the works of art; nothing speaks across cultures and across time as does the human spirit expressed in its works of art. It was through the arts of a past time that we heard its people speak. The architecture of the churches at Chartres and Mont St. Michel is a key to the period in which they were built, a key that opens their time to other works of art and to the art of other cultures of the same time. As we understood more of our own world, we moved with more assurance in the world of art. As Sherwood Anderson said, "we wanted to know if we were any good out there," and we grew respectful of the world we found "out there," the world of times before our own as well as the times in which we were moving. We said to ourselves, "We have to be very good to be any good out there." Henry Adams, as guide, was a great teacher and a fellow student. George and I moved in our own times, in and out of studios: an education.

George and I avoided joining the groups that surrounded the artists and writers we visited. We had found our beginnings in our own roots, and we had found Zukofsky, Williams, and Pound; we were twenty-two years old and full of ourselves. We wanted to observe and learn from the impressions we received as well as from the reading we were doing. Attachments beyond these would have been an encumbrance; we were searching for freedom in which to pursue our own truths. We did not claim the people we met, and I think we avoided also any claim on us. We were the "new generation" to Pound, Williams, and Brancusi, and we may have seemed to hold the future opinion of their work in our hands. They certainly respected us, and it seemed to us that they looked upon us as their heirs as we looked on them as our precursors. We respected them, but our position was different from those who were expatriates. We were thoroughly children of the United States, and we intended no other allegiance. We claimed the United States, but since our education had been interrupted when we met we intended this traveling to be our education. It must be remembered that we were always *two*; we learned from reading and from what we saw, but conversation never ceases between us, and our critical views of our elders kept us from depending on them for our daily intellectual sustenance. We made our visits brief, but discussion of these visits was long, sometimes life-long; we have discussed and discussed again in the light of learning more about what we had already concluded. Our rising concern with politics made us more anxious, especially concerning Pound's reference to "The Boss," Mussolini. He also disclosed that he did not understand that the term "The Boss" is not attractive to American workers.

Pound wrote that he'd be in Paris; we were to meet at a restaurant in Rue de l'Odéon. We had to tell him that we could not continue paying for all the expenses of printing unless a return came to us on the books, and letters from Louis indicated that no money would return. Also, we had read Pound's *ABC of Economics* and discussed it between ourselves; we thought it absurd. Pound wrote, "When I gather chestnuts on the hills of Rapallo I step outside the Capitalist system"—Pound trying to circumvent Marx, Pound who couldn't have read Marx and hold the views he aired. Pound, we knew, lived on income derived through capitalism, and without confronting capitalism he was trying to change the system, proposing as an example his grandfather's system of scrip issued to workers for trade at his grandfather's store. To us this seemed to be the company store of the fur-traders or the tenant-farm system of our southern states, in which workers are compelled to trade at the company store at the trader's or the owner's prices. Perhaps Pound could not think clearly about economics; at any rate, we could not agree to publish the book.

In Berkeley in the 1960s we attended a production of Pound's *Villon* lavishly mounted. In a prologue, excerpts from Pound's works were read by two actors outside the curtain, declaiming dramatically Pound's poetry and including the anti-Semitic curses and indecent language blacked out in the Faber and Faber and New Directions editions of Pound's works. George walked out of the auditorium; the usher, a girl student, said, "Sir, if you go out now I can't let you in again until the intermission."

"I have to kill those actors if I don't leave," he replied, "and I think perhaps that would be wrong."

"Perhaps, perhaps," she said.

The *Villon* itself was attractive, and at moments it was beautiful, especially in a lovely duet. We never found out who made that decision to include Pound's invective—someone with his or her own anti-Semitic hates, no doubt. George says, "Every poet who ever talked to Pound or corresponded with Pound or read him has reason to have loved him; though the madness was real, it was not in him, it seemed—but somehow there."

"The Boss," Pound said, "The Boss," with awe translating "Il Duce." It was the sudden intrusion of a madness, for no man has ever been more pure or more generous than Pound.

The year that we lived in the countryside at Le Beausset we had received a subscription to *Time* magazine. We had never read a newspaper every day and had paid little attention to economics or to politics, but we read *Time* magazine each week and discussed what we read. We were shocked and aghast at the schemes carried out in the last year of Hoover's administration—food was being dumped while people starved. Although we were far from the United States, we had perhaps the advantage of that distance, and our friends the butcher and the hotel-keeper had been educating us. We were innocent of preconceived views, and we looked on at poverty in France, at children so thin and tubercular that they were almost transparent, and our minds began to dwell on politics. Our education was conducted each week by *Time*.

George's father left us a small car that we were to bring back to the States when we came home. It had a removable top, and we could ride along; it was almost like riding in the cart with Pom-Pon, the difference being that we no longer conversed with everyone we met on the road. However, we made friends in Paris with students, mostly Americans, who were of our own generation.

Sylvia Beach's book store in Paris had a lending library, and I borrowed Trotsky's *History of the Soviet Union*, which George and I both read. At first political ideas had seemed to concern others and not George or me, but with Jewish refugees pouring into Paris from Germany in 1932, I could not help seeing their distress and feeling the threat to us, too. I had to try to understand the politics that were affecting events all around us.

Among our new acquaintances in Paris was a young woman doctor, Eva Klein, who because of her presentiment of Hitler's horror was an early refugee. She had opened a summer camp for Jewish refugee children in Paris. Through her and her mate Dan, an American medical student, we met her circle of acquaintances among the refugees and had our first experience of the life of refugees. She took us to a party of White Russian refugees from the 1917 revolution in Russia; here we met a Russian prince, a nervous man who had a sort of tic of shuffling used matches in an empty match-box. George asked him, "What do you think of the results of the Revolution in your country?"

"I would be a traitor to all I was born to if I said a good word for it," he replied. At this same party Chaliapin, the singer, arrived in a magnificent full-length black coat, and as he swept it off and into the hands of a servant, I saw that it was lined with sable.

One Sunday we went into the country with Eva and Dan and stopped at the country house of some of her Russian friends. We were admitted by a servant and shown into a parlor to wait; it was a damp, cold, cheerless habitation. Eva sniffed and said, "Smells like goldfish pee."

Dancing in the park one night to the music of a wind-up phonograph, we stopped dancing and were leaping back and forth over a small iron railing beside the road in the Bois de Boulogne. As I vaulted, my feet slipped on the dew-wet grass, and I hit my head on the iron railing. In no time I was covered with blood, and our two doctor friends directed

George to a nearby hospital. Dan rushed into the emergency room, washed up, and was treating my wound before the bewildered nurse in charge could forbid him. George was left standing after having driven us all there; no one was watching, but we heard a thud—Eva looked around and saw George lying unconscious on the floor.

Before our return to the United States, we made a trip to Venice and to Florence to visit museums and to see a little of a country other than France. In the Piazza San Marco, we were suddenly surrounded by Black Shirts pouring into the Piazza from all the entrances so fast that we could not escape. We were pinned against the monument at the center of the Piazza by the press of the crowd, crying, "Il Duce—pericolo del morte." Mussolini's life had been threatened, and we were trapped in this sudden, impressive demonstration. We saw no differences of expression on the faces of the young men, only a blind fanaticism, in ecstasy and worship of Il Duce.

Roosevelt had been elected President of the United States in November 1932, and in that winter the Blue Eagle was introduced in the States. Blue Eagle posters were pictured on the front pages of Parisian newspapers, and the military-looking symbol frightened us. We were afraid it meant that fascism was rising in the United States too. Germans in Venice, military men, had said to me as they passed, "Guten morgen mein Taube."

It was 1933, and the next war was ominously looming. We could feel more than we could understand of the threat to Jews, to artists, to all freedoms. I was determined that fascism was not going to strike this pigeon! We saw Jews, the lucky ones who had fled early. Born in Germany, they had been citizens, but they were now threatened, bewildered people who did not yet know the worst that was still in abeyance. We began to understand that this threat was portentous for us as well. We returned to Paris and took passage on the first ship home. We had to get home to see what had happened in the two years that we had spent out of our own country.

Eva and Dan came to New York soon after we had returned, and we shared an apartment, a "railroad flat" on Pineapple Street in Brooklyn Heights. All of us were gone from the apartment all day—Dan to work at the Rockefeller Institute and Eva to study for the exams which would qualify her in her second change of country as a doctor. Sharing a living place became our style of living for the following ten years or more. We did not make a rigid system for this sharing; it was conducted very simply, with a piece of paper hung in the kitchen on which each one who spent money wrote down what had been spent. We found it a cheaper way to rent a much bigger and better apartment, we could afford to pay someone to clean the place, and each couple had living rooms and sleeping rooms apart. We shared the kitchen and the cooking duties, and of course we were in agreement as to the amounts to be spent on food, entertainment, etc. I found it a desirable way to live during the years that we were both working, and later, when we had a child, we often shared households in order to extend our family group and to have another child in the group for the sake of our only child.

NEW YORK CITY

1933–1937

The people I see and talk to, the ways they earn their livings, the children I watch, the courting customs, the ways of parents with their children are all to me learning, and I re-evaluate my own ways and my country's ways every time I travel. It is not comfort, ease, or previous knowledge that takes me traveling; traveling is never as comfortable as being at home, and I am thrown out of my accustomed style and habits on meeting situations and people for whom I have no preparation. I think I go traveling in order to be jostled and jolted and confronted with the necessity of thinking faster to meet fast-changing occurrences. Happiness comes in the conversations and the learning that I have to master, even in the barest knowledge of how to get from here to there. It is culturation simply to gain insight to yet one more country or city I never saw before; if I do not learn it well, at least I meet it freshly at the moment I confront it.

In France in 1930, from the art of the Louvre, paintings speaking out of different times, from the streets of Paris which make their patterns and take their names from the earliest use the ancients gave them, from a cafe for writers, tourists, artists, or students, we looked on and tried to absorb the meaning to us of a culture which accepted living artists, writers and students into the social fabric with a freedom we had searched for in the United States and had not found. I think I travel to ask the questions which are hard to formulate about one's own times because one is in the midst, at home, of all that one has seen so often that one does not receive the jolt that might confront one with the uncomfortable but important question. Not with answers—answers are not possible for one's own times and in one's own place. The answer only becomes obvious after time has passed, and we can see, if we have survived it, the predicament that we have passed through.

In Paris the Impressionists were not yet all dead; in 1930 even their art was not yet in the old established museums, and we went to a private gallery to see Picasso's latest show. I noticed Picasso himself watching us to see our reactions to his paintings, which were the first I had seen of women distorted into their social and emotional meanings, beyond the portraits of previous times. Meanings which were painful to accept I later found to be profound class judgments and beautiful in new ways, in their colors and design. After seeing these portraits, women on beaches and bourgeois women in cafes had a different meaning, in which Picasso had caught and held them. His contribution of fifty years as a painter, most of which time I have been alive, has put him on a list of those who will speak for us to a future time.

Apprehension mixed with elation as we disembarked at Baltimore and began the drive to New York City. As we approached the first stop-light, grown men, respectable men—our fathers—stepped forward to ask for a nickel, rag in hand to wipe our windshield. This ritual was repeated every time we paused, until we felt we were in a nightmare, our fathers impoverished.

Manhattan loomed across the New Jersey flats; it grew into pinnacles as sunset lit the windows, and we entered the long tunnel under the Hudson River. In Brooklyn we rented an apartment on Willow Street, the first of many apartments we have lived in at one time or another in that same neighborhood of Brooklyn Heights.

Zukofsky, the slender dark young man, sloping along on his long stalk-like legs, head forward, shoulders hunched, a little close-visored cap on his head . . . Louis so delicate I didn't think he'd live out five more years, Louis in my mind associated with his own *Mantis* . . . but as his long life has proven, Louis is hardy, more hardy than we knew. He has survived with Celia, refusing the attentions of the young who have come admiring him and his place in poetry. He survives, perhaps strengthened by his bitterness and feeling that he must be the only poet or he will not accept acclaim. Louis had not been to Europe; he had only corresponded with Pound, and I think it was Tibor Serly who spoke to us of the importance of Louis' going to visit Pound. The problem was that Louis had no money; the trip required that Louis' friends help to pay his way. Somehow this was done, and several of us made contributions; Williams, Serly, George and I bore the expenses of traveling, and Pound and Bunting provided housing and meals once Louis was in Rapallo.

Lorine Niedecker, a student of Louis' at the University of Wisconsin, followed him to New York; we invited her to dinner, and after waiting for her until long after dinner-time, we ate and were ready for bed when a timid knock at the door announced Lorine. "What happened to you?" we asked.

"I got on the subway, and I didn't know where to get off, so I rode to the end of the line and back."

"Why didn't you ask someone?"

"I didn't see anyone to ask."

New York was overwhelming, and she was alone, a tiny, timid small-town girl. She escaped the city and returned to Wisconsin. Years later we began to see her poems, poems which described her life; she chose a way of hard physical work, and her poetry emerged from a tiny life. From Wisconsin came perfect small gems of poetry written out of her survival, from the crevices of her life, that seeped out into poems.

When Louis went for a passport for his trip, he had to get a copy of his birth certificate, which had his name as Salikovsky. The certificate had been made out by a midwife who probably did not know English, and she may have unintentionally misspelled Zukofsky, but Louis was understandably upset. Misspellings happened often enough in immigration or in birth records, but it was a blow to Louis' identity, and he was intent on setting the record straight; he finally got his passport in his correct name, Zukofsky.

Walking with Louis when *Discrete Series* was in manuscript, George was discussing it with him before showing it to anyone else. Louis turned and with a quizzical expression asked George, "Do you prefer your poetry to mine?"

"Yes," answered George, and the friendship was at a breaking point.

George gave a copy of the manuscript of *Discrete Series* to Charles Reznikoff, who gravely discussed it the next time we were together. Charles pointed to the lines inside quotation marks, "'O city ladies.'" "Now this," said Charles, "is the only line that sings."

George also sent a copy of the manuscript to Ezra Pound, who replied with a gift: the foreword. ". . . I salute a serious craftsman, a sensibility which is not every man's sensibility and which has not been got out of any other man's books. [signed] Ezra Pound."

George's father (also named George) was accosted one day in 1934 in his club in San Francisco by a man who drew forth *Discrete Series* by George Oppen. "Here," he said, "did you write this?"

"No," answered George's father. "But my son did." The man began to sputter. George's father asked him, "What would you do if your son wanted to write poetry?"

"I'd shoot the bastard."

The Gotham Book Mart bought some of the books; very few were sold, and the rest were stored. Politics were dominant and danger was imminent. In German neighborhoods in New York City and New Jersey, right-wing organizations were drilling in fascist military style. Father Coughlin was using the radio as it had not been used before; every Sunday, especially in working-class neighborhoods, the windows were thrown open, radios were turned up full blast, and the voice of Father Coughlin, the Radio Priest, blared divisive, vituperative anti-Semitic fascist propaganda. Many people in the United States were beginning to think about politics. We had seen the beginnings of fascism in Europe, and now we tried to understand the reasons for the collapse of the economic systems of the western world. We were reading leftist papers, and we asked Jesse Lowenthal, a friend of Louis, to take us to meet the son of Daniel de Leon, the founder of the Socialist Labor Party (S.L.P.). He explained their program: when the workers of the United States arrived at the realization that the answer to the collapse of capitalism was the socialization of the means of production, then the S.L.P. members would present themselves—well-read, educated and ready for the great day. The S.L.P. was doing nothing at the time to alleviate the problems of the workers with whom they planned one day to ride to power. We looked on at Trotskyites who spoke publicly of revolution, and sometimes caused police attacks by their provocative tactics. The unemployed were the victims who had no desire for revolution; what they wanted and were willing to fight for if necessary were jobs, food, and rent money.

We found ourselves suddenly involved in these events which swept over everyone. In 1929, when the stock market crashed in New York, a very few men jumped from windows when they found they were no longer rich. By 1934 despair had swept the whole population, from the richest to the poorest, as factories slowed and then stopped production, railroads had no loadings, ships had no cargo, and the country was bursting with products that no one in the United States or elsewhere had money to buy.

The United States was lagging behind many other countries in social legislation. Welfare organizations in the 1920s, before the crash, were mostly philanthropic, and they soon ran out of money in this overwhelming emergency. People were frightened and helpless and in many parts of the country irregular ways of obtaining food seemed the only way to avoid starvation. The propaganda of fascism and the authoritarian state appealed to many who saw no other solution to the economic collapse of the United States. They had been through some hard years with President Hoover—fathers of families had been given apples to sell on street corners instead of useful work or temporary food-orders and rent money. Men felt guilty when they became unemployed and could no longer support their families, and many left their homes in despair. Young men roamed the country.

In the last days of February and the first days of March, 1933, at the moment we returned to the United States, President Roosevelt's first act as President was to declare a bank holiday. In effect the U.S. Treasury was empty as President Hoover went out of office. Depositors had lined up in front of banks to remove their money. Some banks went bankrupt, and the depositors' savings were lost; with no insurance of depositors' funds they quickly ran out of money and closed their doors. Some banks had speculated with depositors' money, and Wall Street had sold them out; but most of them re-opened with the assurance that government would pass legislation as soon as possible to protect deposits in the banks.

During the last days of Hoover's presidency the depression had deepened, and in the election year of 1932, ten to twenty thousand Bonus Marchers, veterans of World War I, marched on Washington to demonstrate to President Hoover and to the nation their demand for full payment of their bonus certificates. Hoover had vetoed that legislation; there was actually not enough money in the Treasury to pay the veterans' demands. The marchers were held on Anacostia Flats, across from Capitol Hill;

they were attacked by troops with fixed bayonets and by tanks, and one was killed while several were wounded.

In the farm country of the middle west, demonstrations prevented foreclosures of mortgages; when the sheriff arrived with an auctioneer to sell the farm and all the farmer's possessions at auction, the neighbors gathered, and with a pre-arranged plan someone bid one dollar for the farm. "Sold!" cried the crowd, and the buyer returned the farm with ostentation to the farmer. All the items were sold the same way, and although the atmosphere seemed festive, the farmers were united and the authorities did not use force. Farmers were tenacious in their hold on their land, they did not intend to be thrown off it, and farm organizations grew apace.

My family in Grants Pass grew closer together during the Depression. At Christmas time they cut trees which they took to San Francisco to sell, and later, as the Depression eased, two brothers continued to cut and sell Christmas trees and to enlarge the project until it could support one family well. Noel then dropped this work and went to work in the lumber industry, piling logs on the big rigs that took the fir logs down to the sawmills. It was dangerous work, and although my brother was a strong man, it exhausted him utterly by day's end. I asked him once, "Why?"

He replied, "A test of manhood."

My mother spent a couple of years during the Depression running a nursing home. Paul was bitterly disappointed in himself, and his wife Julia and his children were prisoners of his desperation; they moved to the woods, where he and Julia could feed their large family by hunting and by a big garden, which in Oregon can be grown year round. In 1934 George and I and June, George's younger sister, visited them. They lived at the end of the road, deep in forest, with no neighbors. Business in Grants Pass had come to a standstill, and my father's store had gone bankrupt; all the lumber mills had closed. Paul and George went hunting, although it was not hunting season. George said afterwards, "We stood at the top of a ridge, and I said to Paul, 'But what if the warden is around?' Paul replied with a sweep of his arm, 'Do you think a warden would be damn-fool enough to walk across one of those valleys?'" We ate fresh venison and garden vegetables, and sometimes Paul sat and played his clarinet or his saxophone. His fingers were so hardened by rough work that they were no longer suited to the instruments, but he still played. Noel was operating a gambling place in Grants Pass. He always gambled, and he always had money. The speakeasy was in an inconspicuous house in a back street. We danced a few dances and tried the gambling, but we were wary of the bootleg gin.

Before his inauguration, Roosevelt proposed that the Blue Eagle symbol on posters be displayed by employers who pledged to comply with him in a promise to keep wages at their previous levels in an attempt to maintain the slipping economy. It was this same Blue Eagle on the front pages of newspapers in Europe that had seemed to us a symbol of possible military significance and had precipitated our return from Europe.

We spent the summer of 1934 in a visit to Mexico with our friends Jack and Nellie from Berkeley. Mexico was the first undeveloped country we had seen, and the steps toward socialization which they had taken seemed an effective way to develop their country. The ten-year-old boys were the first educated generation, and they joyfully fulfilled the responsibilities of being literate. In the square in Taxco, an English lady with a wide shade hat and her watercolor pad in her lap asked a small boy to pose for her. He held up his thumb and forefinger, a little space between them—"Momentito," it meant, I'll be right back. He returned with his watercolor box on his thumb, and he sat for her while he sketched her on his own pad of paper. All the male children of Taxco were artists; Kitagawa, a Japanese artist living in Taxco, helped them to make their own watercolor boxes from gasoline tins. They made their own colors and he gave them brushes. The boy in the square took us to see an exhibit of their works; I still have a program of this show, and the work was beautiful child-art. Kitagawa was concerned that all the boys of the town were artists, and he asked us, "What will become of such a town?" We met these competent children in the public markets, in the streets, in the plazas, beside the adults, helping in any dealings requiring reading, writing, or arithmetic. Children guided us, and they were both avid learners and teachers— neither shy nor bold, they were responsible and proud of their country with a new pride. They were the generation that was taking Mexico from colonialism and "peonage" into equality of nationhood.

We too were learning as we saw the ideas of socialism applied in a poverty-stricken nation. We saw nationalization of oil, railroads, and public education; welfare laws that applied to the whole family of the worker; freeing of fallow land held by absentee landlords to give it to impoverished landless peasants, who formed "ejidos," a form of traditional commune, to improve agriculture and to plant forests in a country that had been bereft of its trees. We admired Cárdenas, the President of Mexico, and we observed that Mexico was coming to a new life. I think it is the only time that artists have been the principal carriers of the ideas of a revolution. Rivera, Orozco, and Siquieras were political artists whose murals covered walls of government, schools, and public courtyards. Hundreds of walls were entirely covered with the message to the people of Mexico of the country's struggles. In the public places in Mexico City, after years of exclusion under the Porfirio Diaz regime, *peones* walked in their traditional white clothes past the murals, stopping until they understood what they saw in the murals. The pictures portrayed the whole pharmacopoeia of Mexico, with the foods which were made available to the rest of the world when this continent was first discovered. Mexico, a gleaming white city such as the *conquistadores* had not seen before, was also pictured in the murals. The *peones* saw foreigners also examining with respect the record of Mexico and her revolution.

We went to California on our return from Mexico. In San Francisco in 1934 a general strike had been called by the Longshoremen's Union, and San Francisco's upper classes were in an exaggerated state of fear. Some had left town, others barricaded themselves in their homes with quantities of food. Gangs of strike-breakers were organized on the Berkeley campus, to break up sympathy meetings and try to frighten families of workers. But on the day we entered San Francisco the bay was quiet—not a ship moved.

For us, this had been a remarkable year. One year before at this same time we had watched sadly as Pom-Pon was led away in Le Beausset. We had visited Ezra Pound and heard him speak of Mussolini as "The Boss"; we had been alerted to the dangers of fascism when we saw Jews fleeing Hitler's Germany, and we had been present at a fascist demonstration in Italy. During this past year we had studied Soviet movies, searching for clues of what socialism might mean in our own lives, and we had just seen in Mexico a degree of socialization applied to the benefit of development in that country. Revolution and socialism were respectable words in Mexico. We returned to New York City from California to find families sleeping on their household goods, piled on the sidewalks in front of their apartments. The city had an air of disaster; the unemployed were the refugees who had exhausted their resources and did not know where to turn.

An appeal was made to intellectuals by the seventh World Congress of the Communist Parties in 1935 to join in a united front to defeat fascism and war. We responded to that call, and in the winter of 1935 we decided to work with the Communist Party, not as artist or writer because we did not find honesty or sincerity in the so-called arts of the left. (I could make an exception for Bertolt Brecht and for some Soviet movies.) We said to each other, "Let's work with the unemployed and leave our other interest in the arts for a later time." Few in the Party or in the Workers Alliance knew anything of our past, and in a short time we were no longer thinking of Paris or of To Publishers, of poetry or of painting. We also left it to our friends and families to keep in touch with us if they chose. We felt that our political decision was not one in which we wished to involve them.

"We are those selfish travelers, happiest in foreign streets." If George and I had come from the working class we would probably never have joined the Communist Party—that was the nearly unanimous decision of the United States' working class. We searched for escape from class. George's experience in the class he came from was one of isolation, and to be a poet who knew no more than that was a bleak outlook; my class background had not led me into an intellectual world. Artists and writers have often looked for ways to escape class and the burden of class mores, and while we did not look for an ivory tower, we did search to find and to understand from the grassroots.

The Communist and the Socialist Parties were the only organizations which were organizing the unemployed to do something themselves about their predicament. When we asked to join, a secretary seemed suspicious of us and sent us to a Brooklyn address, where we again asked to join. The two people in the Brooklyn office also seemed to find us queer birds, and they turned us over to Doretta Tarmon.

Doretta had taken part in the many schisms within the radical left; she had joined with Jay Lovestone when he left the Socialist Party, and she broke away from his group to become a Communist. She came to New York where the Movement was her breath, her sustenance, her life. She had intense black eyes behind thick lenses which flashed as she tossed her head in impassioned speech. She held crowds with her speeches at street meetings—words came to her faster than her mouth could say them. "Prize your fellow worker like the skin of your eye," she said once at a street meeting. Conviction made her a great speaker and a remarkable but difficult friend. Doretta told of herself and of her life-long friend Esther who organized on every job they held; two women, they understood each other and the same passions moved them. Arguing with their boss's lawyer once, they held on to his sleeve while they poured words on him; he pulled and they pulled, and his sleeve came off in their hands. Words failed them, and the lawyer took them to court. The judge listened carefully, and said patiently to the lawyer, "But isn't it possible that the tailor only basted your sleeve to your jacket? Isn't it possible that the tailor neglected to sew the sleeve on his machine and it may have come off rather easily?"

Doretta might as well have moved in with us, as we became constant companions. She was new to our experience, and we were continually surprised, confounded, and delighted with her. She took us to our first street meeting, which we could have gone to, of course, without permission, but she gave us permission and we went like adolescents to a first grown-up party. Doretta wore a leather jacket and a hat with a long red feather; having come recently from Paris, I was bare-legged and bare-headed, wearing a Paris dress. Doretta cautioned me, "You don't want to be sectarian, comrade."

At the street meeting in an Italian neighborhood nearby, a speaker explained to Italians on their own block that fascism meant dictatorship. Italian families were sending money to Mussolini, and wives were contributing their marriage rings. To the Italians, Mussolini was a hero because he was winning the war against Ethiopia, and he was unifying Italy, where the trains did run on time. It was a difficult audience at the street meeting, but Italians too were out of work and were threatened with eviction or loss of homes; and although a few milk bottles were thrown, the day after the meeting a few Italians came into the Workers Alliance for help. A short time later, George and I created organizations of the unemployed through this same Alliance.

Doretta invited us to join a new-members class in the Communist Party. Of the fourteen people in the class, not one was foreign-born. Several of those new members are still our friends, but with these new friends we found ourselves in a very different world, a world in which we were politically exposed. The Communist Party remained strange to us; we threaded our way in the organization, and even the vocabulary within the Party was a different vocabulary than I had known. The older Communists were wearing leather jackets that had become almost a uniform. Most of the older members were Russian, Jewish or Polish immigrants, and they were not easy to understand.

The Socialist Party had organized the Workers Alliance, and the Communists had organized the Unemployment Councils—these two organizations merged to form one organization, called the Workers Alliance. George began work in the Borough Hall area of Brooklyn, in a neighborhood that contained the Philippine, Puerto Rican and Syrian-Lebanese population; it included Atlantic Avenue from Flatbush Avenue to the waterfront and from Brooklyn Bridge to Manhattan Bridge, with all the slums that crowded under the El (the elevated railway). Slums pressed in and around the sweatshops that were now closed. Many single men in this population had come to the United States to work, leaving their women behind. It is hard to understand now the way things were then. Almost no one was working, and the people were in their own neighborhoods, at home or on the street in their own block; the activities of the Workers Alliance in every neighborhood where it existed were the immediate concerns of that neighborhood. George tells in a poem of Petra Roja, who called a crowd together by leaning out her tenement window and beating on her dishpan. When no one worked in a family the rent could not be paid, and if a family could not get "the relief" (as it was called), the landlord gave them an eviction notice and called the city marshal, who with several assistants put the furniture in the street and put a lock on the door. If the furniture was not soon taken from the street, the sanitation department hauled it away to the city dump. This was one of the frequent emergencies for which Petra beat her dishpan. She came down the stairs to march at the head of her little army to the apartment of the family that was threatened with eviction. When the marshal struggled up the solidly packed stairs to the apartment, he found Petra and the other Alliance members filling the apartment. "What's going on here?" yelled the marshal.

Petra yelled back, pointing at George, "It's his birthday!"

When the furniture finally reached the street, the neighbors helped by sitting on it to prevent its being hauled away. One man returned to his evacuated apartment with a big bag of plaster-of-Paris, which he mixed and slowly poured into the toilet, and as it went down through the tree of plumbing the plaster solidified in the pipes of the whole building. It was a war for food and shelter.

George had a bodyguard, a big man named Raf who had been a prize fighter in Puerto Rico and who appointed himself to be George's protector. The membership of George's group in the Workers Alliance treasured George and appreciated the organization they had built together, but they did not think that George was well dressed. A committee was organized to go with George to a nearby men's clothing store. Raf asked to see the manager. "We are from the Workers Alliance on Adams Street," he told him. "We want to buy a new suit for our organizer, and it had better be a good suit or we will come back and picket your place."

A short way out Flatbush Avenue, in front of a big Protestant church, George went one morning with leaflets calling for a demonstration at the nearby relief bureau. As the congregation came out of the church and George was handing out a few leaflets, he noticed that a group of men went back into the church with the leaflets, to emerge in a wedge aimed straight at George. They came swiftly and dispersed the other people who were just standing around; a young police officer directing traffic at the corner moved in fast close to George, who was already belabored. He stopped George from handing out the leaflets, and said, "I'm taking you in."

"But I have a constitutional right—" George began.

"Please," said the cop, and he drew George around the corner. "They'd have slaughtered you," he said as he let George go.

Mary Auerbach and I went to the Bedford-Stuyvesant neighborhood in Brooklyn to form a new local of the Workers Alliance in a neighborhood of Jews, Italians, and many blacks who had just come from the South. In most of the southern states nothing was done for the hungry, and thousands were on the roads, moving into the industrial areas. New York had more liberal laws concerning the relief of hunger, and many Southerners came and stayed in the city, but the settlement laws made it difficult for these people to obtain food or rent orders when they first arrived, and they did not know where to turn for help. Emergency relief was given only in dire cases. Poor people do not usually keep records, a year's residence had to be proven, and these people had been harassed on the roads; starvation was real for them and they were frightened. Mary Auerbach and I went through the apartment buildings, knocking on every door and explaining that it was not the fault of the men that they could not find work and bring home a wage at the end of the week. Many men took to the roads looking for work, while others were just not in evidence, as women and children could more easily get aid if there was no man in the house who presumably should be working. Many women were alone with their children, living in misery. We spent hours every day talking to these people in their apartments. We presented ourselves as members of the Workers Alliance, but our intentions were doubted, and only men came to our first meeting; Mary and I went with these men to the relief bureau, and we did get emergency food and rent orders. We soon had a membership made up almost entirely of young black women with their little children and older women who knew how to run an organization. They collected dues of ten cents a month, visited the sick and talked to neighbors; it was they who really built the organization. We rented a store building next door to the Nostrand Avenue relief bureau, where we talked with clients on their way in to confront the bureau. We found that they usually came to our headquarters after failing to get food or rent orders. The unemployed wanted jobs, and in the demonstrations we asked for jobs, but the purpose of the Workers Alliance was to relieve starvation and to guide people to a realization that government could solve these problems—not with fascism, but with a liberal solution. But as the organization increased in numbers and its successes became apparent to all levels of government there were attempts to break the Alliance.

We "sat-in." I asked George to bring the membership of his Borough-Hall Workers Alliance to picket the sit-in at the Nostrand Avenue relief bureau. We had learned this technique from the auto workers in Detroit; we sat in for a day and a night, holding the relief bureau so that the day's business could not go on. The administration of the bureau decided on the second day to smash the demonstration, and the police came through the big front doors with clubs swinging as our women screamed. I remember watching a young black woman while she screamed, and as the sound continued it seemed to me she screamed that scream for minutes. Manuel, from George's local, was clubbed to the floor and a cop bent over him beating him on the head. I threw myself between Manuel and the cop, Manuel, not knowing it was my hand beside his face bit my thumb! The cop pulled me to my feet by my long hair, and for days after I could not turn my head nor use my thumb.

We were arrested. The plan of the relief administration was to break up our organization by depriving the membership of leadership. The International Labor Defense took charge of our defense; we were accused of attacking the police. The trial began, and it dragged on for two years—a tactic planned to dissipate energy from the organization by making us attend court. The trial was postponed again and again, but every time it was called, our membership escorted us to court. In November of the second year the trial was finally held, and we were charged with felonious assault on the police. As the jury was chosen we watched and speculated about each person chosen, until the defense's challenges were exhausted, and a Jewish manufacturer of flags and emblems was the last jury member called—we would have rejected him. After deliberating for many hours, the jury returned to the courtroom at ten o'clock at night with a not-guilty verdict for all of us except Manuel, who was the only non-white arrested. We went out free to the street, and there, waiting for us, were our Workers Alliance members.

At a later time we met the girl who was secretary to the manufacturer of flags and emblems, and she told us his account of the jury room. The eleven other members had opposed him—they were for a guilty verdict. The compromise was to convict Manuel, and he served nine months in prison.

George and I were twenty-nine years old. The war in Spain had been going on for a year, and George wanted to go, but I would not agree unless I went too. As we did not have any special skills that would have made a difference in the war, we did not try to go to Spain, but friends near us in age or younger, who were single men and women or who had special skills either went to Spain or tried very hard to get there. Mary Auerbach, with whom I worked every day, gave permission for the son of her old age to go; barely eighteen years old, he had never held a gun. In Spain he was rushed into the lines the very day he arrived, and he was killed in his first battle. Our friend Joe Hecht was one of the heroes who swam the Ebro River into fascist-held territory at the point where the Loyalists established a pontoon bridge to move the army across the Ebro. Our friend Conlon Nancarrow, the composer, went to Spain from Boston, at age eighteen. Conlon told us of Bart van der Schelling, a Dutch friend we came to know later in Mexico: "I saw him walking on the deck of a ship on which a group of us were crossing from France to Spain." Bart was German-looking, stiff-necked and red-faced. Conlon said, "Our group talked together and we decided to dump him overboard," but more sober minds prevailed.

Bart tells next, "I had had war experience in Indonesia when I was sixteen, so I was made a commander in Spain. All was quiet at the front, as it had been raining for days, and everyone was miserable; I asked myself, 'What can I do?' I jumped out of my trench and began to do vigorous exercises in view of all the men, then I strode down the line inspecting fox-holes. Conlon was in his fox-hole, dug out of the earth just as everyone's was, but Conlon's hole had an improvised shelter under which Conlon sat with his feet propped up out of the wet; with a niche for books and for cigarettes, Conlon was reading." Bart came close and Conlon's mouth dropped a little as he recognized the "enemy" from shipboard.

"What are you reading?" asked Bart.

"French," said Conlon. "I thought I might as well study French with so much time on my hands." Conlon came home with dysentery, but he came home alive. Joe came home too, to die in the next war as soon as he went into action. These men were convinced that fascism must be stopped. Of 3000 who went to Spain from the United States, 1500 died there. Little news came to us of the war in Spain. The United States government joined with France and England in an embargo of all arms to Loyalist Spain; meanwhile Hitler and Mussolini were supplying Franco with men, arms, and planes.

In 1937 George went to a Party training school for a period of study and discussion. I went to see Pete Cacchione, who was chairman of the Communist Party in Brooklyn, and said to him, "You sent George to school, and now you must send me too." Pete felt pressured, but he agreed, and I went for the next three months to the school. George went on to Utica, where we had agreed to go after finishing the school, which was held in the Catskills at a resort hotel. In the wintertime this hotel was the center for lectures on Marxist economics and political theory, discussions of the women's movement, Negro history in the United States, and trade union tactics.

Pop Mindel was the teacher I loved. Pop was Russian-born, Jewish, a scholar of Marxism. He was acutely intuitive in his understanding of each one of us, and he is the only person I ever met in the Party who I am sure loved each one of us. A young Negro boy from the deep South who wanted to be an artist drew with his pencil every chance he had. Pop Mindel finally told him, "It's the wrong time for you to be an artist—you have set your foot on the path to help your people, and you can help them more in politics than you can with your art."

To me he said, "There are times in your life in which you might choose to be a revolutionary, but there are also times, as when you marry or when you have children, that this is impossible."

George and I had been unaware of our being a special kind of couple until Hitler and fascism made being Jewish a pointed issue of survival. Our interest had been to understand a class not our own and to be part of sweeping changes in the United States. We held close a belief in ourselves as artists, and we intended to find our way back to a life in poetry and the arts. If there had not been a clear need for people like us to defeat fascism, we would probably have dropped the politics as the depression eased, and we would have resumed a life in the arts. But fascism, socialism or a more liberal form of republicanism were the choices: Germany, Italy, Japan, and Spain became fascist, France had a People's Front government, Russia was socialist, and the United States had embarked upon a more liberal form of republicanism with the election of Roosevelt and his cabinet of Keynesian economists and politicians. Events moved us with them, and we believed that fascism meant death to us along with the other Jews of the world, and death to millions who would be caught in the war which actually came to pass. Communists were still, at the end of the Depression, the ones who warned most consistently against this danger.

In Utica George and I found ourselves in an industrial area, where workers were either foreign-born or the first generation born in the United States. A strong thread of radical ideas ran through workers in the foundries and in the arms, copper, textile, and shoe factories. In opposition to this working-class population, a politically organized upper class of owners and elected officials ruled the area. Traditionally, the cities voted Democrat whereas the surrounding counties voted Republican, and Oneida County was no exception. Utica had a Democratic mayor while the congressman and the senator, with district-wide votes, were right-wing Republican. Hamilton Fish was "our" congressman.

Small groups of Communists were in the towns, and scattered about the countryside were people who in some other time or place had been involved in leftist politics or in trade union actions. George and I set ourselves to find and to talk to every one of these scattered radicals. George began by calling a convention of all the Communists to elect a new leadership; and, of course, George was elected chairman. He then organized meetings open to the public with speakers known to these old-time radicals; these meetings were well-attended and drew people who were interested in political events in Europe—Italians from the copper mills of Rome, New York Polish women who worked in the textile mills and who were militant, their men who worked in the foundries, Russians who had come to the United States to work in the mines and coal fields of Pennsylvania and who were now farmers in Oneida County, Czechs who worked in the Remington-Rand arms plant. Friends found friends at these meetings, and there was an awakening in this neglected area. A liberal doctor, three or four ministers, a few businessmen, and liberal intellectuals found us, or we found them. All these people endangered their livelihoods by their interest in the left, but nevertheless they were interested in defeating fascism. The group also attracted people who were accustomed to being alone with their ideas, and they met together and heard reports of the neighboring areas, where young people similar to George and me in age and background were working in other upper New York State communities. These intellectuals joined the League of Women Voters or the League against War and Fascism, or one of the many groups in the more liberal churches. The election of Roosevelt and the work done to alleviate the Depression had stirred people, and a strong liberal tendency was growing throughout the country, due not only to Roosevelt but to all of us who were opposed to fascism.

Usually the vote is more radical in the United States than the apparent opinion of the people, and we met surprises when we went out door-to-door selling the Communist Sunday paper. People were not afraid of us in their own homes—the fear was for loss of jobs—and they asked us in. We made friends, and they trusted us not to expose them. These people knew at first-hand the long and frustrating struggle for trade unions and the continuing struggle to keep those unions honest. The CIO was organizing in this area at this time, and it was making sweeping inroads into the old craft unions of the AFL, which accepted the skilled workers but left the rest of the workers in the same plant unorganized. We were a small force with few allies, and yet we saw first-hand that we obtained results and that achievement came—slowly, but it came. Working in New York City had been frustrating because we lost touch with people and did not see the results directly as we did in this smaller city.

A Methodist minister, an ebullient man from a neighboring church community, came to see us regularly just to talk with us, for he shared similar political ideas and preached his ideas as much as he dared. A Quaker invited us to a Quaker meeting which was really an anti-war group and asked us to take over his little group, but we said that although we shared political ideas and that we opposed fascism, we were neither religious nor pacifist, and in sincerity we could not join his group. Both of these men had graduated from Union Theological Seminary, where Harry F. Ward, a loved and respected teacher, had imprinted his liberal mark on many who passed through his classes.

A minister on the staff of the Episcopal cathedral in Utica came to call late at night, a man with five children who was sure of his job only so long as one of the higher-ranking priests needed him. He was ghost-writing the memoirs of this priest. Our caller was the son of a coal miner, who had been educated into the priesthood, and he risked too much if he raised his voice at the cathedral; but he came to tell us that we were in danger. Hamilton Fish, the Republican congressman, was warning the upper bourgeoisie of the town against us, and George's and my name headed the list that Fish wrote on the blackboard in the cathedral. We were not frightened; on the contrary, we were encouraged to know that we had made such an impact on the town.

Farmers were protesting the prices that they received for their milk from the Borden and Sheffield milk companies, which held a grip on the milk market in the milk-sheds all over the country. Upper New York State was one milk-shed, and there were others wherever there was big dairy production. Some farmers formed a Farmers' Union and held their milk, to pour it in protest in the streets of Boonville, where the road ran white with milk in front of the milk receiving depot. I went to visit Archie Wright, leader of the Farmers' Union. Archie welcomed me and suggested that I help by visiting farmers and asking them to withhold their milk, to join the Farmers' Union, or at least not to endanger the farmers' strike. The farmers in the valleys where the soil was rich and deep were not seriously affected by the reduction in the price of milk; their farms were paid for, and they could weather the price-cutting and perhaps even benefit by the wiping out of the small hill-country farms. Enclaves of Welsh farmers in the valleys, whose ancestors had come to the United States in whole village groups to be weavers in the textile mills and who had in a later generation left the factories to take land in the valleys, had forgotten their fathers' struggles as workers, and were now entrenched conservative rich farmers. I made no progress in talking to them about the milk strike, and after a few attempts I went to the "higher tiers," as the hill country was called. Most farmers in the hills had been industrial workers for years in the mines of Pennsylvania, in the steel mills or foundries, or in arms plants or shoe factories. They had dreamed of retirement to a farm, but they could afford only marginal lands, and they still owed money on their land, for which they depended on the sale price for their milk. They had to oppose the price cuts.

These farm families usually consisted of a farmer and his wife and as many of their sons as could be supported by the operation of the farm. Extra cash came from sons who went to work in the factories. These farmers supported the milk strike, but their idea of action was to pick up their rifles. They took a few pot-shots at tank cars carrying milk, and they frightened strike-breaking farmers with occasional armed threats. They were accustomed to acting on their own, and it was a delicate line that Archie Wright trod in holding the strikers to dumping their milk, while at the same time persuading them not to go out and shoot their enemies.

In the higher tiers I met a strange household. A young German immigrant, alone on his farm, had desperately needed a workmate, a woman. He advertised in a farm journal for a woman housekeeper, and from Florida a stranded circus performer answered the ad. She had been born in Bavaria to a bourgeois family, from which she had run away to join the circus because she loved horses. She was an accomplished horse-woman and had also been the lady who got sawed in half; she had lived twenty years in circus life. She and the German farmer married soon after she came to the farm; she wanted a child and the farmer wanted a son, so they adopted a little boy, a scrawny, pitiful small child. They were, I thought, severe with him, but it may have been that their accents in English made their speech seem rough. They were a strange little family and very lonely. They begged me to sleep at their farm when I was in the vicinity, and I slept on a straw tick on the floor. Supper was boiled potatoes with skim milk to drink and maybe onions to eat raw, but I had found that this was usual fare on the hill farms, except that sometimes a bowl of boiled eggs was set out to eat with the potatoes and onions. One farmer, born in the Ukraine, had earned the money in the mines for the down payment on his farm and had moved to it with his wife and five children. All the children died in a diphtheria epidemic; their graves were near the house. But now there were five more, who sat at table with us.

The women worked as hard as the men; they kept house, ran the dairy, and kept a kitchen garden if they could find time and strength. Electricity was used to run machines—not for reading, there was little time for reading. Farmers rose at dawn and went to bed early. Poor farmers kept twenty cows, the limit the farm could feed, but fewer cows made a dairy farm uneconomical to run. Rich farmers kept a hundred and twenty cows, with electric milkers and conveyors to bring feed to the cows and to convey manure out of the barn. While I was at one hill farm a cream separator was purchased, and they were using it for the first time. These were radicalized people, still very close to their European backgrounds in Germany, Italy, Czechoslovakia, Poland, and Russia, and I found a skein of ideas which intertwined with mine and made these people dear to me. This was not placid country of rolling meadows, but rough country with forest patches where land was too steep and earth too thin for anything but wood-lot. I was driving down out of this country when I passed the local Catholic priest, who motioned me to stop. I stopped and we talked; we were far away from any habitation. He told me that I should get out of this country, that I was not wanted here, and that the farmers were benighted in their demands against Borden and Sheffield milk companies—that I was an arm of the devil and that I was surely headed for hell. I said, "Well, suppose we both go to the Farmers' Union meeting tonight and ask the membership whether you or I should leave this country."

I drove on, but I was angry and drove slowly because it had been a violent, virulent attack. We both were at the union meeting that night. I spoke, then the priest spoke, in the style of Father Coughlin the Radio Priest. Archie defended me and spoke of the divisive role the priest was playing in the strike. He called for a vote, and although the union membership was predominantly Catholic, they voted resoundingly for me to stay.

TRANSITION
1938–1941

In 1938 the war in Spain was ending just as the Second World War was beginning. Chamberlain signed the Munich Pact, giving Hitler the Czechoslovak munitions works, and in the town all around us in Utica the church bells rang, "For peace in our times." Only a handful of Communists and Socialists understood that the betrayal of Czechoslovakia was the first act in World War II.

I was thirty years old and I wanted a child. My attempts had all ended in still births, and I became obsessed with my desire for a child. Some of the tension of those times probably entered into my preoccupation: I had to have a child, difficult as it proved for me to give birth to a live child.

Birth . . . I think I am afraid to try to write of it. In childbirth I was isolated; I never talked about it even to George. He was surprised to learn that giving birth was a peak emotional experience and so entirely my own that I never tried to express it. Exposure of the experience has been attempted, and although I concur with the attempt, I do not think it has yet been told in a form in which it is whole. I would wish it to remain whole, and I have preserved the wholeness of my own experience of birth by not telling it; it is too precious to me. Even now, writing of the experiences of age twenty-four to thirty, I wish to encompass my isolation and the wracking devastation of loss, the sense of being a nothing on the delivery table, knocked out by anesthetic, only to regain consciousness and be told once more, "The fetus is dead." Finally, I was not anesthetized; I labored and gave birth in the delivery room. Back in my room, I asked to see the fetus. If the nurse had carried it in her hands, or even wrapped in a towel, it might have seemed a shred of humanity, but in a hospital pan it was viscera. Another time the fetus lived a few hours, but I never saw it. Months later, in wartime Detroit where George had been drafted into the Army, I received a telephone call: "You have not given the order for disposal of the prematurely born infant that you gave birth to." I thought, a swindle, an ambulance-chasing outfit, and I threatened them with exposure.

Death of the male was conceived in me each time the sperm and ovum joined. One male lived through birth, and at six weeks his death, not accomplished in the womb, overtook him—cradle death. He did not breathe his next breath, and that was death. Of course, every birth is conceived to include its death, but to carry the life and the death of one's own child before its own birth . . . I confronted that birth and that death with every male I conceived.

Our only girl child passed her birth date and was born a small but tenacious infant. The pediatrician stood in the doorway of the cubicle where the baby lay naked. "What a female shape!" he exclaimed.

"How can you tell?"

"Oh, would you like me to tell you more about her?"

"Of course."

"She is an ascetic type, so do not expect her to eat much; but she is a hardy type, her hold on life is strong, although she seems delicate and probably always will seem fragile."

All true, for in her later life this prophecy proved accurate; and as I had more experience with babies I found I could foresee in the newborn a type that continues into adult life. We are what we are from conception; we are influenced by the environment, but we also influence that environment by what we are conceived to be.

With my first pregnancy I could not eat or drink, and in the first months I became emaciated. In the hospital I had visions of water, of drowning, and in hallucination I was submerged in water, and satisfied, I entered my death, but George was there, young, eager, demanding, needing me. And I returned. A priest came by to tell me that his prayers had saved me, and he gave me a little colored card such as good boys and girls receive in Protestant Sunday schools. I recovered spindle-legged, with my belly showing the child within. I have never received an explanation for the males' fetal death after seven months of fetal life. For cradle death some explanation has been offered, and it is now possible to monitor infant breathing. If breathing stops, the parents have two minutes in which to restore it. I don't know if we could have survived that strain and been normal parents. I read of one infant who stopped breathing many times, and the hope was that he would develop beyond this plight. I believe that the deaths I bore were not my fault; even this small sop is a comfort, for the burden of guilt in infant death is almost unbearable.

Later I held another baby, the one who lived, and my fear diminished as she lived and flourished, and as I gradually believed in her will to live. But our fears made us frantically anxious parents. We would rush to Linda's room and shake her, just to hear her cry the cry that meant she was alive.

Our child Linda was an infant when George began training in a government-run school. After six weeks of courses, the workers were sent into defense plants to build planes. George became in a year what previously had taken a seven-year apprenticeship to attain, but on Long Island he still could not get the classification in the union of Machinist or Pattern-maker which he wanted for work after the war. He went to Detroit, giving up his draft exemption—if a worker changed jobs, he was drafted into the armed forces.

Linda and I moved to Detroit too, a crowded wartime city, with rats as big as cats in the alleys where garbage was not collected. Our dog hunted at night, and sometimes in the morning he guarded on our doorstep the rat he had killed in his hunt. Housing was nearly impossible to find. I sat in the newspaper office downtown to get the paper before it was on the stands to look for ads for a house. I found an apartment, but the landlord locked the furnace room door; I broke down the door and turned up the heat. It was an embattled existence. Winter in Detroit is cold, the apartment was cheerless and every necessity was surrounded by difficulties. People were pouring into the industrial centers from the south for war work; families were torn apart, slums proliferated and all of us were strangers to one another. Women as well as men worked long hours; George worked a seventy-hour week those months before he was drafted.

I was with child and lost the child. A young black girl took care of Linda while I was in the hospital; the girl was kind, and Linda was well cared for, but when I came home Linda pressed her body close to mine and could not let go. We were frightened.

WARTIME
1942–1945

George wanted to go to the war. The enemy was fascism, and we agreed that the war must be fought. It seemed to us that the lives of all Jews were endangered by fascism; our lives were in danger, and not to fight in the war was to ask of others what we would not do for ourselves. But it was hard, and I remember those years as strange, unreal, and strained. George had the classification of Pattern-maker in the Machinists' Union by the time he was drafted. He proved to himself that he was as good as any worker, as good as any soldier; when he went to the war, he fought for himself and for Linda and me. That was how we put it to ourselves, and although it now seems a foolhardy and even meaningless decision, it was the experience of manhood in those times. George suffered over his decision to go to the war and leave us, Linda and me, without husband and father. He agonized over this during the war, and I told him, "You must come back alive, do not throw yourself away in any moment's heroism. I want you to return."

Just as George was drafted we found a friendly, even a motherly house-owner, and Linda and I and our dog Vicky were in the new apartment by Christmas time. I wrapped Linda warmly, put her on her sled, and the three of us set off in a snowstorm on Christmas Eve to get a tree and a few decorations. I set up the tree and decorated it. Linda liked it, but she was soon sleepy, and I put her to bed. It was Vicky who loved the tree; he lay near it, nibbled it and guarded it. Linda and I were too deserted to feel merry that year.

We went to visit George in Louisiana, where he was training for the infantry. Trains between Army training and factory centers were overcrowded, and our coach had overflowing toilets; no one cleared them, and the sewage pushed slowly down the aisle until there was no place to step. We drew our feet up on the seats and sat this way all the way to Texas, where we changed trains. It was a clear day, windy, ten degrees above zero. The train we were to board came into the station, but it let down no steps, and we could not get on until I pleaded with the conductor and he let us board the train. When we reached Alexandria, Louisiana, I found a taxi and we set off to find a hotel room. Suddenly I discovered that my traveler's checks were not in my bag. Linda had been playing with them in the dressing room in the train, and there was a chance that I might find them. Back at the depot, the station-master located the car in the yard; I found the car, went to the dressing room, and there on the windowsill were the checks.

We found a room and telephoned to George, who came dressed in uniform. Linda was over-impressed with the uniform, and she felt that George was a little strange. On the streets in Alexandria, blacks, even black soldiers, stepped off the sidewalk to walk in the street when they met a white. Their eyes never met our eyes; I had never been in the South before, and I didn't like it. We walked along the levee of the Red River, which was red with mud that washed from the surrounding land. We saw huts of tenant farmers, black and white farmers living in poverty I had not seen before in the United States. The fields were vast, and the farm families seemed crowded into one corner of the truly enormous planted areas.

On the way back to Detroit Linda had a fever, and I fought for a taxi to get to a hotel, then fought for a hotel room, which I shared with another young woman and her child. I called the hotel doctor and stayed in Chicago until Linda was well enough to travel.

In Detroit Linda stood at our window, and as children we didn't know passed she would say, "Bring me that one." We were not long enough in any one place to invite anyone in, and as housing was very scarce Linda and I shared some of our empty rooms with Israelis who had come to the United States for training in agriculture, planning to return to a kibbutz. When the men volunteered into the U.S. Army, the women set up housekeeping with Linda and me.

I decided to return to New York where I had friends and knew of a nursery school for Linda. We left behind all our furniture, taking with us only a camp bed, a couple of suitcases, and Vicky in a crate. In Grand

Central Station in New York, Linda and I sat in the baggage room to await Vicky, who had been put on a different train. We watched the crates as they arrived, and at last one was set down with a tail sticking up between the cracks. "Vicky," Linda called, and the tail wagged.

Sunnyside, in Queens, had no shortage of houses, and we moved into an empty house. The grocer sent over forty orange crates, and we made a sort of play-house; it was like playing house in Montana when I was not much older than Linda. She was eager to be with other children, as she and I had been almost sole companions. We ate our meals on the front steps, weather permitting, and we talked to neighbors and to all the children. Linda was afraid I, too, would disappear as her father had, and she was afraid to have me out of her sight. At her school I sat with her and reassured her, as did the teacher, who said, "Mommies and Poppies always come home," which reassured me too. We clung to each other. When we arrived in the mornings at the school Linda was still in her sleeping clothes because she refused to be dressed until she could play with the other children. We both soon had friends, and Linda was willing to be dressed and eager to go to nursery school.

One day a young lieutenant stood looking out from a porch near our house where there was a sign for piano lessons. "Is there something wrong with the piano teacher?" I asked him.

He answered, "No, but my aunt is old, and I must move her in with my family while I am away. All this furniture to get rid of . . ."

When I told him our plight, he said, "I'll ask the moving men to move the furniture over to your house when they come." The little music teacher furnished our house, and we loved her marble-topped dressers, her Christmas ornaments, her knives and forks. I think of her sometimes, and of the shock she must have felt to be moved about, just as we had been.

Stella and her little boy Steve shared our house with us. We lived together for perhaps a year while our husbands were both in the Army. But we remained isolated, even from each other; although we shared the household tasks, we were dazed, shocked women.

I worked in an Army Post Office during the war, where I was older than the high-school kids who were working there. I asked one of them, "Do you remember the Depression? Do you remember eating only oatmeal, or only fish for days at a time?" When the girl looked puzzled I asked, "Did you ever sit on the furniture with it piled in the street?"

She exclaimed, "I have always wondered—why was the furniture in the street? I must have been three years old or so. So that was the Depression!"

George came home on furlough and visited Linda at her nursery school. The uniform made the little children envious of a father who was in uniform, and I suppose some mother told her child, "But Linda's Daddy may be killed."

Linda came home in tears. "They say Poppie will be killed in the war."

"Say to them," I told her, "their fathers are not good enough, they won't even have them in the Army."

Attracted to two women alone and in need, men came to offer assistance. Our need was clear to Stella and me: we needed our husbands, and no other man was a substitute. Tension might have been relieved had we been friendlier, but we were determined that our men come home to us. Stella and I, frightened women, lived in a superstition that our resolve would bring home our men, and we would not break that resolve. Our children reflected this frightened, frightening household.

George, meanwhile, was in the Vosges Mountains just south of the Battle of the Bulge. His company had been six weeks in the front lines without replacements; they had replaced a black regiment which had received heavy casualties behind the lines which held the front. For six weeks they went without change of clothing or showers, although they were warmly dressed. George tells, "Some G.I.'s walked around in their sleeping bags, with holes cut for legs. Supplies were ample, they only needed to ask and they received another sleeping bag to sleep in. And of course, our mail came to us wherever we were."

"We came down through the Vosges mountains into a town leveled by artillery fire and which had only a cellar remaining; into it my company crowded—not a good position to be in—and scouts had to be sent out immediately, as shells were still lobbing into the area. We found the town's entire population huddled in the depths of the cellar on piles of coal and sacks of potatoes. They were fearful when they saw us crowding into their cellar too, and to calm their fears I went over and addressed them: a little speech in French as I was the only one in my company who spoke French—'You do not need to be afraid just because you see us coming into your cellar, this is the way we fight!' In the very back of the cellar a tiny, very old man came toward me, sliding down the pile of coal; edging his way among the people, he came up to me and touched my arm, saying, 'A Yid? Speaks English, speaks French—but this soldiering now, that's no business for a Jew.'

"Somebody, probably the company messenger, came seeking me. 'Hurry, Oppen, you have won a raffle—a three day pass to Paris; come quick!' And we crawled and then ran back to Company Headquarters, and he said, 'Run, the truck is just leaving!'"

George ran, clambered in over the tailgate, and with his steel helmet, gas mask and handgun was off to Paris. Dazed, he thought that the Company Command had probably picked him whether he had won the lottery or not because he was the one who spoke French and had been interpreter for the company all the way up from Marseilles. George was the one who loved France, as most G.I.'s did not. The truck stopped in Paris at the Place Pigalle ("Pig Alley" to the G.I.'s), where they were surrounded by the girls who came crowding around, asking for chocolate and soap and offering themselves. George walked through Paris to the Boulevards, where he looked on, incredulous, at the Boulevardiers, who, momentarily safe behind Allied front lines, sipped ersatz coffee and nibbled delicacies concocted of sawdust; as they daintily continued their cafe lives, on the kiosk were large beautiful, extravagant posters advertising Leger's latest exhibit. George says, "I nearly went berserk; there was no way to express my anger at these Parisians who could care about such mediocrity at such a time."

Stella's husband, a Frenchman, was parachuted into France in the first days of the Allied invasion. He was not heard from until war's end, and Stella had months of anguished waiting. The War Department did not notify her of his death, so she hoped he lived, but the fear was monstrous. Our children played an endless game; Stevie rang the doorbell, and Linda answered. Stevie said, "It's a letter from my Daddy." And Stella watched this game. Her husband Pierre was found when Dachau was freed by U.S. troops, and after ten days in the hospital he was flown home. He was alive!

George was wounded shortly before Victory Day in Europe. He somehow mailed me a letter before he reached the hospital, for the notice did not come from the War Department until six weeks later, informing me of his multiple wounds of face, back, and legs. I imagined the wounds and wrote to George, "You are to come home alive, no matter what the scars."

He wrote again when he was able. The wounds were many. An 88 mm. shell had exploded in a hole where he and two others took refuge; the two men in the hole with him were killed, and George lay wounded, pinned down by German fire. The Germans had retreated, and some platoons of Germans had probably been left behind to impede the advancing U.S. troops; they were shelling directly. George lay for hours, then crawled at night until he was picked up, put in a truck and taken to an aid station. He sent me the letter from the aid station before he was taken to the hospital. And still he did not come home. Months passed and our men were not getting out of the Army; the war was over, and still they did not come home. April 1945 was the date of victory in Europe and George did not return until the last of November 1945.

In Manila at the war's end demonstrations were held by soldiers who wanted to go home. In Army trucks they drove to centers where they marched in protest at being kept abroad. In Paris, U.S. soldiers began marching down the Champs Elysées; by the time they reached the Place de la Concorde they were a great parade of 5000 protesting soldiers. At home, those of us who were involved because our men did not come home circulated petitions in the street; we were hugged and greeted by other women who took the petitions and returned them to us filled with the names of women who wanted their men to come home. The demonstrations which began in Manila and spread to other centers were led by men who had been sent to the South Pacific when they were drafted because it was thought they would be in an unimportant sector, men who had been, in the phrase of the time, "premature anti-fascists." Men were being held in all areas where the U.S. Armed Forces had men after the war was over. Both the U.S.S.R. and the United States maintained troops in Asia, where the struggle immediately at war's end became one for division of the Orient. China was now an independent nation to be reckoned with, Japan was a vanquished enemy, and neither the Russian nor the United States government intended to leave that part of the world. U.S. troops boarded ships for what they thought was home, only to find themselves transported to the South China area. The demonstrations by our men abroad aroused support at home; and although to protest in uniform and use Army vehicles to transport men to the demonstrations was mutiny, those men who demonstrated were not tried for mutiny. They were not punished in any way; a regiment of blacks was threatened with court-martial, but the court-martial was quickly dropped because of the atmosphere at home, which opposed any further involvement in Asia and which forced the government to abandon the idea of war in Asia— until the United States became involved later in Korea, and still later, disastrously, in Vietnam. These defeats of the ruling United States government powers were forced by determined action, by people marching, by petitions and by protests against the attempts to conquer Asia.

George was held in Le Havre from June until November. He tells of having their French francs taken from them in preparation for the return home, but months passed and they were still in the miserable Replacement Depots ("Repple Depples") waiting. George and a major with whom he was friendly decided to try to get some money to send cables to wives and families, telling them of their plight. George and his friend took blankets, arms, boots, anything they could pick up around the barracks, and walked toward the gates, where the Military Policemen turned their backs! They knew, and agreed to the necessity of protesting in order to get home. George and his friend sold their contraband on the Black Market and sent wires to everyone they knew who might help them to get home— and the news spread.

In 1974 we met Abe Chapman, who told us another side of the Manila demonstrations. He was in Manila, where the men in the armed services were not being demobilized although the war had ended. A group of G.I.'s understood that the U.S. and Russia were unwilling to get out of the Pacific area and China; these G.I.'s planned to hold a rally in Manila, but they didn't know how to get the information to all the G.I.'s in the area concerning where and when the rally would be held. They mentioned the problem to Abe, a G.I. and editor of the Army's G.I. newspaper, who said, "I'll do something—I'll get the word out." He was free to publish without censorship the stories that came to him from United Press, Associated Press, or Reuter's news agencies, but local stories had to be passed by the Army censor. Abe called the head of one of these news services and said, "I'll give you a scoop on a tremendous story if you will promise to keep it secret where you got the story." Promptly Abe received the news over the wire from the news service; the story of the demonstration was sent to every group in the armed services in the Pacific area in the tallest headlines in the G.I. newspapers. It was that demonstration and that news that swept around the world to George and to all G.I.'s waiting in Replacement Depots and in "lost" groups, while headlines in the U.S. papers proclaimed different numbers each day for the size of the armed services, with news stories that ships were not available to get them home. Men saw with their own eyes ships sail with a few men or a few Wacs (Women's Auxiliary Corps) in empty ships, and when the authorities were questioned they replied, "Oh, we can't put G.I.'s on ships with Wacs."

During those years Linda and I did not laugh much. In pictures we look like refugees—remote, thin and bleak. Linda looked like a little wild girl; she would not have her hair combed. When George came home at last I told him, "Linda does not understand what a joke is; laughter is threatening." George made little jokes for her, and we laughed, but we needed time to recover our spirits. Linda also needed to learn that George and I were equal as her parents—she would turn to me for permission when George had already told her what she might do.

New York City was not a place we understood in ways we needed to understand to bring up a child. George and I visited the school I would have chosen for her to attend in the fall; we tried to imagine what life was like for a child growing up on city streets, and we quailed from it. We needed to get out of New York City, where tension and too much argument had to be faced; we needed to get away from the scene of wartime living and be a family again. We needed to be free of close neighbors and be together, just three of us, free of the tight living of New York City. We needed space, sky enough to see the sweep of it, stars at night, forests, to have a garden and ride horses.

George had been through shattering and at the same time exhilarating years in France. He was emotionally sympathetic with the French and in an intimate conversation some of the time with peasants and with Free French in Merci le Bas, the village where his platoon was fighting toward the end of the war. George returned to a civilian life that knew nothing of the dangers and the horrors of war on home soil. G.I. patience was limited. Once I made out a check on my bank for George to cash; he stood in line at the window and was told to see the bank manager behind a little railing. George stood outside the railing and told the manager, "My wife has an account here, I am her husband, I want to cash the check."

The manager began, "We never cash checks for strangers—"

What!" exploded George, "You won't cash the check—" and he started over the railing. The manager quickly initialed the check.

The stay-at-homes had no idea what it had been like to be a G.I. on a battlefield in a war. George and most G.I.'s were illegally armed; I didn't know any who had not taken hand arms out of the services when they were discharged.

We retrieved an old open trailer from New Jersey. George parked it at the curb in front of our house in Sunnyside and began to build it into a camping trailer for our trip west—we were going to California. Our neighbors were incredulous, and fathers brought sons on Sunday to watch George at work on the little camp trailer, making a place to sleep, a little shelf for a stove and food, a hitch for the car to pull it. They said, "That trailer will never make it over the Rocky Mountains." At war's end these neighbors were buying their first automobiles and learning how to drive them. In March 1946, we drove west. Linda stood behind the front seat and kept up a constant conversation, happy that she had us where she could touch us. We had barely started to be a family when the war came upon us, and Linda had had only stories of a father. Her love was for us, and to be with us was her life.

Mornings we drove until we found a roadside place open for breakfast. We discussed farms, animals, horses; I told Linda an endless story about Hoppy the Frog until she began calling me "Hoppy." We passed horses on the prairie, and George caught one for Linda; he has a poem:

"Horse," she said, whispering
By the roadside
With the cars passing. Little girl welcomed,
Learning welcome.

CALIFORNIA AND EXILE

1946–1958

W e stopped with friends in Los Angeles who were living in a housing project, shared between blacks newly arrived in wartime from the South and whites from the East, also newly arrived. Los Angeles was a strange vast city encompassing hundreds of communities on land which earlier had been planted with orange groves or which had been garden acreage. Our friends had no place for us to sleep, so we drove at nightfall to the foothills and went to sleep as we had slept coming across the country. In the middle of the night police troopers swept up, shone their lights on us and woke us up. I said to them, "Hush, you will wake the child," and they went away.

We drove to San Francisco to visit George's father and stepmother. For George and for all G.I.'s the business-as-usual attitudes in New York City and in George's family when we met them in San Francisco were infuriating. We thought we had fought the war so that anti-Semitism would be defeated, so that the holocaust should never happen again. In a party in San Francisco in George's father's house, a very rich man said to George in conversation, "I just returned from Florida."

"And how was it there?" asked George.

"Oh, it was full of kikes," he said.

George asked our niece how it was that a Jew could speak so, and she answered, "Oh, he thinks that only Jews speak in that way about Jews."

Not a house or a chicken coop was to be rented; housing was all in use, and people were pouring into California. George's father went with us to buy a house trailer. It had a separate little bedroom for Linda with a sliding door, a table and a bench that folded into a bed for George and me at night. It was well insulated, a snug and comfortable place to live. In 1946 trailer living was a comfortable way to travel and a possible way to have a dwelling place at that moment after the war. It suited our needs, and we found it almost a perfect way to live for a year or two. We had strained our emotions too much with the war and with separation—we had to be at home and by ourselves. George and I had had almost no experience of being equally parents, nor had Linda had a father within her young memory.

George had driven trucks of all sorts in the Army; he had always been a fine driver, and he drove the oversize trailer up the winding cliff-side Highway #1 to Oregon. Linda discovered the abalone shells that were on every beach. George rigged a rope to lower her down and lift her up the steep cliffs, and she collected shells. We carried fifty pounds of lovely shells that she couldn't part with.

As we drove up the coast George and I discussed how best to talk to my mother. We decided to ask questions; George said, "Perhaps she will speak more freely now, and you may find out what it is that has made you feel guilty toward your mother." Eleven years had elapsed since I had seen my mother, and she had not seen our child. So much time had passed that I had become a stranger from outside her life, and she could talk to me as she had never talked to me when I lived with her. It was a relief to find that I had not been central in her life. The fifteen years I had been in her house had slipped aside, and she remembered far more vividly the years before she married and the years after my father's death, when I was gone from her life. On this visit she had presents to give us. For George she had a mandolin (George the poet), for Linda she had the little folding enlarging glass she had used for studying botany at teacher's college (Linda studied medicine), and for me she had a biography of women feminist leaders at the time of the Civil War (I am a liberated woman). She could not have known what symbolic gifts she gave!

Wendell found five-year-old Linda enchanting and took her to show her how to make ice cream sodas. Wendell and my mother were running a trailer camp, and they had an ice cream parlor too.

It was the end of March, and the higher mountains were still snowy. The Oregon Caves were strange and wonderful to enter by ourselves—it was too early in the season for guides; we were the discoverers, and high inside the caves we saw light coming through a crevice. We climbed to it and wriggled through, to find ourselves in snow. We sat to regain our sight in the bright light and then slid down the hillside.

I was relieved of a burden of guilt with this visit. Mama lived now in a continuation of her girlhood hopes and ambitions, and I thought of her more happily. My presence had made her uncomfortable when I was adolescent. Now, with her death, I sigh and think of her as I never knew her, but perhaps as she more nearly was.

Wendell came to see me in 1972, and he mentioned that Noel had brought down a truck-load of Christmas trees to San Francisco. He asked Noel, "Come along to visit Mary?"

Noel replied, "No, I guess not, she writes me a letter once in awhile, and that's enough."

It was one letter, which I had written the previous spring, and it could have been written any time in the past forty years. I told him that he had been the one in my life after my father died and until I met George, I believed he loved me, because he thought about me and asked me to live with him and then let me go freely and confidently. I wrote that as he had believed in me, so I believed in myself. I wrote about our father's death, how bereft I had felt and how I had turned to the first man who touched me.

I realize in writing this that perhaps I am also describing my mother. I had interpreted her to myself as not having lived the life she wanted, because she once told me that she had at first wanted my father's older brother. But she lived her life with my father whole-heartedly and with great spirit. For her to have abandoned that spirit at his death would have been death for her too. She was still an attractive woman when my father died, but I thought of her only as my mother. I did not see her attractiveness to men, and I was, in a sense, my father's eyes on her; I was intolerable to her in her house.

In the woods where the sea meets the land it is beautiful, and on first sight we persuaded ourselves we could live in Eureka. We had made an acquaintance before we left San Francisco who told us, "I left Eureka to come down here to write, but my fishing partner needs someone to fish with him; also, if you go to Eureka, please look up my dog Jody and take care of him."

So we looked up the man and the dog. George went on one fishing trip for salmon and came home with a boatload of fish, but he did not like the design of the long and narrow boats used there for ocean fishing. Although it is a beautiful life on the sea at this place on the craggy California coast, it seemed to us to be a hopeless life of hard work. The dog Jody accepted us with dignity, and although he would occasionally go off for a trip to sea on some boat with a fisherman friend, he came home to us tired and hungry and ready to play with Linda or to go for walks with us. He had a passion for swimming, for boats, and for retrieving.

My brother Paul, his wife Julia and their many children were living in Eureka, and George got a job driving a truck. We considered buying land and building a house, but the lumber company town was too violent a community for us. We needed a place that was not at war with itself as this community was. A strike was called in the redwood industry which resulted in violence, threats, and even deaths. Also, the community was insufficient for our intellectual needs. We spent a month or two with the trailer parked under redwoods in an abandoned cherry orchard whose trees gave us ripe dark red cherries, and we absorbed the quiet of the forests.

The house trailer was a haven for us. We stopped almost anywhere— in forest, beside the road or beside the sea. We let down the doorstep and we were at home. I liked living in the trailer more than in any house, but the trailer parks or trailer camps were not pleasant, nor was it easy to find one where children were welcome. As we went back down the coast we inquired of other families in trailers, "Where is there a trailer camp near Los Angeles for us, one that welcomes children?" We were directed to a trailer park in Compton, on the south side of Los Angeles, in a working-class part of town near the new airplane factories and small machine shops. The owner of this trailer park took in only families with children. It was crowded, but for our needs at that moment it was a good place, and in the newly-built school Linda entered the first grade. The project for their work was "My Home," and the first picture she brought home was of our trailer with the butane tank on the front bumper. The teacher and most of the children also lived in trailers.

Howard, a boy of seven, came by our trailer with a large Mason jar. I asked, "What is in the jar, Howie?"

"Black widow spiders, want to see them?" and he unscrewed the lid to show me dozens of black widow spiders. "I'm going to give them to my teacher."

I said, "But Howie, they are poisonous; what if you got bit?" I sprayed them with an insecticide; he wept, and I remembered Raymond's mother who had destroyed the sand-pile park that we had made with ground glass fountains when I was Howie's age.

A stable adjoined the trailer park on the bank of the dry Los Angeles river-bed, where we rented horses and rode in the afternoons. Linda had been in love with horses since she rode her first horse in the desert on the way across the country. Here she loved Babe, a beautiful golden-chestnut mare who was a perfect horse for a child, but Babe was barn-sour—she would turn suddenly and head back for the stable. George bought Babe for Linda and trained her, just for Linda. One day George rented a horse, a new small red Arab gelding named Little Red, and as he was putting him in the corral, the corral horses crowded Little Red, who did not know the horses, though he did know George a little. He stayed at George's elbow, nudging George to stay with him. George bought Little Red for himself, leaving me without my own horse. Then for me George bought the horse I liked best, a big gaited gelding named Trigger. I couldn't sleep that night—I never had thought I would have my own horse.

A small circus wintered in the stable, and Linda and I rode the baby elephant, Zaida. The horses did not like the circus animals; they shied sometimes when suddenly around a corner they met Zaida, and the smells of the caged animals made the horses snort.

Los Angeles encompasses hundreds of small communities, like Compton, which retain vestiges of their small-town identity, although super-highways bypass or go over them. Not a house was available. George worked a short while in a machine shop and then began to build houses with Stewart, a neighbor in the trailer court. These houses were bought before they were finished, usually by Japanese who were returning to civilian life after their internment in the camps where they had been held during the war, or by G.I.'s using the G.I. loan with low interest rates. The houses were on larger-than-usual plots of ground, and the kitchens were well planned and open to the living areas; as far as the banks would allow, George tried to make them attractive. Bank loans for building were based on conservative house plans—no slant roofs, no facing the back of the house to the street or similar slight changes were allowed by the bankers. George and Stewart were on their way to being successful in the building boom that followed the war; hundreds of people were pouring into the state every month, and they all needed houses.

I drove our car a hundred miles a day, taking Linda to school, George to work, and then going to look for a piece of land for our own house. It was strange to me to think of owning a piece of land, a piece of Earth, a piece of our planet. I found an acre of land at Redondo Beach, near the sea and high above the surrounding valley, with two eucalyptus trees on what was called "the soil." It had been a Spanish land grant, with only two previous owners, and tomatoes had been grown there a short time before we bought it.

In 1946, a land-owner in California could write into his deed any restrictions he liked, and they were binding on future owners; it was difficult to find a piece of land which was not restricted to whites only. Our land had only the restriction that alcohol could not be sold from it. All three of us went to look at the land, and then we bought it. The first thing we built was a corral of cyclone fence. We trailered our horses to the land and came every night to feed and ride them, and we soon knew our neighbors.

In the Depression of the 1930s settlers in Redondo had lived in packing cases or in homes they were building themselves. Redondo had vigilant citizens, many of whom attended city council meetings to protect their rights and the character of the community. An airplane was being repaired in one yard, in another an excavation for a swimming pool was being dug, in another a six-meter yacht was being built; and many families kept horses. After work electric saws could be heard from the valley below us—everyone was building. We made friends with a Finnish couple who had come to the United States as cook and butler; they had saved their money and now were building their own house, with, of course, a Finnish sauna. Mr. Johannon also had a horse seventeen hands high, with fancy tack—black bridle and saddle. He said, "I always want to be cowboy, so when I see ad in paper I buy horse and saddle, but horse not know me. I never been on horse and horse not go. I cluck to him, he still not go, so

I knock my stirrups together under his belly. He go a few steps—I do it again, he goes again, that is how I go home. I pass a door with a little boy who yells for his mama, 'Mama, come and see the cowboy.' I happy." Mr. Johannon galloped his horse now, and they made their own rules. Mr. Johannon would yell "Whoa," and the horse would stop abruptly.

Our neighbors across the street had been dusted out of Oklahoma in the Great Dust Storm of the 1930s, and down the street was an old Armenian couple with a grape arbor and a fine garden. Behind us were a Mexican couple, Lupe and Jose, twenty-five years old or so, with four children; their baby rocked in a homemade hammock from the ceiling. They had romantic tales of the fruit-picking and the dance halls that had been part of their lives. Our own friends Raf and Carlin came to live on our street. Raf was learning the printing trade on the G.I. bill for education, and we all helped one another in building our houses.

We could not move our trailer to our land until we had water, a cess-pool and a toilet. George went to the bank to borrow money for the houses he and Stewart planned to build, and the man at the bank said, "But you have no credit rating."

George asked, "How can credit be established?"

"Oh, you buy on credit, and as you make payments you get a rating."

I went the next day and bought a 20′ by 20′ garage on credit, to be built on our land on a concrete slab. With credit established, in one week there stood a little building under the eucalyptus trees on our land. We rented a bulldozer and made a driveway up through the cliff onto our land; we brought our house trailer and installed it beside the little utility building, which was the core of the house we built later, extending the building around a patio of bricks. But we still had no water, and the town did not plan to put in a water line to our end of the street in time for our needs. It took me a long time to find enough pipe to lay our own water line—meanwhile, we used water brought by garden hose from the nearest neighbor's house. These same neighbors had a pig half grown, already a large animal. Only the woman and her daughter were in their household, as the son was in and out of an Army hospital with injuries from the war. The woman asked George one day to help her put the pig in her car. George had never handled a pig, and he knew nothing about how to put a pig into a car, but he went at the task with aplomb. He grabbed the pig by its hind legs and walked it like a wheelbarrow to the car; the pig walked himself right up the step and onto the seat.

I made a list of all the parts necessary for the model bathroom I had chosen from a Sears Roebuck catalog. I then set out on my daily search for parts. Because of the war, house-building supplies were in short supply, and a real search had to be made. At one point I had twenty weekends of work scheduled, filling in my list from parts I found as I drove about the outskirts of Los Angeles, hunting. We completed weekend after weekend of work on our house. I bought a how-to book on plumbing, another for electric wiring; George did the plumbing and I did the wiring on the 20' by 20' service building. It was like solving puzzles. We hired a neighbor who was in the business to put in the cesspool, and except for the difficulty about water, we established on our own land. An acre of land seemed the nearest to farming we would ever come; I said to George and Linda, "If there is any animal you ever wanted, here is the place for it."

Some friends from the trailer camp, a family with five boys, moved to the opposite side of Los Angeles, fifty miles away. They raised rabbits and had many other creatures too, all of them prolific. On Linda's birthday and on holidays they came bringing a pair of ducks, or doves, or pigeons— it was like filling up the ark. The pet-store man bought finches and ring-necked doves from us which multiplied in our aviary. He telephoned one day: "Mrs. Oppen," he asked, "would you please give a home to a gopher snake a little boy can't keep any longer?" I was doubtful, but Linda and I went to the library and read, "The gopher snake is the most domesticated snake to keep for a pet." We went to the pet store and were handed a large brown grocery bag. At home in our garden we opened the bag, and out crawled a three-foot-long handsome snake, who wriggled across to a gopher hole. He went down it, and we never saw him again!

Linda wrote to friends in New Jersey for a box turtle. We also had a large desert turtle named Little Dickens, not after Charles but because Linda saw a roguish look in the turtle's eye, and every time I opened a drawer in Linda's room, I found a horned toad. When we had to move from Redondo we had sixty pets to find homes for, besides the dog and the parakeet who remained with us. The dog, Kinch, was given to Linda by Andy, our niece, when Linda was seven years old; Kinch was the noblest, most wonderful dog I have ever known.

George and I discussed whether we wanted to live the kind of life that his house-building was leading us into. We decided that we did not want it, and George set up a carpenter shop in our garage and began making cabinets for hi-fi sets instead. A combination of components had been recommended by Consumer's Union, and people who bought them needed a cabinet. Each week a new customer would appear in answer to a small ad in the newspaper. George did the designing and building of the furniture, and I helped with the finishing.

In April 1950 a little procession of neighbors came up our driveway with a lit birthday cake for George. The feeling in the neighborhood was friendly, neighborly—but this little party was the last of this neighborliness. The F.B.I. began its visits:

"Whose car is that at your neighbor's house?"

"Do you visit those people often?"

Nagging and persistent, it was clear from their questions that they had a dossier with information about us far back into our lives. They visited not only us, but every friend, every neighbor, every person who had signed a petition, every trade unionist, every supporter of Henry Wallace; Henry Wallace himself was suspect because he was a liberal. Visits from a neat, unobtrusive car with two gray flannel-suited young men with F.B.I. credentials and notebooks became routine. We decided to give no answers to their expert questioning, although their insinuation was: give information, tell all, expose your neighbors, friends, comrades—that is the only way for you to be safe. One young man did the questioning, the other took out his notebook. When I walked around in back of the one who was writing, he looked up and asked, "Are you going to watch to see what I write?"

"I am going to do just that."

We were part of the movement which had begun with the mutiny at Manila. Now with war declared in Korea it was clear to us that Joseph McCarthy and General MacArthur, representing the policy of the Pentagon, sought to silence opposition to this war.

Our friend Raf came to talk to us of his predicament. He was in more immediate danger than we were. He was free on a bail bond. A questionnaire had arrived in the jungle where Raf was working on a United States project to eradicate Hoof and Mouth disease in cattle. Each worker was to sign— "Yes or No! Do you believe in the forcible overthrow of the U.S. government?" Raf had answered honestly "No." Later another questionnaire had arrived; the question this time was, "Have you ever been a Communist?" To which Raf answered, "Yes," because years before, when he had been a student, he had been a Party member. The charge was perjury. It had seemed unlikely that a trial would ever be held, but now with this wave of repression, Raf decided that his trial would probably be called. He decided to leave at once for Mexico, and he asked us to take care of his family and to follow ourselves as soon as we could.

The next day a friend from Hollywood called on us. "What would you think of me if I should leave the country?" he asked.

We replied, "We are going to Mexico next week."

In preparation for going to Mexico, Linda, now ten years old, was reading a child's account of the life of Benito Juarez, president of Mexico at the same time that Abraham Lincoln was president of the United States; he occupies the same position in the hearts of Mexicans as Lincoln does in the United States. Linda was talking in her sleep one night, and George went into her room; Linda sat up in bed, and patting the bed beside her said to George, "Sit down Juarez, you're tired."

As Linda, George, and I drove to Mexico with the parakeet and our dog Kinch, we discussed our attitudes toward living in Mexico. We were quite sure we would be there for a period of years. We had our child, whose culturation and education had to be provided. What kind of life would we find for ourselves and for her? We said, "We will enter into the life of Mexico as it is offered. We do not want to live only within an expatriate group of foreigners in Mexico."

Linda had had to leave behind her mare, of whom she sometimes said, "I think she would take care of me like my mother."

On June 11, 1950, the Great American Desert was hot. We planned to drive only at night, but we couldn't get across the desert in one night's drive. Daytime temperature reached 120°; the tires heated to danger point, and the bird collapsed—he couldn't hang on to his perch, and I rode along with my finger under his beak, holding it up. We all wilted.

Linda had barely recovered from a viral pneumonia; she seemed a fragile child, but she traveled better than the rest of us. Water was for sale at service stations, and at one station the man said to George, "I'll make you an iced coffee in my own glass." It was a quart glass beer mug, and George and I shared it. In the station, which was air conditioned, was a fancy cage of parakeets; when she saw our bird, the woman said, "The last people through here before you gave me these birds, which were not surviving the heat." At another stop a woman gave us cold watermelon—watermelon has never tasted so exquisite since.

We crossed the border uneventfully and entered Mexico with a three-month tourist visa. At Chihuahua, we stopped at a hotel that was patronized mostly by Texans, a sort of spa with a swimming pool, gardens, and a restaurant. We rested and recovered—it seemed a delightful oasis after the desert. But we had not received any advice about hygiene or diet in Mexico, and in our resolve to enter into life in Mexico fully as it presented itself, we ate freely, and within three days Linda and I had *la turista*. In Linda's condition it seemed too dangerous for her to continue on a hard trip of several more days' driving. Linda and I took a plane to Mexico City, established ourselves in a hotel, called a doctor and collapsed into bed. George arrived three days later, came upstairs and fainted into the bathtub. We had arrived.

In a few days we were able to emerge, holding each other up. We drove about the city to discover a *pensione* in which to convalesce. In the dining room the first day, we noticed an elderly gentleman, who eyed George with apparent recognition and stopped just short of speaking to us. George crossed the room, and said, "I noticed you looking at me; do you by any chance know my father?" He was old man Gerstle, from San Francisco, who knew George's father and recognized a family resemblance. He sighed for bygone days in San Francisco, which were in his memory a golden age.

"In what way have things changed?" asked George.

"Why, just the other day one of our girls married a Polish Jew," said old man Gerstle.

"Who was that?" asked George.

"David Sarnoff."

George understood—a German-Jewish girl of merchant class family had married into the family of a second-generation Polish immigrant (chairman of the National Broadcasting Corporation), and it was a lowering of class for the German-Jewish girl in the eyes of old man Gerstle.

In Mexico City we got in touch with a family whose name had been given to us by our movie writer friend. We were received cordially, and with all the information and attention we needed, we began to find our way into Mexico City's United States émigré and refugee circle, in which we lived for nine years. Through friends of these new acquaintances we found an apartment into which we moved within a few days, which had been built from an old wine storage room in the Monastery of Carmen in San Ángel. The plumbing was faulty, so we bathed in the garden in the fountain where water flowed more freely. The garden was the chief reason for living in this place; it was lovely and intimate, with a high wall and a stable for a burro in one corner. Linda immediately wanted a burro, and on our walks and drives to the outlying areas of the city we always asked to see any donkey which might be for sale. We looked at many donkeys and finally bought one that seemed better trained and more willing than any other. He was very small and babyish, and Linda named him Pinocchiore. He became part of our household, greeting each entry through our gate with hilarious loud braying, indicating how lonely he had been for us in our absence. Linda arranged saddlebags across the donkey's back and undertook the daily marketing.

Linda was a small ten-year-old with long brown braids and brown skin from long hours spent on her horse. She was to all appearances a Mexican child. On her first trip home from market, with the donkey laden with our food, she met at the entrance to our alleyway beside the convent a bus-load of Canadian tourists, visiting the Carmen convent. By hand-signs they indicated they would pay her ten centavos if she allowed them to take her picture. She gravely collected the coins and silently stood beside her donkey before racing home to tell us the joke.

We were prepared to receive political refugees, sure that many of them would be coming. A Hollywood family arrived and moved in with us in our convent apartment, and I began looking for a larger place. I found an old colonial house with thirteen rooms; the street floor also housed the San Ángel Post Office and a branch of a bank. Upper floors contained a patio, a ballroom, and a chapel. When we moved in, a young Indian girl was sitting on the doorstep—she made it clear that she had to be hired, that she belonged to the house. Francisca was an intelligent girl, whose grandfather came from back in the hills toward the mountains at which we looked from our windows. Her mother lived in a hovel on the out-skirts of San Ángel, where the servants and the landless people huddled as in medieval times; she came to do our washing and ironing. I undertook the cooking because the severity of amoebic dysentery had made it clear to us that we could not eat carelessly.

Our discussion of taking Mexico as it presented itself and entering its culture came to very little if one could not accept food when offered. The commonest cause of death at this time was enteric infection, and with all our care I think I had every variation of intestinal upset at least once. We were stopped short, for instance, of inviting and being invited in turn by Mexicans with whom we might wish to be friends. Mexico in 1950 did not yet have adequate supplies of pure water available; if pure water were available, and no other precautions were taken, U.N. research had shown that enteric infections would become a minor source of death.

The Post Office and the bank beside our doorway brought everyone in the vicinity to our door. In our first days in the house we ourselves got lost in the thirteen rooms—we met Francisca's relatives abruptly face to face, and we didn't yet know them. We even met a few people wandering on our patio, looking for the Post Office. We had to be firm with Francisca about locking the downstairs door and about having so many of her relatives sleeping in the house. In the old colonial days, if one person from a family were hired, her whole family became dependent on the *patron*. We decided after a short trial that we would have no sleep-in help. The strength of custom was too strong if we let even Francisca sleep in, so she stayed overnight only to babysit.

Our red-paneled truck was noticeable, and as we wanted to be able to visit our friends and acquaintances a little less conspicuously, we had the truck painted a dark blue. When Linda came home from school and looked at it, she said, "You might as well have Georgie Florist painted on it."

Our friends had recommended the Luis Vives school for Linda. We had no knowledge of schools here, and as our new acquaintances sent their children to that school, we enrolled Linda, and I accompanied her to school. The teachers were recent refugees from Spain; they had been educators, and Luis Vives himself had been a noted educator in Spain, but no person in the school spoke English. I spoke Spanish from two years of high school Spanish, which came back to me in this emergency, but for a little child it seemed too hard to be placed in the situation of having to learn the language all at once. The children came and invited Linda, and when she was reluctant to join them they politely stood near her and tried to talk to her. A man and a woman teacher taught in the double class-rooms for each group. The methods seemed admirable to me, but we took Linda out of the school when we found that an American school existed which was qualified in the United States for grade school, high school, and college preparation. The appearance and size of this school made it seem very similar to a big United States consolidated school system. Spanish was taught half the day and English the other half; in the student body were included many Mexicans who wanted to enter American colleges or who wanted to be qualified with the English language and American business training. Before we enrolled Linda we talked with other refugee parents with children to be placed in the school. One parent who had several children talked to the principal for all of us and discussed the problems of children of leftist political refugees. He asked, "Will our children suffer from prejudice of the teachers or the administration of the American School?" He was assured that no prejudice would be allowed to continue if any became noted. We did not, in all the years of our child's education there, hear of any such incident in the school. On the San Ángel school-bus, however, before the parents put a stop to it, the children carried on a fascist-communist vendetta. We made it clear to our children that their parents' politics was not to be carried over as an adventure on the schoolbus.

More refugees arrived every week. We usually had an extra family staying with us until a house could be found for them. In a short time Carlin and her two children joined us, and Raf was reunited with his family.

We noticed two men hanging around our house day after day, checking on us. On one visit from these surveillants, George and I were sitting on the patio with the man who was interrogating us. We were curious as to what questions he would ask. He had the same dossier, with all the same background that the F.B.I. men had had in California and all the same errors, but these were Mexican men, supplied with dossiers that the C.I.A. and F.B.I. had compiled. Little Miguel, an infant fourteen months old, wandered onto the patio with bottle in hand and diaper sagging; while the preoccupied man absently stroked the baby's head, Miguel was saying, "Funnyman, funnyman," which usually got a response from any adult. The policeman did not think, "Whose baby?"—babies are so usual in every Mexican household that it didn't occur to him to wonder. Meanwhile, Raf was on our roof, and at the first sign that the questioning concerned his presence in the house Raf would have been away over the roofs.

At our first meeting with our lady lawyer, we sat in the anteroom waiting until the door opened and her secretary said to George in Spanish, "Perhaps you could help us?" Our lawyer was standing on her desk, from which she was vainly trying to reach the light which hung on a central cord from the ceiling. We introduced ourselves, and George changed places with her and fixed the light. Then we said to her, "Two men, obviously from the C.I.A., are watching us. Can you do something about it?"

She replied, "That's not done in Mexico, we don't have an F.B.I. or a C.I.A.; you must be mistaken."

We insisted, and she said, "Meet me early tomorrow morning at *Gobernación* [the Department of the Interior] and we will see who it is that you say is bothering you."

Next morning we entered office after office, where Carmen, our lawyer, would say to the secretary, "Oh Angela," (or Maria, or Josefa) "may I please look in your files?"

"Certainly Carmencita," was the reply. Whereupon Carmen would call us over to look at picture after picture in the files. We did not recognize our men. "Oh," said Carmen, "this is serious; they must be from the presidential secret police. We will go outside and look for them on the steps of the palace, where they congregate in the mornings."

As we walked toward the steps we saw our men and pointed them out to Carmen, who walked directly up to one of them. "My clients tell me that you are bothering them," she said. "That is very ugly [*Es muy feo*]. I want you to stop at once. I want you to promise that you will not do it anymore. I am instructing them to tell me at once if you do it again. If there is something you want to know, please come to me. I will confer with my clients. I will speak for them." We never saw the men again.

It is remarkable and strange that in the years when we were being questioned by the F.B.I. and the C.I.A., our families were never disturbed, nor questioned. In Mexico we were friendly with many of the Hollywood exiles; George was in a way "their" proletarian, because George and his partner Carlos had a furniture factory, and our acquaintances turned any job they had over to George.

I began to paint, and George and I both attended an art school in Mexico City; George attended because this was one of the ways to collect G.I. job-training money. He sketched and carved in wood while I sketched the model and worked in clay and in paint, but we did not talk to our friends about poetry, our publishing venture in France, or our connection to the poets. One day our friend Alice came knocking at our door. She was indignant. "I have been reading William Carlos Williams' autobiography, and in it he mentions meeting at your house in Brooklyn, and that you were part of a group that published and wrote poetry! You never told me you were intellectuals!" I agreed with her that it was a failure in friendship not to have been frank with her.

On our return to the United States, George and I determined to present ourselves as who we were, with all our past included. The first taxi man George encountered in Brooklyn said, "It's cold enough to freeze the balls off a brass monkey."

George in a previous stage of our "proletarianization" might have replied in kind, but he answered, "The weather is extremely cold."

"Yes," the taxi man replied, "it's seasonable."

We have always felt that our writing required distance from the politics of experience. Even the ideology of day-to-day politics is not a far-reaching truth. Our minds were occupied with these expedients in very material ways, and our stay in Mexico had been forced upon us. We were in exile in a country we had chosen only because we could enter Mexico without a passport when a passport was refused us. Our lives then were occupied with earning extra money in order to live a bourgeois life in Mexico, because to live as the lower classes live in Mexico is a life fraught with danger due to the lack of hygiene in such a poverty-stricken, undeveloped country. We were not expatriates by choice, and we were unrelenting in withholding ourselves from becoming exiles forever. We wanted more than anything to return home to the United States. To be artists in these conditions was impossible to us. We needed to be freely in our own country, to have time to assimilate the violent years before turning them into thought and poetry.

The last year I was in Mexico I was disturbed, and for a longer time than I realized I needed help. My need was for a psychiatrist, but to even say that word was admitting weakness. I felt guilty and feared that my life with George would be threatened by this exposure. My need was finally desperate, and although George was reluctant, I convinced him that I needed help from outside our private world, from which I could not now find my way forward. I found a Mexican psychiatrist, who had recently returned from study in the United States. He was young and intelligent and had advanced ideas of women's freedom. I sat and talked; I thought one began at the beginning, but he cut me short—"Let's get on with it, what is on your mind right now, *now*. We'll take it from there. Write down your dreams, and at the next session we will discuss them. Think hard about what it is that you want. We'll try to get through this very quickly."

I went home and dreamed. I was standing beside a deep black hole at the top of a hill. I drew back from the rim with a feeling of fear and terror. I turned and went away from the black abyss, to where a little man was standing smiling, eating peanuts; he gave me some and ran down the hill, and I ran after him. I did not want to die yet, but what was it that I wanted? I dreamed and dreamed. I thought hard about what I wanted. The psychiatrist and I moved fast through my frustrations and my wild casting about to put blame on others—anywhere but on myself for not being what I wanted to be. Time after time he said patiently, "But no one is preventing you; you are free to move forward, to become whatever it is you decide to become."

I thought about identities within which I had lived and about the frustration of being only wife and mother. So many years! The years were full, and full of meaning, but there was now no necessity for continuing in the old forms of keeping a big house and maintaining an ambience for Linda and George. George had an outside world with his furniture business, and Linda was going away—her future seemed full to her. We were soon going back to the United States, and I was full of fear. My fears were not unreasonable, but they made my future seem fraught with uncertainty and indecisiveness. I was paralyzed. I had been brave with a sort of frontier bravery when it had been necessary, when we had left the United States and danger had been real and immediate. Now my fears were vague; I was suffering anxiety.

The psychiatrist asked to see George and Linda. George had a dream: he and his sister were going through his father's papers after his father's death. In a file marked "miscellaneous" was a paper entitled "How to Prevent Rust in Copper." George thought, "My old man was a little frivolous perhaps, but he certainly knew that copper does not rust." He shook the bed with his laughter, but I did not find the dream funny. Dreams that seem funny are, in my experience, the ones to watch out for; they are the jokers. Sometimes the dream is saying what is so deeply hidden that one's reaction of laughter protects one from understanding what the meaning is. But George tells of driving on Avenida Insurgentes in Mexico City, weaving the truck from side to side, laughing at the dream of rust in copper that he was going to discuss with the psychiatrist. When he sobered and drew up to the curb, he said to himself, "I'll kill myself driving this way," and drove the rest of the way carefully. When he told the doctor the dream, laughing again at its ridiculousness, the doctor stopped him.

"You were dreaming that you don't want to rust," he said. On the way home George stopped and bought a pad of paper and some pencils and started to write *The Materials*.

In 1975 a friend was remonstrating with me; she wanted me to make a return trip to Mexico. I replied, "No, I don't think I'll ever want to go to Mexico again."

"Why Mary," she said in surprise, "those were the happiest days of our lives."

U.S. passports were being issued again in 1958, and we began to plan our return to the United States. We engaged a New York lawyer who had made a public statement that he would take any case in which a passport was refused to a citizen. He wrote a letter for us to the passport division when we found our request for a passport was delayed for an unreasonably long time, and we received the passport at once. A passport meant that our rights as citizens were again being respected—we always had the right to the passport. Joseph McCarthy symbolized more illegalities than this one, but to us a passport meant we were free to leave the United States legally, to go where we chose, to live with all the rights that citizenship presumably guarantees under our constitution—our basic rights of citizenship which had been grievously violated.

SO NEAR

New York had meaning to George for his writing. New York was where he had roots from which to write again; but before we returned to New York to live we made a visit to Linda, who had gone to college in New York. We discussed our attitudes toward our return. We decided to look up everyone we knew and find out what we all made of meeting again; we saw friends, of course, but also acquaintances from twenty or thirty years before—the ancient aunts of George's father's family, his uncles, poets, political acquaintances.

Printmaking seemed to me a remarkable medium, to have the picture that one loved while working on it, and to be able to sell equally original copies. I set myself to return to a discipline of drawing, and to begin the techniques of printmaking when we returned to New York.

In Mexico, Linda and I had talked of being in the United States, where women, in my memory, walked safely even at night, where I would understand all language that flowed around me, and where an evening of conversation would be in my native tongue, and I would not be exhausted from the effort. When we crossed the border to Texas the language flowed; I heard it and I did not understand.

We had neglected to buy automobile insurance for the United States. As we passed the border we said, "Oh well, we'll drive carefully and get the insurance in New York. In New York, George went to see an insurance man and asked, "How do I buy insurance for a car with Mexican plates?"

"Come back tomorrow and I'll have looked up the procedure," said the salesman. Next day he admitted defeat. "Go to the licensing bureau and ask them," he suggested.

George stood in line at the window marked "Information" and asked again, "How do I buy insurance for a car with Mexican plates?"

The man behind the desk wet his finger and leafed through pages of a book. He looked up and said to George, "Do you speak English?"

George turned to me and said, "Let's just drive carefully."

We visited the Zukofskys—Celia, their son Paul and Louis—who were living in Brooklyn. In the course of conversation Celia said, "I don't know what we'll do for a vacation this year."

I impulsively said, "Why don't you come to Mexico with us?" and was immediately stricken by my own words. I had taken on more than I was going to be able to deal with.

Celia replied, "We will."

As we left their apartment I said to George, "I've done it again, inviting them without asking you if you want them, or without knowing if I want them." It was not a good moment to cause strain, but now we were committed. We did indeed want them for our friends, as we had once valued Louis' friendship. But my heart sank.

Our friend Max Pepper, a doctor, laughed at me when I told him what I had done; he laughed at my dismay and my own behavior. Max said, "I can give you Miltown, a tranquilizer—take one each morning and I think you will feel quite tranquil."

"But what about George, he'll have to do the driving, he can't take a tranquilizer."

"For George I have no prescription. It's you, Mary, who asked."

"We'll try to make the trip in five days," said George, who was making the schedule. Indiana was our first stop for sleeping; Celia chose the motel, and I was surprised that she cared so very much about where she slept. There was wall-to-wall carpeting, a heat lamp in the bath and television. Evening in Indiana meant green country, rolling hills, and farmland; the green grass of the motel sloped to wheat fields, and across the highway was a farm center with trees and lawns, cool and moist in the summer evening.

Louis said, "Let's go for a walk."

"I'll stay here and rest," said Celia. Paul, Louis, George and I walked on the paths toward the houses and the one store at the meeting of the roads, and as dusk came on and shadows lengthened the fireflies appeared, first in the fields and then near us on our path.

"Paul," I asked, "did you ever catch fireflies and put them in a jar to light your room at night?"

"No," Paul gravely answered, and I dashed after a firefly and held it in my cupped hands to let Paul see the flash of greenish light that made my fingers glow.

"Here, take it," and I held it out to him, but Paul backed away and the insect escaped. "Too bad," I said, "I'll catch another."

We walked back to meet Celia, who was standing outside the motel talking to a Jewish man. As we came up to them Celia made introductions: "My husband, my son Paul, George Oppen a friend, and Mary who is not one of us." And my expectation of having Celia for my friend disappeared.

We came to the International Bridge to re-enter Mexico and stopped at the customs shed. George got out and walked to the back of the truck with the customs inspector. "How much do I pay if you do not inspect the truck?" asked George.

"Five dollars," replied the inspector.

"But there's nothing illegal in it," said George.

"In that case, one dollar," said the inspector.

After our unsuccessful attempt to buy insurance for the truck in New York it was a relief to be back in Mexico, where as long as the money holds out one can arrive at an understanding with officials.

After our first night in Mexico, George and Paul and I were up first, standing outside beside our panel truck, waiting for the others to come along for breakfast. "Paul," I asked, "can you balance on this curb-strip here, between the cars?" There was a six-inch raised strip separating the parked cars. "You can balance if you tense your belly muscles; you could balance the same way if you were ten feet up. It's a Yoga exercise, try it!" We were laughing at ourselves, balancing with our arms outspread like two birds, being silly.

"Paul," Celia's voice came, "I don't think you should be doing that." With a slight motion of annoyance Paul stepped off the six-inch curb.

We drove deeper into Mexico on long straight roads without a curve for two hundred miles south of Laredo. Paul sat between his parents, bored with us grown-ups, saying little; we watched the desert on each side of the road, where we occasionally saw a man or a woman walking, or a pig or a donkey near an adobe hut back from the highway. A drought held the land; there was no green anywhere except in the arroyos or dry watercourses, where the roots of cottonwoods sucked moisture from deep below the surface. We were all a little sleepy. The road was, in places, on a raised dike between low fields, and driving on the dike made the road even more uneventful, but safer from the flash floods that could in minutes flood the roads. We watched the mountains for a sign of clouds, but there was not a cloud in the sky, no water for this parched land. A young heifer stood dejectedly beside the road on our right hand; as we approached her, George slowed the truck and the cow looked away. George proceeded, and as we drew abreast of her, she suddenly gave a wild leap and landed in front of our car. We hit her, and she skidded across the road and slid, all feet braced under her, onto the left shoulder of the road. We scarcely felt the bump, and I jumped out to inspect the damage; I could see that the car was not injured, but I gave a gesture of dismay. "We are covered with cow shit."

Paul began to laugh, released laughter from days of restrained behavior; he clambered out over his parents' knees and said, "Two thousand miles of driving and this is the first funny thing that has happened!"

We were plastered with a thin coating, and no matter what any of us called it from then on, Paul laughed. We cleared the windshield and the headlights, but we were unable to wash the car until we were at home in our own garden in Mexico City. It was enough to even insinuate the situation with the cow and Paul would laugh, with thoroughly fifteen-year-old humor. He regaled us with his favorite jokes, having to do with orchestra conductors, and with anecdotes of the music school; he laughed at himself, at his own jokes, some of them pretty old and decrepit. We told him our favorite jokes and laughed too.

After we had returned to New York and George was writing *The Materials*, our relationship with Louis was no longer the same. We loved and cherished Louis still from our early friendship and from George's relationship with Louis when George had been the nineteen-year-old poet learning from Louis. "He taught me everything," said George. But now, with George at fifty returned to poetry, and Louis a few years older, the relationship was a different one, one of equals. George was writing out of many years of his life; he was full of his own poetry, and he was about to be published again. And again, Louis asked, "Do you like your poetry better than mine?"

With a lifetime of poetry to be written, George answered "Yes." George, insisting on clarity and understanding, speaking of his difficulty in knowing if the readers would understand; Louis, with a shrug replying, "It doesn't matter, they don't care if they understand you or not." Louis was implying, why don't you write like me—does the reader care whether you have arrived at truth?

Not knowing how to say it without insulting Louis, but implying that Louis used incomprehensibility and obscurity as a tactic, George said, "You're tougher than I am, Louis," referring to Louis' disregard of the reader.

To George "tough" meant an operator, a schemer. To Louis the term probably meant being of a lower class, a street kid. He turned pale and replied, "You would not use that word if you knew what it means to me."

Long before, jokingly, George had once said to Louis, "Drop dead!" and Louis had replied by turning pale. When he could speak, he said, "It's an exoticism."

We went for a few more walks together, but Celia ceased to join us, and then Louis stopped coming. Our friendship was at an end. I think the Zukofskys were moving into a very private world, to which few were admitted.

How does one describe it? We had friendship and love with Louis a long time ago, when Louis was the slightly older, brilliant prodigy. His bitterness which we glimpsed and the stubbornness with which he holds himself aloof from the people in the world of poetry leave only his poetry to tell all that Louis, and perhaps Celia too, wish to be known about themselves. In the poetry is hidden the record of their lives, convoluted and at times impossible to decipher. It was Louis' intention not to be easily or clearly understood—this was the argument between George and Louis. Music is in Zukofsky's poetry, and if that is all one can have from it, one can be grateful that a great deal of his poetry does indeed sing.

In 1968 in Wisconsin, during an interview, the discussion concerned Zukofsky's study of Shakespeare's Bottom, "a metaphysics of cognition" based upon what he conceived to be Shakespeare's definition of love. Louis said, "So much for epistemology . . . the theory of knowledge, which is done away with in *Bottom* . . . when I was through with doing away with epistemology in *Bottom* . . . The interviewer asked, "What do you mean, you got rid of epistemology in *Bottom*? The work seems to me all epistemology." Zukofsky replied, "The questions are their own answers. You want to say 'yes,' say 'yes'; you want to say 'no,' say 'no.'" Asked "Where does the idea of love fit in?" he replied, "Well, it's like my horses. If you're good enough to run or feel like running, you run. If you want to live, you love: if you don't want to live, you hate—that's all . . . it's as simple as that."

Robert Duncan explained to us recently that Louis, Pound, and Rexroth misunderstood our financial position; Louis expected us to help him more than we did, and his disappointment probably colored his relations with us from the time we discontinued To Publishers. Duncan said, "Did you know that Pound was preparing all his works for To Publishers to print?" We had not known.

In 1959, on our return from Mexico, we walked once again with Charles Reznikoff, who had been ill, and who had lost his job when the law book company dissolved. Al Lewin, a friend of Charles' youth who had written poems and read and discussed them with Charles, was visiting New York. Charles told us, "Al's poems were too fancy, he wrote them fast too; I preferred mine, but I benefited from the discussion because Al discussed every word." Al was living at an elegant hotel and Charles, who was going to visit him, said, "I find that one had better be rich if one has a rich friend. Now I am on my way to visit Al, and I must stop in here at this delicatessen to buy him a kind of bread that he remembers from our boyhood days." We entered the shop, Charles pointed to a loaf of pumpernickel bread and the clerk wrapped it; then, handing it to Charles, he said, "One dollar, please."

"You see?" said Charles. "And every time the word *haiku* enters our conversation, Al says to me, 'I think those translations by Arthur Waley are the best; I love that book you gave me, I wish I had the others.' I must buy them for him—I am so poor and he is so rich."

George, now well launched on *The Materials*, wrote to Henry Rago, editor of *Poetry* in Chicago, "Do you remember me?"

Henry wrote back, inviting George to send some poems. George wrote to James Laughlin of New Directions, asking him if he would print a book of poems. George's sister, June Degnan, who was publishing the *San Francisco Review*, offered to publish two books by George with New Directions. James Laughlin wrote to George, "I will publish your book with or without your sister's partnership." The books were published by New Directions with *San Francisco Review*.

Charles Reznikoff was sixty-six years old when we looked him up in New York. His poetry was largely unrecognized, and he was in very low spirits. George discussed with Zukofsky whether he thought Charles would agree to being published if New Directions could be persuaded. Zukofsky said, "I think Rezi does not care about any but a Jewish audience."

George thought for a moment. "But what about Mary?" he asked.

Louis replied, "Oh, I guess he thinks of Mary as Jewish."

Rezi agreed to be published; James Laughlin and George's sister too were pleased. George's book, *The Materials*, and Charles Reznikoff's book, *By the Waters of Manhattan*, were published at the same time. The Gotham Book Mart gave a party at the time of publication, and among the people who came to the party was Sir Charles (C.P.) Snow, who had written, at June Degnan's request, a foreword for Reznikoff's book. Reznikoff had never met Sir Charles, nor had Sir Charles known Rezi's poems before he was asked to write the foreword. At their meeting Sir Charles bent over and said, "Er, ah, you aren't—er, ah—as thin as I thought you'd be." George was introduced next; George, who is tall enough and thin enough for anyone's idea of a poet, left Sir Charles with nothing to say. They smiled and shook hands.

While signing books, in a lull George signed one and handed it to Charles Reznikoff. "Read it in health," said George.

Rezi accepted it gravely and corrected George's translation from Yiddish, "Read it in *good* health."

George and Charles came West together on a reading tour after *The Materials* and *By the Waters of Manhattan* were published. At one of the colleges they sat, after reading, for a discussion of students' work, with each young person's poem making the rounds of the table. When Charles had finished reading one of the poems, he laid it down, folded his hands, and with one eyebrow higher than the other said, "If I come to a poem like this when I am reading, I turn the page."

In Michigan, at a poetry conference to which George and Charles as well as many other poets had been invited in the early 1970s, we found ourselves, men and women, housed in a women's dormitory with one bathroom for both sexes.

Charles had forgotten to bring soap, and when I supplied him I watched while, with his towel over his arm, Charles set out for a long walk to a dormitory where he had found a bathroom for men only. At this same conference, young people showed their love for Charles and for his poetry by a standing ovation after he finished reading. As Charles bowed and accepted the ovation, he was murmuring what he had planned to say: "I hope I haven't taken up too much of your time."

The students teased him thereafter; after talking to him about a poem, as they left him they said, "We hope we haven't taken up too much of your time."

In San Francisco Charles was invited to read, and George and I went to his hotel to accompany him to the reading. He was not there; we waited, and presently Charles appeared, looking very much the New Yorker in black overcoat and astrakhan hat, carrying his briefcase in one hand. "Have you had breakfast, or do you want lunch?"

"No," he replied, "I had breakfast at seven, and I've been out walking."

On our return to the United States, we paid two visits to William Carlos Williams. On the first visit his wife Floss cautioned us not to stay long, that Bill had difficulty in talking since he had had the strokes, and that he tired easily; we assured her we would leave when she thought we should go. Floss remained in the room to help Bill remember the words which came painfully to him now, but soon she left, as Bill was talking easily and was exultant that he was having no difficulty with speech. George was soon to read at the Guggenheim Museum (I think it was George's first reading), and Bill asked George to read to him. George read "Population":

> *Like a flat sea,*
> *Here is where we are, the empty reaches*
> *Empty of ourselves*

Where dark, light, sound
Shatter the mind born
Alone to ocean

Save we are
A crowd, a population, those
Born, those not yet dead, the moment's

Populace, sea-borne and violent, finding
Incredibly under the sense the rough deck
Inhabited, and what it always was.

Bill said, "George, promise me that you will read that poem slowly, and that you will read it twice at the Guggenheim."

George replied, "I wouldn't dare."

Bill said, "Tell'em I told you to."

As we stood up to go, Bill stood up too, wavering and fragile where he had been straight and tall; but when I kissed him it was a young man's kiss.

OTHER
WRITINGS

RE: MAINE

our boat makes a way for us
a free passage
on a sea of glass
or held in the surges
our words move toward
each other

I

The anchor flukes strike down through ooze to rock. This island can be entered up a bank of drifted wood and worn round stones on a path as small as a deer's trail, but it is made by humans. The firs and spruce stand thick, occasional birch, maple, and oak bring light and movement into dense shade in August, on the forest floor. We walk on moss, and ancient stones flat as masonry, make steps. We climb beside trunks of trees, and through branches we see our boat below, the water smooth, glassy, clear. Stones below us enter water, green stones, great rocks of an upheaval more recent than the ancient stones of the steps up the cliff.

A chick-a-dee infant discovers us, he comes chirping down branches, hops from tree to tree—comes close, flutters his wings, asking for food. His parent calls—mouth full of bugs, calls and flies from branch to branch, baby follows, follows for food, hops near us again to see.

A cairn to mark the turn. Probably the piles of rocks mark the path to be cleared anew each spring, rocks stacked make precarious sculptures, sharp angled slabs and shards of the most ancient stones. The cairns are lichen-covered, stained with circles, colors spread and grow on the rock surfaces. Soil is made of fallen spruce needles, birch-leaves, rotting stone; tree's roots are covered with moss, inches deep and various in kinds of moss and shades of green, the pile of this carpet is close-grown, or clustered stars, resilient where the foot falls: we leave no mark. A plank shaped by a carpenter for some other use at some other time, found on the beach, is now a bridge, and nailed to a large root, it makes a firm crossing. Berries and leaves of Bunch-berry are red on each side of the path where we come out of the forest to stand on a narrow, high end of the island above the water; nearly silent water in no wind, water surface is glassy, it swells and recedes—it does not break, it soughs—hsssss—hwww. We stand quiet, we hear it rise and recede.

The path divides and we climb high; steps cut in rich mold, held in place by cedar roots: cedar trees, trunks smooth with fans of cedar branches hang quiet, ferns grow up through the moss. We climb into the sun. Above the tree-tops steps are cut in the rock, we feel beneath our feet the back-bone of the island, back-bone thrust up from the ocean floor deep in Penobscot Bay. Great Spruce Head, from whose top we can see the islands of the bay: Eagle Island in the distance, across from us Dirigo and Bear, and off to the south North Haven Island, but between them all are the rocks, spits of sand, and pebbles; Scrag Island is a crag with two trees and piles of stones like slag, where a fisherman has a snug all-year house with storm-windows still up in August and a complex television mast stayed to stand in the winds. The sea still lies glassy, but in the center of the small islands we see on the water that the wind is coming. Southwest wind is turning the water dark blue and streaks of darker blue riffle and sweep in some logic they find among the islands. To the north, east, and west, the mountains rise blue, Blue Hill, the Camden Hills, and off to the east Cadillac Mountain, purple because its rock is rosy-gray granite. Now it is a deeper blue than the other mountains, it shows its sixty miles' distance from us here. We retrace our steps. Back-bone, cairn to cairn. Maine forests are impenetrable without a man-made path. We've tried to walk or climb into forests here in Maine, but exhausted, confused, assailed by black-flies and mosquitoes, we've been lost in dense forest growth pervading as jungle and as fast growing. At the feet of spruce are spruce trees one inch high, up through the moss the new trees start from seed, next year they grow first branches, rise in height, with lichens and dead branches in the lower levels of the forest where light is scarce, their roots in gloom, their branches are nearly black, their green is so dark against the sky. Two ospreys build their nest in the top of a tall, old, broken spruce. They find a current of air and lie against the sky above the cliff to watch over their fierce young one who sits like a phoenix in the nest: he fixes their gaze, whistles his piercing cry: they answer. We find a long black feather—a raven's feather; nearby are shells, a perfect large sea-snail shell, clam-shells, and mussel-shells lying with both halves open, emptied and cast beside the path or scattered on the moss, far above the beaches. We've seen ten different mushrooms, and a yellow and brown velvet lichen like a velvet hat left lying on the ground beside an old tree-trunk. Flowers grow in the moss and ferns, faces turned down, petals thrust face down to the moss—Pipsissewa, used by the Indians as a medicine.

We near our beach, retrace our path over the plank-bridge to our orange, inflated canoe. We carry it to the water's edge, step in and float on water. We are beside the island, no way is now visible to penetrate it.

II

We flew kites that year, kites that flew high and steady. An engineer and his family visited us that summer and we all made kites. I put them in the barn when the engineer left and Marge and her little brother Samuel came in the afternoons, put the baby in the shade and flew one kite or another in the field beside the house. Marge caused more anxiety to her parents than all the other children. She would go to Boston, she would go to Washington D.C. They drove her there, but she beat them home both times; couldn't deal with the big world she was unaccustomed to. She made friends and then fell in love with a Black Portuguese boy who took her home to his mother. They married and she tried to live with him in his mother's house in a Boston slum. "I got up when he was sleeping, I slept when he was awake. When we walked I was a few steps behind him—he never heard a word I said and I didn't understand their speech. He played cards or practiced his music with other young men. He played the drums, and he shipped out in the Merchant Marine to earn money, and was seldom at home."

"Why did you love him, Marge, what was it about him?"

"He looked like Belafonte," she said in her low, slow, reluctant speech. She came home. Still almost a child herself, she now has a child, a child half-Black, half-Portuguese Black, a glowingly beautiful dark child on these islands of descendants of Scotch-Irish pale people.

"I mean," said Marge, clapping her hands for the baby to dance with her first steps, "she has *Africa* in her veins!"

Marge walked with me that summer, took me to her favorite haunts where Mumma shot the deer. We walked on a logging-road fast disappearing in the fir forest that grows fast and thick. She says, "Over there is an old silver mine that someone tried to work." She showed me a miniature graveyard. "Samuel and I made it for all the pets." In a circle of trees in deep forest, small blocks of native granite marking graves. "My bird, our dog"— with a stone, *Duchess* scratched on the polished fragment of granite, "Duchess went deaf and was run over on the highway."

She and Samuel, the youngest boy, felt close and intimate that summer. Marge tried to talk to us that summer, tried and the effort failed. She tried hard. She came from such shy and quiet people who talk little of what is important to their lives. They keep secret how they feel, how they feel toward each other, what they want in their lives.

Our friend Steve was visiting us and we were talking of Russian Roulette when Marge and the baby came to visit. Steve explained the game to her. . . . She sat, silent as usual, but I heard her murmur, "I could play Russian Roulette and not lose." She is a little wandering spirit—when we first met her she said, "I will get to Peru."

Now in another summer she is married to an insistent suitor, she has a second child, but she lives a strange life. The children reflect her strong, strange adventurous spirit. Not a strange spirit to someone out there adventuring, but she is an adventurer who must live at home. But where Marge is life is not ordinary. One year she couldn't bear to be in the same house with her husband. She took the children and moved into a cabin in deep woods—in Maine, in winter! But it is her country, and they survived. Her husband worried about her, begged her to return. Perhaps she is his spirit of adventure. He bought her a car, made her kitchen modern and shining, but she stays outside, works all the land anyone offers her, plants gardens that grow. Even in a year of drought Marge's gardens grow. She is dear to her husband and very much trouble. The children are bright. "Little devils," their grandmother says. "I would rather have all my other grandchildren in the house at once than Marge's two." The little girl is in school now, the outstanding child in her class, and the teacher loves her. She is a diffcrent child to the teacher than she is to her grandmother, or to her mother's husband. Her own father loves her too, calls her on her birthday, and on Christmas. This year, her third at school, a child called her *Dirty Nigger*. Neither of the children knew what the words meant, but Marge comes to us for comfort and to plan her strategy for protecting this wonderful child, for in the future there will be more, more name-calling, and here in the islands the child may suffer. "Beautiful, she is so beautiful, with a father who calls her on her birthday. He loves her too, even though," Marge says, "he couldn't take care of us down there in Boston, so I came home."

III

Captain Frank sits out in front, almost sightless, nearly deaf, smoking the little corn-cob pipe that George brought him at the beginning of summer. From my bicycle, I shout, "Hello, Captain Frank." He raises his arm in greeting, peering to find someone to connect with my voice. Captain Frank came to Eleanor's birthday party, everyone was there, everyone she still remembers. (Everyone, that is, who is still alive.) Captain Frank stands in the doorway, leans there until he has the attention of the roomful of people, shouts, "Eleanor, another eighty years and maybe you'll be all growed up!"

She came one summer from upstate New York, a girl—Hudson River-Dutch. A tall, lank woman on an island of short, wide women, she married that first summer, a son of a farmer on the island. He had come to meet the steamer that brought Eleanor to Maine. She had sailed down the Hudson on her father's boat, a working boat, the last of the sailing-barges on the Hudson River, New York to Boston by steamer, on a smaller steamer to Portland, and smaller still, the boat from Portland to Rockland, and then to the Penobscot by one of the many little steamers that were the means of transportation for the islands. A dirt covered promontory of jagged granite blocks made the landing, where every summer a hundred people came for their summer vacations. They came, each to a favorite spot, "a camp," or a rented room in a house opened to summer visitors, or to their own houses. A summer population that was lively, vacationers who brought employment to the islanders to augment their income from fishing or from lumbering, or from shipping out on lumber-schooners or as captain or as crew on the yachts of the rich. The island young people met the steamer at the landing, walking or coming by horse-carriage to meet and to view the new arrivals, and to escort them to their summer homes. Young people greeted friends from past summers, they flirted with boys and girls who arrived with these families. Some families even brought their own horses and carriages in order to have their own transportation on the island. Summertime is the busy time in the islands, summertime means work for those who live year round on the islands, for the women as well as for the men. For the young people it means also the return of the dances that are held in a great barn, a boat builder's barn, used for their dances during the summer; picnics, swimming at ponds warm enough to allow swimming; or trips to places of particular beauty.

Eleanor married into an old island family, and her young husband took her to live in a small house near his family's large farm-house whose acres stretched down to the bay—but Eleanor had no children. She knew, at last, that she would have no children of her own, all her young friends had their first baby, then a second, even a third and she had none. She was barren and desolate. A sister back in New York State died suddenly, leaving three boys. Her sisters were willing to take one boy each, but Eleanor wanted all three. She asked her husband if he was willing to take the boys. "We're too young to take on all that responsibility, Eleanor," he said. "They aren't ours." But Eleanor was persistent, it was her chance to have children, and they were her own sister's children, close to her by blood. She was persistent, she tells. "When I baked, I'd say, 'Isn't it a shame the three boys can't have some of this?' Or when we went sleigh-riding or skating or picnicking, I'd say, 'How the three boys would enjoy this.'" Until one day her husband said, "Eleanor, you'd better send for the boys."

Her husband is long dead, now, and her loyal "boys" visit her in the summers where she now lives again in the little house near the water's edge, the old farm-house and most of the acres sold long ago to summer-people.

IV

In thick fog by the time we passed the bell-buoy, we noted the time, measured the distance on the chart, took a compass-reading on our heading, guessed at our speed and the speed of the current, and waited for Sylvester's Cove to show up out of the fog: vaguely it appeared, but we were almost on it before we saw it. I chose to return on a reverse course, and to wait for the fog to lift. We waited at our mooring until two o'clock when the fog lifted suddenly and we set out again, but with an adverse tide. Visitors, headed for the 4th of July picnic on our island, waved to us from the mail-boat. We were near the bell-buoy for an hour, held by the current and the tide, but the day was fine and we were glad to be in the boat, on the water. The wind freshened and we sailed to Stonington, anchored near the old granite-polishing site under the quarry-derrick, and went in search of a room and a meal. After dark we walked to the main street to watch the fireworks, but the fog returned. The little street was jammed with people and with cars.

Next morning after breakfast we sailed down Stonington Reach past West Mark, and past Scraggy Ledge, past the big red bell out in the middle of the crossing in open seas to Vinalhaven. We tacked back and forth with a southwest wind; on the oceanward tack heading out to the great granite tower which marks the entrance to Penobscot Bay, tacking back to Vinalhaven Island where we were becalmed as we approached land. On every tack we were stopped, although we could see the wind dancing on the water. The tide was sweeping us south where we wanted to go, but when we approached land we were stopped, we couldn't move—a sea of glue. I put up our big, new, light jib and we worked out to sea to sail fast, but each time we returned to land—the sea of glue. In Vinalhaven at last, we anchored in front of our acquaintance's house. He came out in his little sailboat to advise us on our mooring, and offered his pier for our landing. We left our canoe on Mr. Moyer's pier and stayed for a drink. I asked him how old he had been when he played his first concert, "I must have been eleven years old, it was in San Francisco, three weeks before the great earthquake." He played for us on his little spinet.

In the night I awoke, thinking about the sea of glue, and realized that an upward pressure had made the water dance and that the landward breeze lifting over the high island had left a vacuum, creating the dancing waves.

In the morning in a ten-mile wind, after a swift get-a-way like a runaway horse (we nearly ran down a moored boat that was hidden from our view by our sail)—we were in Vinal Reach with a beam-wind favoring us through islands: narrow passages, wondrously beautiful water with birds, islands, trees, vistas.

Sailing day after day, the first sensations of sailing each year merge with other trips: the foggy day into Stonington on the 4th of July mingles in memory with the 4th of July when we had arrived in Stonington in thunder and lightning, in downpour, and the grocery-store lady, Mrs. Bartlett, found us a room. I awoke, in still another summer, not having slept soundly, in a room in Mrs. Robinson's guest-house in Camden. The wind had blown hard all night. It was four-thirty in the morning, and there was some visibility. "Would you like to sail home now?" I asked George. The weather report had predicted heavy fog for two days, and it seemed to me to be not yet impenetrably thick. We left the harbor at five, wind still south to southwest, a favorable wind for home; the tide until eight would be in-coming. We sailed fast in a ten-mile wind for Job's Crossing. We decided on compensation of 20° for safety's sake. Fog became dense, we sailed fast, and suddenly there was an islet, low in the water on our right hand and a wooded island on our left! I am the navigator, and in such moments I must decide in a split second—hold off or continue, port or starboard—decide, fast, fast—remember which island is low in the water, which island has a long sand-spit out from it, which island has that bent tree? "We are down-wind from La Selle's Island. Haul in the sails and hold up for Job's Crossing!"

George called out, "There's a bell—on our right—"

"Quick, George, quick! Hold up, hold up! This is Job's Crossing and we are too far down wind, we can't cross the bar so close to the sand-spit, we have to be at the five foot spot." The current had been even stronger than we had calculated, or I had not held a true course when I had been steering. (The second time that summer I had allowed that to happen.) The egg-shell we sail in, the little Day-Sailer held up valiantly, we swept through the opening and held our course for home. Fog cleared suddenly, and as we neared Northhaven Island we could see clearly: Channel Rock, Fling Island, Eagle, and even Hard-head beyond Eagle and both Porcupines—

and there was Robert Quinn, our friend, out hauling his lobster-pots. He hailed us with an arm uplifted from work, and we were home.

V

We wake to the raucous clatter and din of a hundred eider-ducks, crows, and gulls. The beach is theirs at dawn and by the time I have watched the sun come up behind Hard-head, and have set foot on the beach, I can see who has walked here before me since the last tide erased all marks. I like to say that my feet make the first marks, but mine have never been the first. This morning a large deer's tracks pointed up the beach with each step out of the water, to disappear into the trees: probably a buck to add to the does we counted in the early morning in the field below our windows, or in the dusk last evening, when they did not yet know we were here. This first morning a deer's face appeared at our bedroom window, gazing in. On the beach bird-tracks and bird-noises are still loud, but the birds quickly move out, onto the water. Eider-ducks with flotillas of ducklings are quack-quacking in an interminable conversation between mamma and babies. They sit on the floating seaweed and dive below the surface for their food, the mother anxiously trying to keep her little ones close. If danger threatens the ducklings climb aboard mamma. Gulls attack them, seals attack them, sea-crows and cormorants too. If a mother duck brings two or three to adolescence from a hatching of twelve or fourteen, she is a good mother.

To line the nest with eider-down, the mother duck plucks down from her own breast, and as this is also a time of molting for all the adults, while the babies are helpless, they too cannot fly.

From the top of the island which is flat and cleared of spruce and pine, the maples, the oaks, and the birch and alder growth, I look out, turn slowly, survey the bay in a 360° uninterrupted view: after many summers here I can identify and name all the islands I can see. Into the far distance islands lie spread out in silvery water. Far away dark shapes are scattered across an expanse of Penobscot Bay as wide as one's eye, reaching the limit of vision—islands forever, too many to count. I see Isle au Haute, pronounced here Isle "Oh Holt," and there is even a small brown lump of a rock named Colby Pup, a reminder to me that my family sprang up here long ago during the great migrations from England. At the end of Merchants Row, a clear almost straight course for sailing east or west, the wind is abeam, and I can see on any day both sail- and motor-boats of summer visitors making their way homeward toward Portland and Boston, or sailing east to a summer-world that's heaven. I look to the mainland and can make out the prominent peaks. The further distant are the mountains near Bar Harbor: Mount Desert, Cadillac Mountain. To the west are the Camden Hills.

Almost as accurate as looking at the calendar, fog tells us it is July, fog makes an enclosed world, no one hurries and it is a time to talk. Helene comes to visit, to tell us of her life in the months we have been away. Fog encloses us, no one looks on and we talk, while our eyes are searching, searching, looking, seeing as far as vision permits: the sea, the wind, the fog are present in our vision and in our minds. As I write this, remembering, I return to that white light of fog and that deep, almost dreaming, almost unconscious state of being.

On the mainland land surrounds us, land-peopled, busy. On our small island we are surrounded by sea until our opinions, even our prejudices seem altered, perhaps because the sea comes first, second things are touched and altered as are the ways of the sea in its tides: if not this tide, then the next will surely come again in a rhythm that requires my rhythms to change in some way too, a slower and surer order in my mind.

We sailed to the island at the end of one summer to ask if a place could be found for us. Yes, the camp that was called "Two Bits." We will put it together as three bits. Three 8′ x 8′ cedar rooms left behind many years ago by a summer visitor who could no longer come to the island. The three-room miniature camp was put together with aluminum foil insulation on the inner ceiling, and with bright green fiber-glass roofing that can be seen, a landmark for the mail-boat or other passing boats; a fine old wood, coal, and canned gas stove, a gas refrigerator and electricity, two water tanks, one on each side of the end of the building, to provide water—when there is rain enough, or we carry water from a fine spring on the lighthouse beach. Lighthouse Beach, where at one end at low tide we could see the pilings of the lighthouse pier, from the days when the lighthouse had been inhabited. The family had been provided for many years with good anthracite coal, unloaded in baskets and carried from the boat up the hill in baskets. In rough weather and with accidents a great deal of coal must have spilled into the sea, for on any day we can gather a bushel or so of coal, enough to keep our fire overnight when it is cold. George and I glean wood from the beach, from the forest, and with a sharp little Finnish saw we cut wood, trying to keep ahead of our daily needs.

Our camp is an acre or two of Maine in dense fir and spruce woods, growing so thickly that we can be lost when we step a few yards into them. We have tied pieces of white cloth to the trees to mark a path to the landing. In the old farm clearing, of which only the foundations of the earlier buildings can now be made out by depressions in the center of the field, eighty-year-old apple trees still bloom, and in a tangle of raspberry vines and tiger-lilies, we make out the garden of the old homestead. In the severe winters of Maine, a house that is not lived in and cared for disappears as rapidly as a house in the tropics. Nothing of the house and barn of this farm remain. The row of seven magnificent locust trees stands, and sprouts spring up each spring everywhere, and must be cut back if they are not to become forest again in a very short time. We built soil of seaweed and mulch from the floor of the forest, where there was no soil, only stones, and in the first year grew vegetables that helped to feed us and our few summer visitors. I have lived most of my life in cities, but in my early childhood I had a garden and when I can have a garden it is a return, it awakens memories I did not know I had.

In the fog of July, George and I have been transplanting flowers and plants, a clump of Evening Primrose. (The moths like them because they stay open at night.) We took the most beautiful path on the island yesterday: the path to the lighthouse, where we dug a clump of Monk's-hood for Joy Stewart. Later I washed them and separated the roots, put them in a mailbag, and sent them off on the mail-boat. They will be beautiful near Pumpkin Island lighthouse.

One fine evening, sailing from Swan's Island into a fiery sunset, we sailed on as the full moon rose, sailing toward the blinking light which we saw all the long, almost windless night, flashing SOS—SOS, until at dawn we anchored in the little harbor of Pumpkin Island.

Just to say "Island" brings to my mind the feeling that I love, cut off from the mainland, water on all sides, view unbroken in any direction. Sailing to strange islands we make acquaintances, who in subsequent visits become friends. The people in the outer islands in Maine have a sweetness— I use the word not in its present cliché, but to mean an attitude that prevails. On the islands in conversations we find this sweetness. Sometimes we anchor because fog has made it impossible to know where we are. The fog encloses us and we go ashore in an isolation as total as though we are visitors from another planet, and if we meet a citizen of this unknown place we talk in a privacy that makes conversation somehow without risk. I think that people who live their lives on islands, especially on small islands, live in a meditation, thinking about the world out there. The miracle of being here envelops them and makes for the sweetness I feel in them.

George has written a poem called "Ballad":

> She took it that we came—
> I don't know how to say, she said—
>
> Not for anything we did, she said
> Mildly, 'from God'. She said
>
> What I like more than anything
> Is to visit other islands . . .

Two winters in Nassau with June, George's sister, in an arrangement we agreed to try as we were casting about for a way to get away from New York winters, a way of trying another place than New York. It was a step toward our eventual abandonment of New York, but a joined household in Nassau proved to be an impossible arrangement. We don't flourish in the lap of luxury.

George had a native sailboat from Turk island waiting, tied to the dock, when I arrived. We sailed with the owner and his wife aboard. Local sailing boats are from each island, each with its own characteristics, all made of native woods, sails are sewed by hand, still made of heavy canvas, these boats are sailed with great skill, and, of course, with the local knowledge necessary in these coral-filled waters. These boats are sailed long distances. Boats from Haiti come with reels of braided grass for the manufacture of hats and bags to sell to tourists, food from every island, fish for every day consumption, these boats came in every day through the entrances to Providence Island to unload at the town market, boats without motor, they were the craft of very poor people who made the boats themselves or by barter, exchanged labor or their labor's products. Sails were cut deep, with an overlap that swept the cabin-top, every time the boat came about, the sail had to be helped overt the cabin-top. A man or woman stood forward keeping an eye on the bottom which changes continually with the currents and the growth of coral-heads, in the strong currents that sweep around and between the islands a sailboat needs every bit that she can gain on each tack, but the person in the bow says, with a calm voice, "Go-o-o back," and the helmsman sweeps the tiller because one more yard would mean catastrophe. The person forward lets go the jib, someone, usually a child, helps the sail over the house, and the boat goes slowly over at the very last minute, to the other tack. Sails slowly fill and she veers away from the shore or from the underwater coral-head.

For a week we sailed with this boat. Linda and Alex sailed with us, Alex and I fished. When a fish was caught it was quickly gutted, scraped and thrown on a bed of coals that was kept glowing in a box full of ash forward of the cabin where a pot of beans simmered. A fish caught and cooked immediately on hot coals has a taste I've never tasted since.

For the rest of the season we sailed a fine little *Snipe*, a borrowed boat. I learned to read the bottom by the color of the water. If it was clear as the lines on my palm, I knew the depth was at least four feet—yellow, then green, then shades of green out to blue indigo, deep, deep blue at ocean depths, five hundred feet deep in front of the reefs of coral. We sailed around the two islands, in the channel, and occasionally we poked out into the ocean. A trade-wind blows strongly every afternoon, it is to be depended on, and the strength of the wind for our little boat made very lively sailing. Our second winter in Nassau we found a sixteen-foot O'Day day-sailer, very modern and fast. We bought it and began to learn all that it already knew of fast sailing.

Three of us lived in the large house in a garden on Hog island across from New Providence island. During the holidays we invited our friends and family and made a small society, at Christmas, Linda and Alex, June's daughter and her child, Andy, our niece, and her four children. We swam, snorkeled, and collected shells from the myriads that wash up on the beaches, conch was the most common shell as it is a staple in the diet of the people. Conch is a fast growing mollusk that travels on the bottom in colonies, feeding. The discarded shells pile up in dumps which, in time, wear away to become the famous pink sand beaches of some of the islands. In other places pure-white bleached old conches wash up to form white sand beaches. A fresh dump across from Nassau near the tip of Hog island was bright pink with fresh shells dumped daily on the Queen's land, this place was called the "Queen's Bottom."

June bought a little red Triumph automobile that was fitted to become a boat, two propellers drove it in the water, waterproofed and sealed underneath, it was a better boat than car, but as it had been planned for fresh water so it deteriorated very fast in our use of it. It was a very stable boat rather like a small raft, but with great power. When it touched sand the wheels helped it move over ground until one could shift back to wheel-drive. The headlights of the Triumph at night as the craft came across the channel caused a stir, little boys raced on bicycles to see the Triumph creep into or out of the water. On land the propellers caused the same excitement, boys pursued us until we lost them, hoping to see us enter the water.

We had brought our bird, a parakeet, named Bird, who always traveled with us in a tiny cage that Linda had made for him. I carried him in my purse. When we arrived at the airport we put him in a locker until plane time to insure that he was very soundly asleep in the dark place. He sometimes squawked during take-off, but by then it was too late for the stewardess to do anything about his being on board. He remembered places he had been before. When we released him from his cage he zoomed around the room through doorways and back to his cage, never knocking into things. We had to hang something over windows for a day or two until he discovered that there was glass. June had a cat and even though we kept our bedroom door locked and only let the bird fly in that room, somehow the cat sneaked in and George hearing a commotion, turned to see the cat swallowing Bird. George hit the cat, the cat fell off the table and Bird flew out, daunted but unharmed, lacking a few feathers, but alive.

I spent my days fishing: little golden fishes ran in schools in the canal off the beach of Hog Island. Larger fish were in the channel off the end of the dock facing Nassau. Needle-fish rose to my cast in the shallows on the North side of the island. Fish were visible in the waters everywhere.

Many evenings we spent playing parlor games. We also became acquainted with a family at the other end of the island in a very remote house, reached by water or by a long and primitive path through rough coral on the ridge of the island. In the summer the family lived in Connecticut, and every fall the trek to Nassau began by train and then by ship from Miami to Nassau, with many pets, children, and servants. They all came to this remote island every year. Communication to the larger island was only by their own launch, their house was indeed their castle, it was simple, but extravagantly isolated. This life was, for us, all that we had fled from when, much younger we had left San Francisco to find a life of meaning for ourselves, and we found it necessary once again to flee because this life endangered us, we lost ourselves. Perhaps we exaggerated, going to extremes to avoid this stasis, but we fled. We could not afford another winter spent in this way, the cost was too high in time-out of the life we had now to get on with, George of writing the poetry that had formed within him in twenty-five years of not writing—for me to find out what was to be my path in and around George's writing, with some expression of my own to make a stand for myself of my own development and abilities. We had to be in control of our own lives, and now that our child was grown we could not spend more time in appeasing our remaining childhood problems. George valued New York, his roots there, his childhood, but for me it was not a place that in any way reflected my childhood, it did not arouse in me the basic childhood myths, memories and experiences out of which to build a beginning in art in some form. Going to Maine in the summers, living at Flossie Powers house began my first writing, the account of Flossie herself. I felt replenished and I understood her difficulties and the meaning of her life. In Brooklyn I had no clues, no childhood spent on city pavements to tell me about our neighbors. Even our friends in the arts were strange and mysterious, hard to understand, though I loved some of them. Charles Reznikoff especially. He took us on long walks which were like my long walks in the forests of Oregon. They were close to earth. For Charles I think the earth was formed mostly of New York City concrete out of which bloomed and blossomed the moon, the parkway trees, the bushes and blowing papers of which he made his city poetry.

After our return to Brooklyn the solution came to me. San Francisco! We were now the oldest of George's western family, we could move there and live as we wished, without threat from his father and his way of life. Let them now watch out for us, we were now the elders. George could return as he wanted to New York on trips to keep in touch with the streets and friends there, to renew that experience as he felt he needed it.

In 1965 I flew out alone to visit Andy, our niece, and her children. As the airplane began its descent from the high Sierras my excitement grew. I sighted the bay from the southern end and I saw the salt flats lying red, purple, and shades of orange, drying salt out of this bay water, but the bay seemed shockingly smaller. I remembered a much larger body of water, and there had been no bridges. At the airport I planned to take the helicopter to Berkeley. I wanted to see more from the air, but its battery needed charging, it was not running. I engaged a taxi with some other disappointed travelers and we were driven over the new San Mateo bridge to Oakland where Andy and her little boy were waiting. We passed a few stranded old ranch properties on the east side of the bay, with old machinery rusting in the dry grass, barns tumbling, houses abandoned. The eucalyptus trees grandly over-towering the wreckage. In Berkeley I felt strange, grandmother age to all these young children of Andy's, Andy who by her age could have been my daughter, her children, the oldest about eleven, the youngest Paul, a very little boy. My grandmother Mary may have felt like this herself, but when she arrives in the family of her children who live far away they say, "Grandma." And I didn't even know these children yet!

DECLARATION OF INDEPENDENCE

Absurd, absurd, we were desperately searching for "the world" and they desperately tried to help us build a wall, a fortress. You were so young, so young and your legs so long, you were afraid for me, you kept taking care of me—tenderly, passionately. The jewel, you thought I was, the warrior, the infinitely precious, the vulnerable phallus. And of course you were right, are right: who but those who stand behind him are in greater danger or more helpless, than the warrior.

He was handsome, women loved him, I never heard of a meeting between him and a woman in which he did not charm her, at least at first, depending on what she wanted her relationship with him to be. His success with women was so nearly complete that he did not notice that I was not charmed by him. I was under stress. I knew before I met him the difficulty for George in his struggle for independence from this powerful and charming father; and insidious power because it was generous and his father was witty and intelligent, as well as charming. My armor in this battle was my love for George and his love for me, and this battle was our first; it was a dangerous hazard, and one we had to meet and win.

George's father, almost at once, rented the house next door for George's older sister. We mentioned that we were thinking of getting a boat—George's father found and bought for us a forty-two foot yawl, and joined the yacht club for us to use it too. (We might have rigged up a row boat with a sail, or we might have bought a twenty-foot boat.) My father-in-law was in and out of our two houses often until we had established ourselves with our friends in such a full life that he didn't feel comfortably dominant among our student friends. Our houses overflowed on week-ends with friends we hadn't seen since we left the year before; Nellie and Jack, our most intimate friends, shared their friends with us, their friends soon were our friends too (Jack, the psychologist; Nellie, taking her

---

* Editor's note: See George Oppen, *The Anthropologist of Myself: A Selection from Working Papers*, edited by Rachel Blau Duplessis (Eastern Michigan University, 1990).

degree in anthropology). We came together on the weekends to share our interests. The work we each pursued during the week piled up a need to discuss, to tell what we had been thinking during the time in which we had not been together, by the weekend we were bursting with all we wanted to share. We formed a community, and although George and I have lived in joint living arrangements at other times in our lives, this was the first and we threw ourselves into it without reserve—perhaps the threat of being engulfed in George's father life, so near at hand, was part of our reason, for we impelled this intimacy, a protection that excluded him and his life, and in which we were strengthened—our own group in which we had status (a counter to his power), and in which we were accorded prestige and love.

My father-in-law proposed a trip up the Sacramento River on the new boat: he would bring along George's little sister, and we would spend several days on the trip. This was his first trip on the boat, although George and I had sailed the boat and knew her quite well, and could handle her by ourselves. At The Brothers, rocks which jut up in the northern part of the bay, we stopped to fish; striped bass were running and we caught a fine big fish for our supper.

"But how will we eat it?" my father-in-law asked.

"I'll cook it—I know how to cook," I replied with a little scorn, and we turned eastward, sailing briskly up the river with the wind behind us and the tide pushing us along.

"Let's anchor in the first good place we come to," said George. "It's almost supper time." George said to me, "Drop the jib and I'll round up to anchor over by the shore there, where I see a pier on the riverbank." Coming up to anchor with the wind and the tide behind us, I stood by the anchor which hung over the bow of the boat, the chain coming up through a hole in the deck with a notch in the housing which allowed the chain to be stopped. The end of the chain was securely fastened around the mast below deck. When George yelled, "Let her go!" I picked up the anchor chain and let it slide slowly through my hands until it hit bottom. I was paying it out slowly to give the anchor more scope, when my father-in-law, impatient man, ran forward, and before my astonished eyes took the chain from my hands and began throwing it out—the boat picked up speed in the wind and in the tidal current which was now running fast, but when he tried to stop the chain from running, he could not hold it against the boat's weight. George yelled to his father, "Let it go, let it go, Dad, it's fastened on the end." But his father could not hear. George came running up and grabbed the chain too, to help his father. George's father, taking a new hold on the chain, put his hands behind George's hands, until it reached its end, and they could then extricate their mangled hands. George's hands seemed to be a bloody mass; his father's hands were injured too.

Ashore, hands bandaged in a hospital which fortunately we had found nearby, and back on our boat again. The little sister, all this time, looking on, terrified, quiet. And as I cooked the fish for our supper, both men lying in the bunks, with their helpless hands lying out beside them, I said to my father-in-law, "Do not meddle in our lives again, we will live our lives as we want to live them, not in your shadow, stay out of our lives."

AFTER A CONVERSATION WITH G.

(dated 12/4/75)

I say we make the choice and call that luck.

The times in which I live (G. too) are not divorced from the choices we have made. Our first break from what our families expected of us was to choose each other. Luck? or choice. The next was choosing to go hitchhiking—(I have written of this at length so here I'll only mention it.) The choice was to escape from the somewhat fragile ties that class holds on youth in the US. We had to make that break and it was a real trauma, no question it was mostly new ground for George out of his German-Jewish, upper-class background. With my father's death and my life in Grants Pass I had already been through most of that trauma. I was already free and I blamed my mother and my brothers for my freedom and for not realizing their own potentials. Why did I think they were not doing what they *chose* to do? I think now that they chose to do what they did. I think I chose to do something quite other than my family's choices. Therefore I think I chose. I think George chose.

At each step of the way I have felt a cultural surrounding that was there or was developing in our society for me to be in—in my choices. We found a Bohemian world when we said *Artist*. When we found the Communists we found a world that would have rejected Bohemia, or our class backgrounds. When we returned to writing, George, in 1958, found a reception, a world that included him. His first book had not been neglected, the Beats, Duncan, Creeley had looked up Zukofsy and he had mentioned the others of that tenuous group, Objectivists. Rago, of *Poetry* magazine knew and remembered George's work. Pound was a recognized poet in 1958 and George's first book had a foreword by Pound. All this made a time and a place and an audience for George's poetry when he began to write again.

I left the plastic arts when I understood the meaning of the Art world in New York, the hold the dealers had on that world, the role of the museum of Modern Art and the flourishing of Dada, Surrealism, Happenings, Found Art, (giant Campbell soup cans, the American flag on the seat of Levi pants, etc.). The disappearance of the real in the natural world. Of course I know that the surrealists are also real. The Art which has emerged in the last twenty years has become the Art of that period by destruction of what went before. It is hard to think that a flower, or a human face or a figure will ever be portrayed again as Rembrandt painted, nor do I think that Art should repeat what has been done. The artists of the last twenty years did make something new and that art represents the cultural period as much as it came out of it or as much as it helped to create the period: an art of alienation, a dithyrambic art, wild and bois-terous Dionysian participation. For me to be an artist in the plastic arts is impossible now, it is a world I am not at home in. I am not alienated from the real.

I started to write with the rise of the Women's movement, although I have not been active in a political way, but I fully appreciate the victories of the women. I find I have an audience and when I write I am thinking of them. I know who will appreciate what I am saying. I count on men too, but without the women's movement my writing would not have been respected, in the first instance, enough to break through the male writing world. Again, I (we) have chosen. I have chosen to write at the time culturally prepared for me. I also helped prepare the culture. My political years still reap victories. I think that those seeds planted in the thirties have borne fruit. With the rise of the Third World whose seeds were also planted and culturally nourished we may be overcome, (I'm sure we will be swamped), by such ways do we choose. We rise, and we see the change brought about, in which we choose again. We have in our own contribution throughout our lives contributed significantly to what exists, we have no great complaints. I am happy to be writing, very pleased with the loss of shyness that took almost sixty-seven years to accomplish. I feel that my faculties are available to me and that gives me confidence, and I find my memories and my thought interesting.

"DOES SHE THINK SHE IS A LEGEND?"

I looked up the etymology of *legend*: to collect, to speak. Perhaps, "One who speaks magic words." Back to the Greek, *lingo*; live. Back to *logos*; speech, word, reason.

A young man said of *Meaning a Life*: "Does she think she is a legend?"

What I was writing was my autobiography, but yes, I suppose George and I are a legend. We have been here so long now that we qualify.

Yes, of course George and I are a legend—"thrown here" we have enlarged the space we and our spirits make, into a recognized place in the culture of our times. A book is a monument, a record put forward, and if it is a work of art it is the only way I know of speaking to other times than our own of what meaning is to us in our time; speaking to times to come as well as to our peers who recognize and who form a circle around us. A small thing? But the meaning is not small. The young man, though he has not yet been able to write poetry that has meaning, wants the life of a poet, but it is without the poetry that must come from within him, from his own life. His position is false, but it is, fortunately, almost impossible to arrive at poetry without the life that caused that poetry, or to write poetry out of a life only lived in order to be a poet or a writer. A poem if it has a life of its own, if it is new in the world will take on a life of its own. The human who made the poem searches to find from whence it came. I think all that one can arrive at, in the wonder of this event of a poem, is to say, it came out of my life. The poem stands by itself. It has its own position in the world as a work of art, with its own voice: this voice speaks or the poem has failed.

I am not unkind to the young man, I even found him interesting to talk to; bright, handsome, but afraid for his manhood. He is living his life in protection of that spark of manhood, this protection maybe the very thing that prevents taking the risk that a poem is, the exposure that allows the eyes and ears of the world to see into his life. Not the spark that is poetry. If he does not expose himself as an artist he is not a legend nor will he be, and attacking a legend in no matter how small a way and in no matter how small a way that legend is a contribution to the meaning of our times, does not speak well of his spirit.

Existential as defined by Simone de Beauvoir speaks of living each moment with its own import, fully, giving oneself to its meaning. Meaning for whom? Well, at least to that person who is doing the living; to feel fully the position of being human—"thrown here" out of the Void—to live, to *be* until the Void closes for us, that is the meaning I want for me, for me and George, for Linda, my daughter, and Alex, for those close to me, for any humans who think. To make their time here on this earth as full a living as they can—to live and to come out as well as they can.

George says *Courage*—that what we had was courage, true, and I think that we were courageous but I am not "being courageous." I am *being*—I am, for almost any moment I can conjure, being myself, living my life as fully as I can. Sometimes I falter, sometimes we faltered and then I'd say, "Courage"; that it took courage to go on—to find a way through to confidence in being. To live fully.

ON A DARK NIGHT

(Saint John of the Cross)

On a dark night
With love-longings aflame
Oh, unearthly adventure!
I went out without being noticed
My house being now still.

In darkness and secure
By the secret ladder
Oh, unearthly adventure!
In darkness and in ambush
My house being now still.

On that night foreknown
In secret, for no one saw me
Nor did I glance at anything
Without other light and guide
But that in my burning heart.

This guided me
More certainly than noonday light
To where he awaited me
Whom I have known so well
Where no one else appeared.

Night which itself guides
Night more lovely than the dawn
Night that itself unites
Lover with beloved
Loved in lover transformed.

On my flowering breast
Which I kept for him alone
There he stayed sleeping
And I caressed him.
Fanned by the cedars

The wind from the turret
Blew through his hair.
With his serene hand
On my wounded neck
And all my senses suspended

I remained myself and I forgot myself
My face rested on my lover:
Everything stopped, and I was outside myself
Leaving me watched over
Forgotten among Mary's lilies.

IT IS A LIFE

1

It is a life
mind takes me where it will go

happy?
strange   full of doubts and fears
shakes my love for myself

something happens to me
a stumbling
concealed from view or flashing

deep hidden
my own powers frighten me

BEGIN
(my voice in my dream)

strangers
apprentices

wandering to perfect our skills
disaster draws us and a kind of happiness

I borrow my first breath
ancestors   sound in my voice

but what I see and what I feel
happens to me

concealed from view or flashing
the occulting light leaves me in darkness

but the door I push
opens toward me

2

as a bird
a place her own
to which she will return

"but I have no home
for I have set on fire the forest
in which I was enchanted"

a stranger
as were all my mothers
ask

this path
now
receive an answer in sleep

what thickening fog tears my gaze from myself

where all the silenced
speak in my voice
shake my love for myself

but deep within
"the forest shimmers in a lovely light"

deer run wild in
words of beauty

she finds her soul with words

Love for another has shaken and
perhaps destroyed
herself
part of herself
left behind   a stranger
no remembering
rid   be rid of those   lapsed images
impostures
dreams and words

in sleep she disappears
she tells it
it changes
but what has been is not entirely gone
herself she takes forward

Love for another has shaken
perhaps destroyed
herself different
herself left behind
no remembering
rid   be rid   lapsed images   impostures
dreams and words she disappears
in sleep
she tells
it changes but it is not entirely gone it
is herself she takes forward

our boat makes a way for us

        it is a free passage
held in the surges

or standing on the sea of glass

our words move toward
each other

I come as a guest
entering my own life

and the tree that leans   lends
me   its strength

what my mothers said,
the dreams
I disappear into in sleep

in safety   I dream danger
I   open my eyes
startled that I am safe

we walk in autumn   stubble
the field not ours
small houses   unfurnished   empty
we enter
and it is our home

MOTHER AND DAUGHTER AND THE SEA

no sign of their paths through the air
from ancient times birds know the paths of birds
twisting their necks cropping new growth
running   stretching their necks   flying   looking about
enticing their young to flight

a daughter   a shadow   outside
herself a troubled river

lovely and comely she stands by the river
her darkness amazes
her hidden darkness a vine in her blood
turning again she broods on that strange vineyard
the mother in her blood
like a wild vine   and the tree said to the vine
Come!

silent her words are a burden
caught by the spinner
in the web she has surmised
love as a leaf drops

beyond the river
springs rise
brooks in the hills   river in the valley

sun and air   dark and her darkness
dark
shore   sand   and rock
a reedy place   a woodland
and the river
nears the sea

as the river flows

I walk the years
in the sedges by the river I walk
I bare my legs   cross over the river
as dawn lights the way

warning lights on mountain tops
lights of cities
but I have no path   the common
hope of my generation
is disenchanted   violent
wind carries a leaf
and a wind answers

CONVERSATION

silent
no bird moves a wing
no bird
moves

in my own darkness   obscure
secret places
shadowy   sombre   sometimes

afraid
from darkness   a glitter
luminous   opens
we talk   we hold
the key

MUSE

like a bird flying through the air
the path of her flight is not to be found
she steps out of my presence
brings no word
her lips move but she is silent
hand covering her mouth
she turns
looks back
belongs to no-one

I grope at noon-day
as if I have no eyes
the door that was open
closes
I hide in secret
dark   although the key
is in my hand

Is there a woman who knows her own way

as a bird folds her wings
or makes her way by flying
in the way of birds

the bird   the singing
bird has not asked long
life   deep
deep   *my center's in a sphere*
no eyes no hands no wings   no time no space

outside myself the way was long

in flight we met
        noise of the wings of living creatures
        sound of beating wings
we met   and found
ourselves in flight
and now I'd say
the wings were love

Mary Oppen (1908–1990) was born in Kalispell, Montana, and spent her adolescence in the Pacific Northwest. She was a writer, artist, and activist, and the lifelong partner of the poet George Oppen. Besides her singular autobiography, she published two collections of poetry, *Poems & Transpositions* and the chapbook *Mother and Daughter and the Sea*.

Jeffrey Yang works as an editor at New Directions. He is the author of the poetry books *An Aquarium, Vanishing-Line*, and *Hey, Marfa*, and the editor of *The Sea is a Continual Miracle: Sea Poems and Other Writings* by Walt Whitman, *Time of Grief: Mourning Poems*, and *Birds, Beasts, and Seas: Nature Poems from New Directions*.